The Friar in Fiction
Sincerity in Art
and Other Essays

JOSEPH SPENCER KENNARD

THE FRIAR IN FICTION
SINCERITY IN ART

and Other Essays

Essay Index Reprint Series

BOOKS FOR LIBRARIES PRESS, INC.
Freeport, New York

First Published 1923
Reprinted 1968

LIBRARY OF CONGRESS CATALOG CARD NUMBER:

68-20313

PRINTED IN THE UNITED STATES OF AMERICA

FOREWORD

MOST writers who have lived long, have studied, read and meditated, are likely to possess a quantity of literary baggage. A trunk in the garret, a box in the cellar, neatly tied and properly labeled packages of "thoughts" on the top shelf of some unused closet. The present selection of essays is, in part, derived from those tin-boxes in the garret; a few samples selected from many. Others have already known printer's ink, but are no longer to be found in the market. They represent many years of reading and meditation. I hope you will like some of them, gentle reader; I hope you will treat all of them kindly, noble critic, even more kindly than they deserve. As I am on the other side of the world, I cannot supervise their progress through the press; but you may be sure that my publishers will give you a book that will be typographically well done.

Benares, India
1923

CONTENTS

SOME FRIARS
IN ENGLISH FICTION

SOME FRIARS IN ENGLISH FICTION

THE friar occupies a very prominent place in every phase of the life of the English Middle Ages, and could be considered in many aspects. In the intellectual life of the Thirteenth Century, a great creative and distinctive century in all Europe, the influence of the friar was great. In England it may with truth be called "the age of the friars."

The Franciscans, Dominicans and other mendicant orders, attempted the reform of the monasteries, carried the vow of poverty to the extremest point, rejecting corporate as well as personal property, and chose the most squalid parts of the towns for their abode. They were confessors and preachers, and soon became scholars, largely influencing the intellectual life of the English Universities, possessed excellent libraries, and were so eager in their search for books that in 1257 the Archbishop of Armagh, Fitzralph, wrote to the Pope, "In the faculties of Arts, Theology, Canon Law, and, as many assert, in medicine and Civil Law, scarcely a useful book is to be found in the market, but all are bought up by the Friars, so that in every convent is a great and noble library, and every one of these friars who has a recognized position in the Universities, and such are now innumerable, has also

3

a noble library." The same was true in the University of Paris, in which, as decreed by the bull *Quasi Lignum* and subsequent bulls of Pope Alexander IV, in 1255, the friars were for a time placed in control.

And the educational work of the friars was not confined to the universities; wherever there was a convent there was a school. Their learning was spread throughout Europe, as the friars passed from one university to another.

When we remember the hatred of St. Francis for book-learning, it is indeed remarkable that, besides occupying some of the highest positions in the Church, one being Pope, the Franciscans were for a time the most learned body in Europe, and some of them the greatest scholars of their age. Roger Bacon and Alexander Hales and Duns Scotus were Franciscans, and Thomas Aquinas and Albertus Magnus were Dominicans. Hardly do we associate these learned friars with America, and yet Friar Pedro de Sante, who accompanied Cortes to Mexico, and opened the first Christian school on the Western Continent, was only one of many. An interesting bibliography of books on geographical, historical and ethnographical subjects, by Franciscan friars, is that by Father Marcellino da Civezza, published in Prato in 1888. There are nearly a thousand titles of such books in Spanish, French, German, English, Italian, Portuguese, Turkish, Arabic, Japanese, Chinese, Siamese, Latin, Greek, and other languages.

And yet the promotion of scholarship was never

even a part of the vision of the founders of the great friar orders, nor was it for this that the Pope gave them his formal sanction. It was a time when over Europe hung a pall of famine, misery, despair, disease, and death; and the land was thronged with outlaws and beggars, and for the remedy of this condition religion did almost nothing. The cloistered monk, intent on saving his own soul, far from the haunts of men, engaged in study or the illumination of manuscripts, or in gluttony and idleness, gave no thought to the rabble outside his convent walls. And then the friars came and changed the character of the age.

To all the world they were *Brothers* (*Fratres*) or, as we say in English, Friars. To the masses, to the poor in spirit and poor in purse, to the beggar and leper and downtrodden, they came and said: "We too are poor, very beggars, and we have come among you to live with you, and share your life, and wash your sores," and the Dominican friar-preachers, to preach the gospel. Sorely were both Dominican and Franciscan needed in England, where after the eight years of excommunication, the churches were desolate and in large districts public worship of God had ceased. For the next three hundred years the friars were the evangelizers of England.

With the Fourteenth and Fifteenth centuries, came the corruption of the friars; and it is these later friars who are depicted by the writers of fiction who use them as characters. Just because the friars were such an extremely important part of the whole social fabric of those centuries, they occupy a most important place in the fiction of those times, and for the same reason they are chosen as the subject of these essays. You cannot understand those centuries, unless you understand their friars.

Anything like a complete review of the friar characters found in the vast mass of literary material of a fictional character which has appeared in Europe since the coming of the friars, would be a task as futile as it would be enormous. In these essays all that is attempted is a selection of a few such characters from that fiction which is most familiar to the average English reader, and thus not attempting to touch the friar characters of the *Fabliaux,* the Italian *Novelle,* the Heptameron and *Cent Nouvelles Nouvells,* or the *Contes Devots,* of Camus, Bishop of Beley, to whom Cardinal Richelieu wrote, "I find no fault in you, except your writings against the friars and monks, Without that I would canonize you." All of them, without exception, present the friar character as deceitful and immoral. And, after allowing for all literary exaggeration, we are obliged to conclude that, in its broad lines, this picture does represent the typical friar as found in real life during those centuries.

Among the earliest literary references to the friar in England are those of the *Robin Hood Ballads,* and these are elusive, as if a face gazed out at us for a moment from behind a curtain, and was then withdrawn. Few, if any of the original ballads have survived; practically all that we now have are ballads about Robin

Hood ballads that were. Thus, the "Ballad of Robin Hood's Golden Prize" begins:

> I have heard talk of Robin Hood
> And of braw Littel John
> Of Fryer Tuck and Will Scarlet.

And another:

> I heard my grandad sing a song
> And in that song he told:

About all that can be said is that the authenticity of the Friar Tuck of the earliest ballads probably depends on, and is equal to that of the authenticity of Robin Hood himself, whatever that may be. But we find such abundant mention of jolly Friar Tuck in the other literature nearly contemporary with the Robin Hood Ballads, that our imagination is not taxed in accepting him as a historic character, as Drayton accepted him when in his Polyolbion he writes

> Of Tuck the merry friar who many a sermon made
> In praise of Robin Hood, his outlaws and their trade.

Vague also are the references of Stowe in his *Annals,* and Skelton, and George Peele and Munday and Chettle, in their plays.

If we turn to William Langland's *Vision of Piers Plowman,* however, we have something substantial. Langland was a churchman who loved his church, and loved all men, and from the whole tone of his poem we know that he was sincere. The *Piers Plowman* poem most evidently tells of real life; in that consists its chief value for us.   There is in it no sense of exaggeration, or a preference for dwelling on the blacker side of life.   And the picture of the friar which we achieve from it, is of a gluttonous, lying, envious, ungracious caricature of the life the founder of his order intended him to live and which was required in his vows.   And yet William Langland was probably educated by the friars.

The Friar Tuck of the Ballads was merely a large-hearted vagabond, who seeing the rotten condition of the social world around him, says, "If I must rob, I will openly rob the rich.   If I must preach falsehood and flattery, I will preach it to robbers who will appreciate it at its just value."   He saw that *"Falseness,"* when in fear of justice, fled to the friars, and *"Lyer,"* when banished from all other company, was sought out by all four orders of friars, and "for knowing of comers was coped as a frere."   *"Envey"* was dressed as a frere, and so was *"Wrathe,"* whose aunts were a nun and an abbess.   And though Lady Meed was a woman so immoral that no decent priest was willing to shrive her, a confessor, "coped as a frere," tells her, "I have heard of all your sins this fourty winter.   But I will assoil thee for a measure of wheat. I will be thy bedesman and set thee as pure among knights and kings."   The Robin Hood ballads sang of bold robbers, and a friar robber preaching to robbers. Langland pictures the actual friar as he saw him in real life.

If we come now to the immediate predecessors of Shakespeare, we find in the *Faust* of Marlowe, a friar as Elizabethan England saw him; and he is again revealed in Marlowe's *Jew of Malta,* in which the Jacobin friar Jacomo, and the Franciscan friar Barnadine, who have hitherto worked in harmony, now plotting against each other, in the interests of their respective monasteries, with the resultant death of both. The corporate covetousness of the Itinerant orders, founded in poverty for the help of the poor, while they themselves were to possess no wealth, is here well represented. And their personal morality is revealed in the sinister innuendo of these words from their own lips:

Friar Barnadine—The Abbess sent for me to be confessed,
　　　　　　Oh what a sad confession there will be.
Friar Jacomo—And so did fair Maria send for me.

In the *Faustus* play, Faust says to Mephistophilis:

　　I charge thee to return and change thy shape,
　　Thou art too ugly to attend on me,
　　Go, and return an old Franciscan Friar,
　　That Holy Shape becomes a Devil best.

Could words convey a picture more sad of the degradation attained by that once holy Order?

Another side of the friar character has been painted by Robert Greene in his picture of friar *Roger Bacon.* Greene was a contemporary of Marlowe and seeing the great popular success of the latter's *Faust,* determined to construct a play which should surpass that which had immortalized the German conjurer, and in which the hero should be the greatest Englishman of his time. It was indeed a daring task to put upon the stage and praise a friar, in that age, when friars all were hated. A cloistered friar, in the eyes of the multitude, endowed with the worst of all sins—witchcraft. Greene's Roger Bacon entirely conforms to the popular tradition. The friar is described as he was, to the people a great necromancer, to Greene a great scholar and patriot.

Says King Henry to Vandermast:

> In Oxford shalt thou find a jolly friar
> Called Friar Bacon, England's only flower.

And here is Vandermast's opinion:

> Lordly thou lookest, as if that thou wert learned,
> Thy countenance as if Science held her seat
> Between the circled arches of thy brows.

And King Henry's opinion, is accepted to-day also:

> Bacon, thou hast honoured England with thy skill
> And made fair Oxford famous with thine art.

The final scene is so strong, quite worthy of Shakespeare himself, as to make Greene's *Friar Bacon* a worthy portrait in the gallery of the Frairs in Fiction. After seven years Friar Bacon has achieved the purpose of his magic art.

> I have framed out a monstrous head of brass
> That by the enchanting forces of the devil
> Shall tell out strange and uncouth aphorisms
> And girt fair England with a wall of brass.

So the wizard falls asleep, after bidding his servant waken him at the first motion of the brazen head.

The head speaks, "Time is," but the servant does not heed. It speaks again, "Time was." Then in the midst of thunder and lightning, and roaring as if all Hell had broken loose, the Head cries, as it is smashed by the phantom hand of Fate: "Time is past." The Friar now awake to the shattering of his ambition, cries, in a strong soliloquy,—

> The turrets of my hope are ruin'd down.

As with the breaking of the brazen head the Bacon of the play beholds the failure of his dream; so the real Bacon instead of realizing his dream of revolutionizing the learning of the Church, and broadening the world of science, finds his work condemned by the powers at Rome. And in like manner the author of the play, Robert Greene, was completely obscured by the glorious noon-day sun of the genius of Shakespeare.

CHAUCER'S FRIARS

> Der betler sack wirt nimer vol:
> Wie man in fult so bleibt er hol:
> Der geiz ist apt in iedem orden.
> (From a German Satire, 1520)

> You ne'er can fill the friar's sack,
> The more you give the more 'twill lack,
> In ev'ry order greed holds rule.

With only one exception, of all the friars in fiction, previous to Shakespeare, those of Chaucer are the most important. They are well worthy of a more extended study than is possible within the limits set for this volume.

Chaucer's *Pilgrimage to Canterbury* is referred to the year 1383, 150 years after the first arrival of mendicant friars in England. In Chaucer's time there were, as there are still, four mendicant orders, Franciscans, Dominicans, Carmelites and Augustinians, and they all had English establishments.

The Franciscans (Friars Minor, *Fratres Minores*) had for their founder that great enthusiast of nature, humanity and divine love, St. Francis. More than any other man he realized the ideal soul-life, as it was preached and lived by Jesus, twelve hundred years before; and more nearly than any other man fulfilled in his own life the counsels of the Master. His Order, while it inherited his name and fame, was not heir to his virtues; and his loved poverty became for his professed followers only a name to conjure with. Before long "Franciscan" became in common speech the synonym of "impudent beggar" and "religious mountebank." St. Bonaventura, one of his most faithful disciples, publicly charged that the Franciscan friars were such shameless beggars that they were more to be dreaded than highwaymen.

The Friar St. Anthony of Padua was the leader of that faction of the Franciscan Order which most nearly observed the principles of St. Francis. St. Anthony would have no compromise with "the world";

and when men spurned his doctrine, he preached to the fishes. Abraham, a Sancta Clara, an Augustinian friar, was the author of *Judas der Erzschelm* (Judas the Arch-rogue) which has been translated under the title of *St. Anthony's Sermon to the Fishes,* of which these are the last two stanzas:

The sermon now ended
Each turned and descended;
The pike went on stealing,
The eels went on eeling.
  Much delighted were they,
  But preferred the old way.
The crabs are backsliders,
The stockfish thick-siders,
The carps are sharp-set;
All the sermon forget:
  Much delighted were they,
  But preferred the old way.

The Dominican and Franciscan friars came to England about 1221. The Dominicans settling at Oxford and the Franciscans at Cambridge University, while the Mendicant friars pursued the ideals of their founders, relief of the distressed and religious ministration to the neglected poor. Alms poured like a mighty stream into their treasuries, and the "Poor Friars" began the erection of conventual establishments that vied in splendour and magnitude with the abbeys and minsters of the ancient wealthy monastic and episcopal foundations. It was indeed a far cry from beggary at Assisi. The friars were everywhere, not perhaps

yet in such numbers as a hundred years later, when
Chaucer's *Sompnour* says of them

> a flie and eke a frere
> Wol fall in every dish and eke matere.

But as early as 1293 Parliament was obliged to
frame laws for the repression of the disorders of
religious mendicants. Fitzralph, archbishop of Armagh, declares that in a few years the number of
students at Oxford fell from thirty thousand to six
thousand because of the unwillingness of the parents
to subject their sons to the influence of the friars. And
he also says the friars got control of the book market
because of "the endeles wynnynges that thei getteth
by beggyng": and one cannot purchase "a profytable
boke of the faculte of art, of dyvynyte, of law canoun,
of physic, ether of law civile, but all bokes beth bought
of freres."

Chaucer, in the *Canterbury Tales*, feigns himself to
be one of a company of pilgrims on a visit to the shrine
of St. Thomas à Becket at Canterbury.   In the company are two friars, namely, a Limitour or mendicant
licensed to beg within certain limits; and a Pardonere, a pedlar of indulgences and of relics, and also a
Sompnour (Summoner) or process-server for a dioce-
san court.   He is no friar, but he is past-master of
friarly tricks.   These are rogues, all three, and rivals
in business.   Chaucer's Limitour is a friar, and presumably of the Franciscan Order.   He is the barefooted friar of the old ballad:

Ne'er shall you find, should you search till you tire,
So happy a man as the Barefooted Friar:

.   .   .   .

He can roam where he lists, he can stop when he tires,
For every man's house is the Barefooted Friar's.

Chaucer's Limitour is a wanton and a merry, and
has the gift of oily speech.   He is a welcome guest of
all the country gentry and of their women folk; for
he possessed extraordinary powers of absolution; and
besides,

Ful swetely herde he confession
And pleasant was his absolution:

And there was no need of penance at all, if the sinner
made a liberal offering to "the poure ordre":

Therefore in stede of weeping and praires
Men mote give silver to the poure freres.

The fellow was a minstrel, and he knew every inn-
keeper and every tapster of his begging district, and
he would even beg of a pauper:

For though a widewe had but a shoe
Yet wold he have a ferthing or he went.

The object of Sompnour and Limitour and Pardonere is ever one and the same—pelf; but their means
of attaining it are different; the first wins by threats;
the others by cozening; but they are all equally shameless and hypocrites by trade.   True, they are sons of
St. Francis, and the friars observe the rule of his Order sacredly, but it is always *"Exceptis excipiendas,"*
says the feigned hermit in *Ivanhoe,* "as our old abbot

taught me to say when laymen should ask me if I kept every punctilio of mine order." The friar is first and last and always a beggar. He specially pleads for money for trental masses.

At last this friar arrives at a house where he was wont to be received with more than common hospitality, and finds the goodman lying sick and like to die. Here is the opportunity to employ all his tricks to get money from the sick man. In vain does the zealous friar urge him with reasons from scripture, from legend, from Seneca. The dénouement of the tale may not be told here. The manners of those mediæval times may have been more stately, formal, courtly than those of the present age; their humour is the humour of stableboys and swineherds.

The road-outfit of the Pardonere, this pedlar of indulgences and of miraculous relics, is wonderful. Among them he has the veil of Our Lady, and also a snip from the sail of St. Peter's fishing smack, and a glass casket full of the bones of martyrs and confessors. This Pardonere is quite free of his confidences. "Think you," he asks, "that I will live in poverty, so long as I can earn money in this way?"

Compare these exaggerations of Chaucer with the living, breathing, rollicking Friar Lippo Lippi, of Robert Browning. Fra Lippo is a scapegrace; and though he is for the nonce an inmate of Cosimo de Medici's palace, he slips out at midnight and is found by the watch prowling in an alley, "Where sportive ladies leave their door ajar."

One of the patrol seizes his throat and hustles him off to his convent, the Carmelites! Soft and easy! "What will you do when you get there? Will you make a rout of the rats there, and nip every wee little white mouse, ye find there, *weke, weke, weke?* O you know your betters!" The merry friar is of course the best of friends with the patrol and he tells them the story of that night. Lippo is leaning out of a window of the palace, and hears a pattering of feet, little feet; hears singing, playing of lute, laughter; a face looks up at him:

> Zooks, sir, flesh and blood!
> That's all I'm made of. Into shreds it went,
> Curtain and counterpane and coverlet—

There was a ladder! and Lippo in a moment "came up with the fun." He was returning well pleased with himself, and all the world, when he is seized by the watch.

He now tells the story of his life. He is an orphan from babyhood and his first eight years are spent on the street, living anyhow. On fig-skins, melon-parings, rinds and shucks; by thieving, of course. But one day his aunt took him to the convent and the friars took him in. He vowed "to quit this very miserable world," and so became a friar. At the mature age of eight years, he "renounced the world, its pride and greed," *et cetera.*

But

> You should not take a fellow eight years old,
> And make him swear to never kiss the girls.

And thus throughout the whole poem; every trait of character that is drawn, every vice of monasticism that is hinted at, every act done, every word that is spoken by the ne'er-do-weel great artist-friar, has the air of truth and actuality.

No consideration of the friars of English fiction can omit the Friar Clement of Charles Reade's great novel *The Cloister and the Hearth,* and the Fra Savonarola of George Eliot's *Romola.*   Of all such friars they are the two most familiar to readers of English fiction, and Friar Clement is perhaps the greatest friar in any literature. So frequently have these two novels been reviewed by masters of criticism, and their several characters compared, that it would be difficult to say anything new upon the subject, that would be of value.

Says Mr. Besant, in his review, which is so just and so filled with a sense of proportion, yet so virile and filled with enthusiasm, "Comparison between *The Cloister and the Hearth* and *Romola* is forced upon one. Both books treat of the same period; similar pictures should be presented in both. Yet,—what a difference. In the man's work we find action, life, movement, surprise, reality. In the woman's work we find languor, tedium, and the talk of nineteenth century puppets dressed in fifteenth century clothes." . . . "I do not say that the whole of life, as it was at the end of the Fourteenth Century, is in *The Cloister and the Hearth.* But I do say, that there is portrayed so vigorous, lifelike, and truthful a

picture of a time long gone by, and differing in every
particular from our own, that the world has never
seen its like. . . . As one reads it, one feels in the
very atmosphere of the century; one breathes the air
just before the great dawn of learning and religion.
. . . There is plenty of fanaticism but no faith; under
the tiara the Pope yawns; under the scarlet cloak the
Cardinals scoff. . . . "

"There is, however, plenty of activity in certain
directions. Soldiers fight and great lords lead armies;
there are court ceremonies. . . . A fine picturesque
time, with plenty of robberies and murders; vast quan-
tities of injustice. . . . With gibbets, racks, red-hot
pincers; and every possible stimulus to virtue; yet a
world in which virtue was singularly rare. All this
—and more—is in *The Cloister and the Hearth* not
described but acted. . . ."

"But besides, there runs through it the sweetest,
saddest, and most tender love-story ever devised by
the wit of man. There is no heroine in fiction more
dear to me than Margaret. . . . 'Oh, my love!' cried
the lover-priest at her death-bed, 'if thou hast lived
doubting of thy Gerard's heart, die not so, for never
was woman loved so tenderly as thou this ten years
past."

" 'Calm thyself, dear one,' said the dying woman,
with a heavenly smile; 'I knew it; only, being but a
woman, I could not die happy till I heard thee say so.' "

All that Mr. Besant has written, more fully than
we have had space to quote, in praise of this great

book, has also been echoed by other writers of merit. We cannot but feel the justice of Mr. Swinburne's comparison when he writes:

"A story better conceived, or better composed, better constructed, or better related, than *The Cloister and the Hearth,* it would be difficult to find anywhere; while the most enthusiastic devotees of *Romola* must surely admit the well-nigh puerile insufficiency of some of the resources by which the story has to be pushed forward, or warped round, before it can be got into harbour. . . .

"The superiority of the male novelist is so obvious, and so enormous, that any comparison between his breathing figures and the stiff, thin outlines of George Eliot's phantasmal puppets would be unfair, if it were not unavoidable. . . . *The Cloister and the Hearth* must be ranked 'among the very greatest masterpieces of narrative.' "

It is impossible within reasonable limits to give an adequate résumé of this vast picture of the Middle Ages and the vital characters which live and march and speak in its pages. They are not described by the author; they are there, in flesh and blood, and we see them act and hear them speak. The Burgundian soldier; is he alone not enough to fill a novel? And little Kate! And Margaret Van Eyck! Bless you, Mr. Reade, for having in your pages given us a woman so normal and real and yet so great of soul, and so true a lover! There are novels a plenty who show us the other kind. And there are half a dozen other characters, out of any one of which could have been made a book. And ever through the book moves Gerard; true lover, rover, hermit and priest. Holland and France and Germany and Rome of that time, live before our eyes, and their men and women talk to us.

As it is pleasant to praise, when praise is deserved, so it is not pleasant to blame, even when one cannot praise. The inadequacy of *Romola,* results from the fact that George Eliot attempted to fill in a canvas that was too large for her brush and with pigments too thin to give substance and form and vitality and fire and movement to the rich teeming fulness, the glow and the palpitation of that marvellous age; teeming with grand anomalies and great contrasts; of the fine arts and the spirit that fed them, in the same city with wild beasts in human form, though often with silken speech and velvet touch. So too, her agnostic philosophy was an empty reservoir, a void in which there could live no true conception of the influence of the powers of the world to come on daily life as then lived. The great battle that at that time shook religious souls, was to her a dead intellectual conception, or at best a mental aberration. Hence her conscientious and laborious study of Savonarola is invertebrate; a marsh-light and moonshine spectre, without real ardour and depth of soul. How could she grasp the secret of his power to sway the people of Florence, as the wind sways the trees of the forest?

In nothing that George Eliot has ever written, or indeed in what other author, is there anything to compare in elevation of sentiment, in nobleness of feeling, in pathos, in the presentation of great love and great courage, of Christian resignation and self-sacrifice with the concluding pages of *The Cloister and the Hearth*.

As has been truly said by another writer, the soul of Friar Clement was the soul of his author. The love-life of Gerard was the love-life of Charles Reade. If Gerard had married, he would, according to his belief, have lost his soul. If Reade had married, he would have starved, since he would have forfeited his fellowship at Magdalene College, Oxford, which was his sole means of support. It was this personal experience, his own suffering, which enabled the author to so graphically describe the loss of love and home, and to make of Friar Clement, the greatest of all the friars of fiction.

> "Girard, Friar Clement, Charles Reade,
> Are they not one and the same?
> Since their tragedy was the same."

THE FRIAR IN
GERMAN FICTION

THE FRIAR IN GERMAN FICTION

IN Germany, as elsewhere, the friar first came to be recognized as a fit subject for treatment by romance writer and satirist when the severity established and the piety practised by the founders of the various friar orders had been relaxed; and when the seeds of decay and death which exist even in the conception and are hidden in the very birth of the most perfect human institutions had germinated and fructified.

As long as the friars were what they professed to be, the helpers, the guides, the teachers, friends and brothers of poor suffering humanity; living examples of self-sacrifice and of service, they compelled admiration and respect. But when instead of the man being swallowed up in the friar the friar was too frequently lost in the man; when the cowl and the gown were used to cloak a multitude of sins, then the members of the friar orders became the butt of the satirists, and appropriate characters for fiction.

Before that time the friar had been the subject of much discussion and dispute among churchmen. About him they had written ponderous tomes. Thereby, but also chiefly by observation, the shortcomings of the friars had been brought home to the German laymen who were not of such an emotional nature as to be able to show to the cowl that respect which they did not, could not, feel for the wearer. And the dull layman is a keen and redoubtable critic when the follies and foibles of the clergy or of any religious order are under discussion.

We could not expect that contemporary popular fiction would mirror the actual friar without distortion, and it does not. The object was too near for that; the subject too intimate and important; the peculiarities too striking; the weaknesses and vulnerable points too obvious; the feeling too intense. It was a subject polemical rather than academical. Therefore it was only natural that satire and exaggeration should prevail over fair discription. Besides the public had to be considered, and then, as now, the detailing and exploiting of the faults, weaknesses and sins of a person or class was more attractive and popular than an impartial account of the best or even representative features. Then, as now, the public cared more that a story should be spicy and witty and perhaps "naughty" than that it should be true. And it is the readers that mould the writers, not writers the readers. The wart on Cromwell's nose has always been more interesting to writers and readers than the rest of his face.

Nevertheless the most ardent defender of Friary must confess that the abuses and evils in the system were omnipresent and omnipotent. Ridicule might have been the bitter medicine to work a cure, had not the disease been beyond remedy. The thoughtful and devout among the friars must have been roused to effort at reformation not so much by the virulence as by the truth of these popular pictures of friar life and friar character, but the great body of friary was gangrened to the core and no physician could avail, no medicine work a cure.

The evils of German Friary were the evils of Roman Catholicism in Germany. But to those evils were added all those possibilities of evil inherent in the friar system. For a long time in Germany there had been a latent ferment and finally open revolt against the nepotism, the sinning, the corruption of the Roman hierarchy. The fact that the Church claimed and essayed to dominate all spiritual, intellectual, governmental and domestic life, explains the intensity and extent of the revolt, when that revolt came. Explains why it occupies so large a place in contemporary literature. Great scholars and humble writers, saint and scoffer, found here a subject of perennial interest and inspiration.

Twenty years before Luther's appearing, two men loomed large in the religious world of Germany. Erasmus of Rotterdam, whom Charles Reade has enshrined in that greatest of friar novels, *The Cloister and the Hearth,* and Johannes Reuchlin. Neither claimed to be a theologian, yet no other men of their times so influenced contemporary religious thought. They were Luther's precursors. Erasmus by his issuing the New Testament in Greek and Reuchlin by publishing the original Hebrew text of the Old Testament made possible Luther's translation of the Bible into the

German. The trial of Reuchlin for heresy caused the storm of indignation and sympathy which culminated in that famous book the *Epistolae Illustrium Virorum ad Reuchlinum*[1] and the still more famous *Epistolae Obscurorum Virorum*.[2]

So important was the influence of this latter book, that it demands notice in any attempt to consider the subject of the Friar literature. Treating as it does chiefly of the Dominican friars of Cologne, yet it is a general arraignment of all friary. It may fairly be called an historical novel. The Reuchlin heresy controversy forms the historical foundation. It takes the form of letters, wholly fictitious, written in the common Latin jargon, so as to imitate the language employed by the ignorant friars and theologians. The language of the book is doubtless one of its chief claims to consideration, and the intended illusion that it was actually written by various friars of Cologne is so perfect, that some English friars, failing to comprehend the satire and believing it to be a defence of their orders, requested the Dominican prior at Cologne to send them copies for use in their convents.

The first letter describes a grand feast supposed to be given by a newly created Doctor of Theology; it details the various viands and delicacies, wines and beers, reveals the ignorance, shallowness and sophisms of the theologians. Another letter depicts the dilemma of a friar who, in eating an egg on Friday, happens to

[1] Letters of Illustrious Men to Reuchlin. 1514.
[2] Letters of the Obscure Men. 1515-1517.

swallow the yolk which contains a little chicken. We have the pros and cons as to whether he has sinned in eating meat on a fast-day. Whether it may be classed as one of the fishes, as are worms in cherries and cheese, or as actual meat. Other letter writers pose as poets and send their poems to the teacher Gratiamus for correction. It is true the metre of their poems is barbarous; but are they not spiritual poets!— how absurd to expect them to be bound by the same limits as these new-fashioned poets who take their pattern from Virgil, Pliny and other modern (!) authors.

These "letters of the obscure men" indicate how thoroughly they enjoy life, and that they have no shame in saying so. Eating and drinking are of paramount interest, but the ankle of a pretty woman, a "sacred" kiss and a little love, never comes amiss. And if their consciences presume to reproach them they always have a text of Scripture pat: "Rejoice, O young man in thy youth" (Eccl. xi. 9). "Let us eat, drink and be merry." Says one: "I am not stronger than Samson and not wiser than Solomon, therefore let's have a good time and drive away the blues. Afterwards we will confess and God, who is merciful, will pardon."

The *Epistolae Obscurorum Virorum* was the work of scholars. To the learned it appealed as a picture of the pedantry, sophism, vanity, fondness for fruitless argumentation, barbarous Latin, and gross ignorance of the supposed friars. But the immense influence of the book over the common people was its revelation of the moral and spiritual decay in the priesthood and in the friar orders.

Scarcely less destructive to reverence for the Church, and especially to the friar orders, were the writings of that "good churchman" Erasmus. His *Praise of Folly,* which is fair fiction, flays monks, cardinals, bishops, popes and mendicant friars. The latter he calls, "Brain-sick fools . . . who make a good profitable trade of beggary, thrust into all public houses, come aboard the passenger-boats, get into the travelling waggons, and omit no opportunity of time or place for the craving of people's charity; doing a great deal of injury to common highway beggars, by interpolating in their traffic of alms. . . . A great part of their religion consists in their title: some will be called Cordeliers, and these subdivided into Capuchins, minors, minims, and mendicants, . . . as if the common name of Christian were too mean and vulgar." "And the Judge of all the earth," he continues, "at the last day shall shut them out from His Father's kingdom, which was prepared only for those who are true of heart." "And when these friars shall see ploughmen and mechanics admitted into that kingdom, from which they themselves are shut out, how sneakingly will they look, and how pitifully slink away."

These writers were Churchmen all; the true friar of German fiction is best seen in the popular literature, written for the people and by writers from the people.

Neither in Germany nor in any part of Europe do we find in such writings an impartial picture of friary. We find nothing to indicate those friars, the chosen few, who out of all the multitude must have existed, those simple God-like men who strove to maintain the best traditions of their orders. Every word written may be true, but it is an unfriendly witness who is testifying, and we shall not get a fair likeness of the friar, though we doubtless have a correct picture of a type of friar, a lay-figure carefully labelled with all the faults and vices of his order itemized. The description compares with reality just about as does the phrenologist's chart with the average head. That the friar limned is no more a real friar than are to-day many self-called Christians true followers and imitators of the meek and lowly Jesus.

The earliest of these popular descriptions of the friar are to be found in the *Fastnachtspiel* (Carnival Play). This was largely of the character of a take-off; the most favorite Sixteenth Century method for burlesquing and caricaturing. Subjects of general interest were handled very much as they are to-day in certain minstrel shows. The foibles of classes were exhibited for the entertainment of other classes. In consequence all had their amusement, all had to take a dose of their own medicine, and all had the much sighed-for privilege of seeing themselves as others saw them.

The earliest of such interesting carnival plays is by Niklaus Manuel, produced in 1525, *Der Ablass-Krae-mer* (The Indulgence Pedlar). The arts and devices and quackery of such as Tetzel are well known. Naturally the Indulgence pedlar is discomfited by the crowd of women and rustics, for Manuel, poet and artist, was an ardent reformer, a co-worker with Luther. We feel, however, that it is rather a particular rascally friar presented to our view, than a type of the order. Manuel has not tried to misrepresent, but, detesting friars, he has searched for a sorry specimen.

In 1536 Hans Sachs, the shoemaker poet of Nuremburg, wrote a Carnival play entitled *Die elf elenden Wanderer* (The eleven miserable Wanderers), in which he dealt at some length with the friar. In 1539 he wrote *Die funf elenden Wanderer* (The five miserable Wanderers), in which the friar figures even more conspicuously. The play exhibits little dramatic development and no profound analysis of character. Yet it will always possess literary and historical value, and easily surpasses similar contemporary productions. It is rough, humorous and picturesque withal; shrewd and sarcastic. You will search far and wide to find an equally vivid and fairly accurate picture of the times; each character is a portrait, each scene is taken from real life. The humour is coarse but genuine; the dialogue broad but sparkling; a spade is called a spade, when not something more emphatic.

The characters are a waggoner, a horseman, a gipsy, a grocer, a mendicant friar and the host. Each one gives a description of himself (and incidentally of his class); blows his own trumpet, and with the exception of the host, tells all that he knows, or can in-

vent, derogatory to the others. The dialogue is in vigorous verse which at best can only be parodied in our
attempt to render into modern English.

Except in his modesty mine host resembles nowise
the landlord of to-day. He is indeed too good-natured
for this earth. With him virtue is indeed its own reward, and those who have nothing wherewithal to
pay, seem to be his especial care.

> Though many came here ev'ry day
> I never turned a guest away,
> But, when he ate and drank his fill
> And stretched his tired limbs at will,
> Gave him a sleeping cup at night
> And tuck'd him to bed so warm and tight.

You may imagine that all the paupers of the country-
side know the address of this jolly Boniface, and as he
finishes his monologue of self-commendation the five
wanderers enter and put his philanthropy to the test by
appealing for food and shelter gratis. They think
that only one will receive his charity and therefore
as each in turn recites his tale of misery, he endeavours
to increase the chances in his own favour by decrying
the others. So with what they say about each other,
a pretty complete picture is obtained.

Quoth the friar:

> Now hear, O host, my sorry plight.
> I tramp the land from morn till night,
> Though many hamlets I traverse
> There's not a penny in my purse.

Must raise much flax and many pence.
The peasant women drive me hence.
They call me names, a lazy fellow,
An ass, a blockhead, coarse and shallow;
I too should work, they rage and storm,
And talk of Luther and reform,
And every damned peasant stinkard
Calls me a Venus friar and drunkard.
Still some old darlings are not averse
Else I'd be surely treated worse,
These dear old girls will take my side,
With flax and tit-bits me provide.

.   .   .   .   .   .

If I do not collect enough
My prior treats me hard and rough.
He has a temper hot as hell
And puts me oft in prison cell.
I' the convent is both pain and dread,
My food there is but water and bread,
The fastings very much me tease.
I often have to watch and freeze
At high mass, vesper and "complet,"
And never sleep in a down-bed.
Keep silence oft without cessation,
Get hard and frequent castigation.
  My host, you surely see hereby
  Most wretched of them all am I.
  Thou should'st give shelter first to me,

      The host:
Well, I agree to shelter thee.

But to this the horseman, who is the next fellow, does
not agree.   He completes the picture of the friar's

life, by the addition of a few details which the latter
has forgotten to mention.

> The friar leads a life of bliss,
> St. Urban's plague [1] is nightly his.
> He fills his greedy belly well,
> And hoards a surplus in his cell.
> He has no wife or child to keep,
> Hence gets a sound and quiet sleep.
> If he goes out for begging's sake
> A pleasant walk he seems to take.
> On farms he sneaks about all places,
> The servant maids awakes and chases.
> Of cash he steals full half the sum
> To serve him as viaticum.
> He's got more money than we four—
> Obey me, turn him out of door.

The good host, however, does not obey but takes them
all in and thus all's well that ends well.

For many a year this play of the "five miserable
wanderers" was as well known and popular in Germany as is the "Punch and Judy" show in rural England. And though the friar character was always
received with glee and always recognized as a familiar
friend and must have been true to the life of many a
mendicant degenerate follower of St. Francis, yet we
feel that there is lack of that light and shade inherent
in every true delineation. He is not the type, presenting the good and the bad of his order, but a marionette
labelled "friar." As the children cry, "Here comes
Mr. Punch," so we imagine the good German folk

[1] Drunkenness.

used to smile and clap their hands and say, "Here comes the friar."

In the friar literature contemporary with the friar and the Reformation, the characteristic tone is that of contempt, ridicule and detestation. He is held up to scorn and pilloried for his vices, his irreligion, his idleness and his ignorance. So uniform is this testimony, so many the witnesses, and so thoroughly did the people among whom the friar lived and moved and had his being, Protestant and Catholic alike, accept the portraiture as correct that we must also accept it as substantially accurate and believe that the friar had fallen indeed from his high estate and become an incubus upon the community.

The Hans Sachs story is so representative of the mass of German friar fiction of the Reformation era that without giving further examples we may pass at once to Nineteenth Century German fiction dealing with the same subject.

Modern German fiction more seriously attempts to understand the psychology of the friar character. Not so much to tell us what the friar was as to understand why he was so. To recognize the fact that there was a serious side of friary. That within the orders there were some men, doubtless many, good and true; deeply deploring their own estate and lamenting the vices and immorality of their brethren. Such is Brother Martin, the Augustine friar, in Goethe's popular *Goetz von Berlingen.*

Immensely admired for the force and fidelity with which German Fifteenth Century manners and life is depicted, we find here fading knighthood and revolting peasantry, gipsies and merchants, bishops, the Emperor, court and domestic life. That the picture should be true to the times, a friar is necessarily conspicuous among the *dramatis personae*. Friary, the most conspicuous vocation of that era of ferment, and the religious revolution, as the dominating intellectual movement, could not be omitted if the picture was to be at all complete; and so Brother Martin is presented, a friar of the Augustine Order.

Though the fact is not expressly stated, Brother Martin is supposed to be Martin Luther. Not Luther the matured and well-equipped reformer, but that first phase of his life; still within the Church, still struggling between healthy instinct and conscientious scruples. He is of course in sharp contrast with Hans Sachs' friar; not willing to revolt from the discipline to which he is subjected, nor complaining of the difficulties of making a living. He is full of unrest, he chafes against the iron fetters of his environment, he realizes the futility of his vocation, he is filled with questionings, yet does not venture to confess to himself the extent of his doubts, nor to cast from himself the crushing burden. It portrays Luther at the time when his soul was storm-tossed, seeking for rest, striving to solve doubts. Although a friar in name, he was not one at heart, for he was not in sympathy with his order. He was in a condition to analyze and criticize rather than to do, whereas the work of the friar was to only do good.

Goetz, the man of war, drinking to Martin's happy return to his convent is answered by the friar: "I drink that only in compliment to you. A return to my prison must ever be unhappy." And Goetz, perceiving his sorrow, says: "I grieve for him. The sense of his condition preys upon his heart."

Goetz: "Why do you look at me so steadfastly, brother?"

Martin: "I am in love with your armour."

Goetz: "Would you like a suit? . . . Were you less sacred I would give you a suit and we would ride out together."

Martin: "Would to Heaven my shoulders had strength to bear armour and my arm to unhorse an enemy. No vows should keep me from entering an order founded by the Creator Himself."

Martin perceives that this man of war dares to be "conscious of his courage and strength," dares to rejoice in his manhood and in all that invigorates his mind or body. Martin: "When thou has drunk wine thou art double what thou shouldest be! Twice as ingenious, twice as enterprising and twice as active, but we [friars] on the other hand, when we have eaten and drunk are the reverse of what we should be. Our sluggish digestion depresses our mental powers and in the indulgence of luxurious ease, desires are generated which grow too strong for our weakness." Above all Martin loathes idleness, though conscious that his vocation is an idle one. "What is not toilsome in this world?" he replies to Goetz. "But to me nothing is so much so, as to renounce my very nature! Poverty, Chastity, Obedience! three vows, each of which taken singly, seems the most dreadful to humanity—so insupportable are they all; and to spend a life-time under this burthen, or to groan despairingly under the still heavier load of an evil conscience. What are the toils of your life compared to the sorrows of a state, which from a mistaken desire of drawing nearer to the Deity, condemns as crimes the best impulses of our nature, impulses by which we live, grow, and prosper."

Despite its popularity in Germany no critic would rank the *Goetz von Berlingen* of the great Master with his *Faust,* nor would "Brother Martin" be generally ranked as one of the great friars of fiction. Yet he has significance to us, and importance among the friars of German fiction, because in contradiction to the friars of the *Epistolae Obscurorum Virorum,* of Reuchlin, of Erasmus, of Hans Sachs and other writers of the *Fastnachtspiel* (Carnival Plays), to all of whom the friar is an object of satire or scorn, a sorry lazy dog, and a glutton if nothing worse, a subject for ridicule and contempt, a character which either misrepresented friar life or at best only represented its most sordid and unworthy aspect. In Goethe's picture there is no satire, no scorn, no prejudice, no hatred for the institution, no effort to hold it up to contempt by an attack upon some particular vice of the exceptional unworthy friar. For these reasons Goethe's friar is doubtless more impressive. His genius has comprehended the profound psychological characterization of the problem. The signification of "Brother Martin" consists in that he is a personified and pathetic condemnation of the friar orders in general and not simply of their abuse. This man does not desire amelioration of friary. He revolts with mind and soul and every human instinct against its very essence.

Though to Friar Martin has not yet been revealed his God-given work, nor does he yet perceive the end of that path upon which he is entering, yet he is plainly in the Way and at the psychological moment he will hear the words: "The just shall live by faith" and the end of that path is The Reformation.

In thinking of a character by Goethe, instinctively we seek for a comparison or contrast in Schiller. Schiller affords us this contrast and comparison in the friar who bursts upon the stage in Scene VIII of *Wallenstein's Lager*. This Capuchin attracts and rivets our attention from the moment he enters. About him there is no moralizing, no complaining of the decadence of the orders, no disquisitions as to the possibility of having made mistakes. He is distinctly a man of action, anxious for the salvation of the souls of his fellow men, consumed with a desire to do his duty, convinced of his right to interfere everywhere and in everything. He gains our sympathy, even something of our enthusiasm by his energy. Although not a complete study of a friar, what is portrayed is well portrayed.

His entrance is dramatic. It is Sunday, soldiers are dancing and rioting with servant girls and market women, when the friar bursts upon them. He commences with sarcastic words of approval but soon changes to earnest rebuke. As he stands there fearlessly denouncing the wrong doings of those whom he is addressing, we seem to behold an Old Testament prophet. The long sermon which he delivers does not smell of the midnight lamp, the words come burning from the heart of one who is inspired by his message.

Skilfully he presents a picture of the lamentable condition of the country—the dogs of war let loose on the Danube; Bavaria overrun; Regensburg in the enemy's hands—is such, he asks, the time for our army to be lying at its ease in Bohemia, dancing, rioting, profaning the Sabbath, fattening and sinning and neglecting all religious duties. Scathingly does he rebuke the soldiers for their many and flagrant shortcomings, which he enumerates and upon which he moralizes until one can see the dark cheeks of the rough soldiers grow still darker with suppressed rage at the friar who thus fearlessly beards them, and scolds them like a crowd of naughty schoolboys.

All the evils which overwhelm church and state are, he declares, to be directly attributed to the vices of the soldiery. Officers and men alike live like heathens, pillaging and brawling; and sin, he points out, invariably brings its own swift punishment, just as surely as streaming tears are caused by strong onions. His comparisons, illustrations, quips and cranks are happily suited to his audience; to more refined listeners the friar's broad humour might be disturbing, as also his evident fondness for puns, which somewhat weaken the force of the address.

The woman in the Gospel, he says, after diligent search found the piece of silver which was lost; Saul found his father's asses; Joseph his brethren; but any one searching for fear of God, good conduct or sense of shame among the soldiers, even should he light a hundred lanterns to aid him in his search, would have little success.

Vividly he contrasts their life with that which they ought to lead, his censure being levelled at officers and men alike; whereupon one of his hearers interjects with the request that he limit his remarks to the rank and file, and leave the officers alone. His only answer is a yet fiercer denunciation of those at the head of affairs, which leads to more interruptions, and finally to an attempt to do him bodily harm. But two Croats take his part and bid him finish his sermon while they stand off his assailants, so, retiring slowly, and speaking slower and yet more slowly and louder and louder, he ends his message, calling forth admiration as a man and a friar.[1]

[1] It must be borne in mind that in German literature the distinction between friar and monk is not always observed. Both being often classed under "Mönch."

FRÈRE JEAN
DES ENTOMMEURES

FRÈRE JEAN DES ENTOMMEURES

Car vous mesmes dictes quel 'habit ne faict le moyne.

IT is impossible rightly to treat of the character of Friar John des Entommeures without considering the character and environment of his author, since the story, of which this friar is so important a part, contains the author as perhaps does no other book: and Frère Jean des Entommeures is Friar François Rabelais. The mocking, *riant,* yet sometimes serious, sometimes almost holy face of Friar Rabelais peeps from the pages of Gargantua and Pantagruel and cries, "What think you of me?"

Rabelais is the Sphynx of Literature. Approached from any direction he is indefinite and immense, and his book is grotesque, droll, pitiful and wise.

The year of Rabelais's birth set by most of his early biographers is 1483, the same year in which was born that other and more formidable enemy of monasticism, Martin Luther. They were both for a while friars, Luther an Augustinian, Rabelais a Franciscan. Rabelais outlived Luther seven years. It is remarkable that in his great satire he nowhere makes allusion to the Saxon reformer, unless indeed the redoubtable Frère Jean des Entommeurs is Friar Martin Luther, as Motteux conjectures.

Rabelais's father, according to the old biographers, kept the inn of the Lamprey at Chinon in Touraine, and owned a small vineyard, the product of which Rabelais misses no opportunity of celebrating. The vineyard adjoined the Benedictine abbey of Seville, and it was in the abbey school that the great satirist of monachism learned to read and write. From this Benedictine school he passed to the convent school of La Basmette, a Franciscan establishment, and thence to the Franciscan convent of Fontenay-le-Comte in Poitou, where he entered the order of Friars Minor or Franciscans and in due time was ordained priest.

But Rabelais was out of his element among the Franciscan friars and doubtless he was free in expressing his contempt for the rules of the order: at last his brethren condemned him, so the story runs, to life-long seclusion in the convent prison underground—the *In Pace,* as it was called. But he had a friend in the governor of the province, André Tiraqueau, who procured his deliverance.

Of course he did not go back to the convent or to the Franciscan order after his liberation. But he was still held subject to the Franciscan rule and it was not until thirteen years afterward that Pope Clement VII released him from the obligation of the Franciscan vows and permitted him to enter a Benedictine house and to hold a church benefice. But before long quitting the Benedictines, he entered the household of the Bishop of Maillezais as his secretary. At the age of

42 he bade adieu to his generous host and went to Montpellier, to study medicine.

Great was the renown of the Montpellier medical faculty at that time; yet this freshman on his first day in the city, showed an intimate acquaintance with the Materia Medica of the ancients. The story goes that on the day of his arrival in Montpellier there was held a public thesis or disputation upon medical botany, and Rabelais being in the audience attracted notice by his odd behaviour, as he signified by extravagant gestures assent or dissent. At last the dean invited him to take part in the discussion, which he did with such effect that without more ado he was matriculated and six weeks later was admitted to the degree of bachelor of medicine. Here we come upon the sure ground of history, for the register of the university contains at the date September 16, 1530, the entry of his admission to the school, and at the date November 1 of the same year record of his receiving the degree of M. B. Forthwith he opened a course of lectures upon the *Aphorisms* of Hippocrates and on one of the works of Galen, in both cases using the original Greek texts instead of the corrupt Latin versions till then employed in the schools.

But the riant humour of Rabelais was not to be repressed by the solemnities of the professorate. The professor of *materia medica,* no less than the Franciscan friar, must have his play. Rabellais composed a comedy—a *comédie morale* or comedy of manners— "The Man Who Married a Deaf-Mute," and had it acted by eight of his fellow bachelors. Rabelais himself says, "Never did I laugh as at this skit": it had the honour of being imitated by the great Molière in *Le Médecin Malgré Lui.*

Rabelais, despite the high favour which he enjoyed in the University, did not continue in residence, but left Montpellier before the term of study for the doctorate was completed. In 1532 he brought out at Lyons Latin translations of medical treatises by Hippocrates and Galen, and published a corrected edition of the Greek text of the *Aphorisms.* But these publications were profitable neither to the printer nor the editor; so "By Jupiter and Styx," cried the disappointed scholar, "by the name I bear I will repair your losses"; this was addressed to the printer Etienne Dolet: "and I swear to you that Rabelais, known now to few, will soon be in the mouths of all and in the hands of all, so that his fame will be as great abroad as at home." He kept his word, for, as he says in the prologue to *Pantagruel* "of the *Gargantuan Chronicle* as many copies were sold in two months as of the Bible in nine years."

By these books and by many indiscreet and *viva voce* strictures upon the friars and monks, the pope and the Church's doctrines, rites and practices, Rabelais was daily inviting his enemies to an *auto da fé* in which the principal figure would be none other than himself. Yet he had no ambition to be a martyr of free thought and scepticism. He was fortunate in always having powerful friends in the high places of

Church and State, who stayed the arm that wielded
the church's thunderbolts and who scattered the fagots
of the heretic's funeral pyre before the torch was ap-
plied. In May, 1537, he takes the doctor's degree in
the University of Montpellier. In 1550 he was made
curé or parish priest of Meudon in the diocese of Paris
and held that charge till his death April 9, 1553.

The priest who attended the great humourist on his
death bed asked him, before administering the viat-
icum, whether he believed in the Real Presence.
Rabelais answered: "I believe it, I am happy to say;
for methinks I see my God such as He was when He
entered Jerusalem in triumph and borne by an ass."
And when the attendants put on him, toward his last
moment, the Benedictine habit, he must have his little
pleasantry, and so repeated the words of the psalm,
Beati qui moriuntur in domino, blessed they who die
in domino (in the Lord). And he made his last will
in this burlesque form: "I possess nought; the rest I
give to the poor." One of his powerful friends, the
Cardinal du Bellau, or the Cardinal de Chatillon, having sent to ask of his state, "Tell Monseigneur," replied the joker, "in what a merry mood you find me:
I go to seek a great Perhaps. He is at the magpie's
nest, bid him stay there: as for you, you will never be
anything but a fool." Finally, at his last gasp, he exclaimed, "Draw the curtain: the farce is played." The
priest who attended him gave out that Rabelais died
drunk.

These anecdotes are repudiated by some modern biographers of Rabelais. They may not be historically true but they are thoroughly *Rabelaisian:* if not true in fact they are eminently true in spirit.

Rabelais is the satirist of the whole social fabric as it existed in his time—not only of the Church and the religious orders but of the law and the schools. But he is tender of the vices of royalty and the great.

We have already noted that Rabelais never mentions his most eminent contemporary, Martin Luther. They were both of them friars, one an Augustinian, the other a Franciscan. They both put off the friar's habit and ever after denounced the monks and friars as lazy beggars, cumberers of the earth, sots, libertines. There are passages in the *Table Talk* of Luther as daring in their defiance of the proprieties as anything in the writings of Rabelais. Thus Luther and Rabelais were congenial spirits and the mission of both was the overthrow of the Catholic religion. But with this difference between them, that Rabelais sought destruction pure and simple of Catholicism and Christianity, while Luther's purpose was only to do away with what he held to be the accretions of superstition and paganism, that in the ages of ignorance had attached themselves like barnacles to the nucleus of pure religion.

The hero of the *Pantagruel* is the Frère Jean des Entommeures not less than its *eponymus* the Prince Pantagruel. Frère Jean is doubtless in the satire what Rabelais would have wished himself to be in real life and in the warfare against Catholicism and the received institutions of society. In a few places Rabelais makes a sham profession of respect for "Evangelical religion" and the "pure word of God"; but he is at heart an unbeliever in Christianity. Had he believed that the Reformation sought by Luther, Calvin and Zwingli was the religious reform needed, he could not have failed to extend the hand of fellowship to Luther and Zwingli at least, if not to the sour-visaged John Calvin. The Saxon ecclesiast and the apostle of Zurich were iconoclasts like himself and hot-blooded fighters; and their assaults upon the Church's dogmas and practices and on monkery—Luther's especially—were made with the same weapons which he himself employed, broad humour and scintillant wit: indeed, it may be said that the *buffon* humour of Luther, ably supported by Hutten, the writers of the *Epistolae Obscurorum Virorum,* Hans Sachs and a cloud of minor and minim satirists, not forgetting the pencil of Hans Holbein and of Lucas Kranach caused such an explosion of laughter throughout western Germany as to throw down the walls of all the convents. How could "Rabelais laughing in his easy-chair" pretend to be indifferent to the truly Rabelaisian humour of Friar Martin's story of how he could always drive the Devil away whenever the fiend was too importunate in his solicitation: "Satan, I said to him"—what Brother Martin did say has to be expressed in French—"*j'ai fait dans mes chausses.* D'ye hear? Add that to the number of my sins."

Rabelais, like his own Panurge, understood and

spoke German: hence Luther's etymological exegesis of the papal Decretals needed no interpreter to make its meaning plain to Rabelais. Chapter 53 of the fourth book of the Frenchman's great satire is devoted to a humorous mock-laudation of the Decretals, and the author in one place gives a feeble imitation of Luther's play upon the word Decretal, Dekret, Dreck. If it were permitted to cite the whole passage from the Table Talk, even in German, it would be seen how far superior in this line the Saxon reformer with his homely Saxon language is to the French satirist with his effete latinish words: *Prenez moy ung decretiste. Non, non. Ie diz ung decretaliste. O le gros rat, dist Epistemon.*" The *Table Talk* was not published till 1566, thirteen years after Rabelais's death. We have no right to assume that Rabalais had report of the feast of reason and flow of soul that were enjoyed by Friar Martin and his *bons compagnons* at the Black Eagle in Wittenberg nightly from 1525 to 1540. The case is therefore to be regarded simply as a coincidence.

Had Rabelais had as fair a field as Luther with the whole power of the state backing him he would no doubt have assailed Popery and Monkery with the same vigour as the Frère Jean assails the host of King Picrochole: he would have attacked them openly and in plain speech, not in enigmas. Frère Jean des Entommeures is introduced in the 26th Chapter of the first book. The Frère is "young, gallant, fresh, lusty, bold, adventurous," etc., absolutely fearless: "every

inch a monk," says Rabelais, but for all that a despiser
of monkish mummery.

He has broken the bonds that bound him to the
abbey, to the order, to the church. He is a strong man
armed. The miseries and calamities that are everywhere befalling *"Les pauvres diables d' Capussins et
Minimes, les pauvres beat peres Jacobins et Mineures"*
do not trouble him. *"Je ne m'en soucie d'ung bouton,"*
he says.

*"Si tout le monde mesdict d'eulx, Je n'y pretends
nul interest."* In other words, "I have given them up.
I have thrown them over, and trouble my soul with
their vagaries and wickedness no more."

Picrochole's army are ravaging the vineyard of the
brotherhood. While the foragers of the enemy are
gathering the spoil and hacking and trampling the
vines, the holy brethren are intoning prayers, litanies
and psalms in the Church, invoking supernal aid *ad-
versus hostium insidias,* against the wiles and designs
of enemies, and chanting supplications to Heaven to
beat back im-im-pe-e-e-tum-um in-i-i-i-mi-co-o-o-o-o-o-
rum-um (*impetum inimicorum,* as chanted in choir).
Brother John loses patience and interrupts the solem-
nity with "O' God's name, why not sing Pannier's
farewell, vintage is over? Not a vine will be left us
and we shall go dry for years to come." The Prior
orders the disturber of the divine service to be locked
up. "Nay," retorts Brother John, "it is the wine service that is interrupted. And you, yourself, my Lord
Prior, love to drink of the best and so doth every honest

man." Frère Jean, for his part, will not stand by and
see their precious vineyard ravaged. So he seizes the
staff of the processional cross—it is the wood of the
crab-apple tree—and sallies forth to rout the enemy.
These were as numerous as the Philistine host that
Samson confronted. Frère Jean falls upon them, turns
them over like swine, thwacks them athwart and
alongst, till the pitifully disjointed members of their
mangled bodies cover the ground.

In vain they beg for mercy, vain are their appeals
to the saints—Our Lady of Succours, of Loreto, of
Good Tidings; Saint James, Saint This, Saint That:
such appeals are for Frère Jean only stronger reason
for making an end of them. When the battle is nearly
over the Prior and the brethren come forth and begin
shriving the wounded. But some of the little monkitos
rallied to the side of the gallant Frère Jean and offered
their services; who directed them to cut the throats
of all the wounded. Some of the shriven ones made
effort to escape out of the enclosure, but Frère
Jean stood there and felled and quashed them
with blows of his staff, saying: "They have confessed and are penitent; they are absolved; they now
go into Heaven as straight as a sickle or as Crooked
Lane."

Frère Jean here imitates the language of Simon
de Montfort in Languedoc, "Slay, slay, the Lord
will know his own." Rabelais may also have had in
mind the exhortations addressed by Luther. But
Frère Francis Rabelais and Frère Jean des Entom-

meures in this warfare with fictions of the imaginations are at least pleased that the souls of the slain are
saved; the Frère does not pursue the objects of his
vengeance beyond the grave and into the viewless
realm of spirits. Contrariwise Brother Martin: *All
ihr Blut ist auf meinem Halse, aber ich weise es auf
unsern Herrn Gott, der hat mir das zu reden befohlen.
Welche seynd geschlagen worden sind mit Leib und
Seele verlohren und ewig des Teufels:* that is, "All
their blood is upon my head, but I give it over to the
Lord who gave me command to speak this. The slain
are lost, body and soul, and are the Devil's own forevermore." Neither the Friar in Fiction, Jean des
Entommeures, nor his creator, Friar Rabelais, could
harbour so vengeful a sentiment as is cherished by
Luther, the Friar in Fact.

This was Frère Jean's first feat of arms, by which
he won the unbounded admiration of King Grangousier and his son Gargantua. The Frère is made the
guest of honour at a royal banquet. This banquet
affords to Rabelais opportunity to laud in Frère Jean
every trait that least befits the character of a professed
friar, and in particular to glorify wine as the monachal
beverage by pre-eminence. Before the bout commences, "Off with his frock," cries Gymnastes. "But
the rule of my order forbids: let me alone with my
frock," pleads Frère Jean; "I'll drink the better that
it is on; it makes all my body jocund; if I should lay
it aside I shall lose my appetite; but if in this habit
I sit down at table I will drink to thee and thy horse."

The Frère had already supped, but what matter? he will eat never a whit the less. He has "a well-paved stomach as hollow as Saint Benedict's butt at Boulogne and always gaping like a lawyer's brief bag."

Then after proposing a most obscene question, this *frère émancipé* though not *défroqué* extols the goodness of God in giving us this exquisite juice of the grape; and he most profanely couples the vine with that stem of Jesse (radix Jesse) of which Isaiah prophesies (xi, 1): the passage is one of the scripture texts in which the coming of the Messiah is foretold. Such shockingly profane allusions are very frequent in Rabelais: with him and his Frère Jean and his Panurge they are indeed *matter of breviary,* words and phrases from the Church's service-books, very familiar to them in the time before they renounced the vows of the monastical rule; but now forevermore the playthings of their frolic humour.

Frère Jean turns for a moment from praise of wine to tell how blessedly ignorant and unbookish he is. "For my part," says he, "I study not at all. In our abbey we never study, for fear of the mumps. Our late abbot was wont to say that it is a monstrous thing to see a learned monk." "Monastic establishments," remarks Eudemon, one of the company, "are the world's cesspools, and their inmates are hated and abhorred of all." "Ah, but," interposed Grangousier, "they pray to God for us." "Anything but that," replies Gargantua; "with a tingle-tangle of bells they trouble their neighbours; and they mumble out psalms and prayers, understanding not a word: that is mockery of God."

Frère Jean des Entommeures in the war which ensued between Grangousier and Picrochole, plays an heroic part and in reward of his gallantry Gargantua founds an abbey, of which the frère is appointed abbot. The abbey of Thelema is in every respect the precise opposite of the monastic foundations. Monasteries have ever been strongly walled around to insure complete exclusion of the outside world. But the abbey of Thelema has no surrounding wall. There are certain convents or monasteries (e. g., of Carthusians) where if by chance a woman comes in, the ground or floor where she has stood is forthwith swept and cleansed: the rule of Thelema prescribes that should friar or monk ever enter the abbey, there shall be a thorough purification of the premises through which they may have passed. The rule of this abbey is throughout a trenchant satire not only upon monachism but of the whole theory of the religious life as conceived by Catholicism. Thelma is in fact a convent of Epicureans.

The name of the abbey expresses the spirit of its rule—θέλημα, Will, Voluntariness, and more plainly is it expressed by the inscription over the main portal, *Do what thou wilt:* indeed that inscription contains the whole rule of this singular religious order. In Thelema "the sweet convent bell" is never heard: it is mere waste of time to count the hours, and it is folly to be directed by the sound of a bell and not by one's own judgment and discretion. The inmates of

Thelema are of both sexes. The buildings are a hundred times more sumptuous and magnificent than any palace or château in the kingdom and their appointments of the greatest splendour. The provision for elegant amusements leaves nothing to be desired by the Sybarite. It was Heaven on earth. The Thelemites had nothing in the world to do but to enjoy their pleasures.

Friar Francis does not forget to mention among the delights of this Paradise the divine service— the wine service. If any of the gallants or ladies should say, "Let us drink," they would all drink. Or if one said, "Let us play," they all played. Indeed from morn to dewy eve these blest Thelemites were at play.

Such is the scheme which Friar Rabelais proposes as a substitute for the religious orders of Catholicism. Rabelais introduces at the end of his story of the foundation of the abbey what he calls a "prophetical riddle" in verse. "The enigma teacheth," says Gargantua, "the progress and carrying on of divine truth." Frère Jean scouts that interpretation and says the verses contain simply "a description of a set of tennis in dark and obscure terms." Perhaps that is so: but perhaps also it is as Gargantua understands it; and perhaps neither of these is the true meaning: in short, the meaning is what you please. The abbey of Thelema is simply a sty of Epicurus, a confessed *porcus de grege Epicuri*. Horace would disdain such a porcine Paradise. The only God worshipped in the abbey of Thelema is the deity spoken of by St. Paul (Phil. iii, 19) *quorum deus venter est.*

The abbey is a figment of the brain of the emancipated frair—of the friar who has renounced his vows and with them the moral law. Frère Jean and Panurge are of that category. In the Sixteenth Century, on the suppression of the monastic establishments, Europe swarmed with these unfrocked and dishonoured friars. It was a time of revolution in the religious, moral and intellectual world, and in the confusion of all things men lost their bearings.

Limits imposed upon this meditation prohibit even a brief review of the many characters and teeming incidents with which Rabelais has filled the pages of his great work, or even to dwell upon many of the adventures of Frère Jean. There is, however, sufficient here to reveal the opinion of his creator as to the religious orders as he knew them in France. The satire is bitter, the exaggeration is great: but allowing for all this, we are compelled to recognize that the abasement of the friars and monks in France was as low as it has appeared from these other studies to have been in England and Germany and Italy. And Rabelais spoke from intimate knowledge, not only living and dying as a churchman and priest, but as having been friar and monk of two different religious orders.

In the visit of the voyageurs to the *Isle Sonnante* there are nine chapters of fierce satire on all orders of the clergy. In it the priests appear under the guise of birds of passage in many plumages. The comment of the Frère is characteristic.

"Watching these devilish birds," he says, "is rank blasphemy,—compared with this the emptying of bottles and glasses is praising God,— 'Venite apotemus.' " The visit to the *Isle of Cloisters* where the "Fredon Friars" have their monastery, affords opportunity for further attack on all friar orders. Friar John is the favourite character of the author; the sort of man that Rabelais would have wished himself to have been. There is a fine description of a storm at sea, with a contrast of the chief characters. Panurge is in horrible fear, he weeps and bellows, prays to saints, devils, the sea-god and Jupiter to protect him. Pantagruel hides himself, after *"avoir preallablement implore l'ayde du grand Dieu Servateur."* Brave Friar John, however, takes command of the boat and works like a galley-slave in the struggle against the roaring elements. To the howling of Panurge he cries:

"Panurge, you calf, you would do better up here helping us than crying like a cow down there."

"Oh, Brother John, my spiritual father, hear my last confession—I drown, I drown. See me here, my good friend, on my knees. *Confiteor votre saincte benediction?*"

"By thirty legions of devils, get on your feet and help us."

"Do not swear, Brother John. It is a sin. You are damning yourself eternally,—but hear my confession—I drown—I drown." And so on through two chapters until the tempest passes and the ship is saved.

There are other sympathetic scenes in the book, of which Friar John is the hero. The author's opinion of him is expressed in the words of Gargantua,—he is not a bigot, he is not at all close-fisted, he is honest, joyous and good company. He works; he tills the ground; he defends the oppressed; he comforts the afflicted,—and to sum up all, he guards the Abbey Close. Friar John of Entommeures is Frère François Rabelais. And he is something more. He is Jacques Bonhomme, the toiling peasant, the citizen soldier, the labourer, the worker in all fields of endeavour. He is democracy.

Of the book itself, the life work of Rabelais, it should be noted that it is without a plan; it grew from the author's pen. It begins in the middle, and the first book was written last. The author in his prologue to Gargantua says plainly that his book is an allegory, has a meaning hidden under a foolish cloak. That if we open the box we may find within celestial and price-less medicine; that if we break the bone and suck out the marrow we will discover in it a very different taste and much deeper teaching both in regard to religion and political and economic life. What that hidden meaning may be, it is not within the scope of this study to try to discover.

Panurge, whose anxious desire for solution of the question whether he shall marry or not marry brought about the expedition to Lantern Land and the Oracle of the Holy Bottle, makes his first appearance in Book

2, Ch. 9. Panurge makes reply to the questions addressed to him by Pantagruel: "Who are you? Whither go you?" first in German, then successively in Arabic, Italian, English, Biscayan, Dutch, Spanish, Hebrew, Greek, Gascon, Latin and at last in French. Rabelais had a weakness for such display of learning and erudition.

The incident in Rabelais's own life which suggested to him this polyglottic feat is described as follows by Paul Lacroix in his *Notice historique sur la vie et les ouvrages de Fr. Rabelais;* having arrived in Paris on a mission from the University of Montpellier to the Chancellor Duprat, Rabelais was denied an audience. But he was not to be foiled. Disguising himself in an outlandish costume and wearing a pair of spectacles on his Armenian cap (bonnet), he paced up and down in front of the Chancellor's lodging. A crowd quickly gathered round him and their shouting and laughter attracted the Chancellor to the window. He sent a servant out to learn who the man was and what his business. The reply was "I am a calf-skinner," which piqued the Chancellor's curiosity and he sent the servant again to put to the man further questions. But Rabelais answered in Latin. A latinist was then found to interpret the answers: but now Rabelais answered in Greek, then in Italian, etc. At last he came into the Chancellor's presence and delivered in most perfect French an eloquent harangue which so delighted Duprat that he accorded all his requests. The story of this mission has been discredited by some modern commentators, but it is traced back to authorities contemporary with Rabelais.

But whether true or fictitious, the story is fully in accordance with Rabelais's itch for notoriety as a great scholar; and hence in this scene Panurge is none other than Friar Francis Rabelais himself. Whether Panurge throughout his whole career is Rabelais is another question. His "case of conscience" with regard to marriage would fit very well with the situation in which Rabelais was all his life—that of a friar, a priest, vowed to celibacy, but certainly a free thinker in all things and a libertine if we can judge him by his writings. To repudiate his vows would be to invite the extreme penalties of the law, civil and ecclesiastical: and we know that Rabelais had no hankering after martyrdom. To wed or not to wed was a serious question for Rabelais: no doubt the wavering inclinations of Panurge had their origin in the heart of Rabelais. In the end Panurge is still a bachelor, as are Frère Jean and Friar Rabelais.

THE FRIARS OF
DANTE, BOCCACCIO
AND MACHIAVELLI

THE FRIARS OF DANTE, BOCCACCIO AND
MACHIAVELLI

IN the Vision of Dante the glorified spirits of the great Divines and Fathers of the Church were shown to him in the Fourth Heaven, the heaven of the Sun. With Beatrice as his conductress he ascends from Purgatorio to each of the ten spheres or heavens successively—the heaven of the Moon, Mercury, Venus, the Sun, Mars, Jupiter, the Fixed Stars, the Primum Mobile or Crystalline Vault, and the Empyrean Sphere, conceived to be fixed and immovable, the eternal realm of the Divine Presence.

In each sphere is shown to him a different order of glorified spirits, but he leaves us distinctly to understand that the local separation of the orders was figurative and emblematic, not representative; the spirits were visualized to him in space, in condescension to the feebleness of mortal man's intellectual power, which thus only could conceive an idea of the order, grandeur and splendour of the Court of Heaven. The choirs of the glorified, like the stars, differ each from each in glory, and this difference is shown to Dante by local distribution, sphere above sphere: the spirits shown to him in the heaven of the Moon are as truly, really and eternally denizens of the highest sphere of all, the empyrean, as is the highest seraph, or even the Virgin herself:

> Of Seraphim he who is most enskied,
> Moses or Samuel, and either John,
> Choose which thou wilt, and even Mary's self,
> Have not in any other heaven their seats,
> Than have those spirits which so late thou sawest,
> Nor more nor fewer years exist; but all
> Make the first circle [Empyrean] beauteous, diversely
> Partaking of sweet life, as more or less
> Afflation of eternal bliss pervades them.
> Here were they shown thee, not that fate assigns
> This for their sphere, but for a sign to thee
> Of that celestial farthest from the height.
> Thus needs, that ye may understand, we speak,
> Since from things sensible alone ye learn
> That which, digested rightly, after turns
> To intellectual. For no other cause
> The Scripture, condescending graciously
> To your perception, hands and feet to God
> Attributes, nor so means. (IV. 28 sqq.)

Having entered this Fourth Heaven, so rapt in ecstasy is the Poet,

> That in oblivion Beatrice was eclipsed.

Presently luminous figures appear—lights he calls them simply, not venturing to attribute to the glorified spirits of the Church's great Teachers any semblance of bodily form or shape. He has vision of

> a bright band, in liveliness
> Surpassing, who themselves did make a crown
> And us their centre: yet more sweet in voice
> Than, in their visage, beaming.

They are like rich jewels set and shining in a crown,

> So dear and beautiful, they cannot brook
> Transporting from that realm;

like a halo round the moon they circle Dante and his conductress, with song and dance, or with measured and agile step. But vain were the attempt to describe it in the language of mortal man.

Dante wrote in an age of faith when men were on more intimate terms with the blest in Heaven than those of our day. In Dante's time the choirs of the blest, the world of Angels and Spirits Glorified, were realities as indubitable as the starry firmament itself. In those middle ages people could without a thought or suspicion of profanity, take liberties, so to speak, with God the Father of all: for example in the Miracle Plays without giving offence to religious minds.

And now commences the action of Canto X of the Paradiso. The tuneful band having come to a pause, a voice issues from one of the "lights," which thus becomes the mouthpiece of the whole glorious company. And who is the intelligence that is singled out from the entire host of the Fourth Heaven, from the innumerable multitude of divines, apologists, fathers, doctors of the Church, to welcome the visitants and to resolve his questions? A friar, a simple friar, who never rose in churchly rank above the order of the presbyterate: whose whole life was spent in a narrow conventual cell, whence he never went forth, except at duty's call, when summoned to give counsel to the Church's rulers. It was Thomas of Aquino, the Angel of the Schools. Does it not seem a strange error of perspective for Dante that the forms of more celebrated if not greater Divines are quite shut out? It was at least an unavoidable error. Thomas, in the year 1300, imagined date of the Vision of Dante, had been for seventy-five years a denizen of Heaven, and his authority in the schools was supreme: in systematic theology he had no peer either among the ancients or the mediævals. His *Sum of Theology* was in those days and is still, in the words of Milman, "the authentic, authoritative, acknowledged code of Latin theology."

Dante made no mistake when he chose the Friar Thomas Aquinas to be spokesman of the great Fourth Heaven. But aside from the choice of Aquinas for spokesman there is an almost ludicrous error of perspective in Dante's choice of the eleven other "lights" forming the circle surrounding the Poet and his conductress. One scans the circle in vain for an Augustine, greatest of the Latin Fathers; a Chrysostom, most famous of the Greek Fathers (but we shall find him in Canto XII in another circle of Divines); an Athanasius, champion of the orthodox faith against Arius; a Basil, leader in the same great contest; Basil's brother, Gregory of Nyssa, "Father of Fathers"; a Gregory Nazianzen, surnamed "Theologus"; a Cyril, whether of Jerusalem or of Alexandria; a Justin, the Apologist; a Jerome, Translator of the Scriptures; a

Bernard, the Church's great luminary of the Twelfth Century.

But Dante, instead of these great Doctors, chooses as representatives of the Teaching Church in this first duodenal circle two Dominican Friars, viz.: Thomas Aquinas and Albertus Magnus, belonging to his own century; and the subject of Thomas's discourse is mainly the eminent services rendered to the church by another Friar, St. Francis of Assisi. And the case will be found little different when we are admitted to contemplate the second circle: for there, too, the spokesman will be a Friar, St. Bonaventura and the theme of his discourse will be eulogy of the Friar, St. Dominic.

These two saintly men, having gathered around them a few followers of like mind with themselves, sought and obtained from Rome authority to enroll in their companies everywhere postulants who should manifest a will to serve God and the Church under the severe rules of the founders. But as the eulogists of the two institutes, Thomas and Bonaventura, admit and lament, the Friars of both orders all too soon departed from the ways prescribed by their saintly founders, becoming themselves as corrupt as had been the secular and regular clergy whose vices they were under vow to rebuke by their own blameless lives.

It is time to return to the Fourth Heaven of Dante's Vision and to listen to the discourse of Aquinas as he lauds the virtues of the Founder of the Franciscan order of Friars.

Now what are the means appointed in the councils of Heaven to keep the Church in the right way? The institution of the two great orders of Begging Friars —Franciscans and Dominicans! Perhaps Dante thought of that saying, "God chose the foolish things of the world that he might put to shame them that are wise; and God chose the weak things of the world that he might put to shame the things that are strong; and the base things of the world and the things that are despised did God choose, and the things that are not that he might bring to nought the things that are: that no flesh should glory before God." Dante sees in the history of the Church in his day, as its most noteworthy phenomenon, the apparition upon the world's stage of the two friars, Francis and Dominic. These two did God, according to him, ordain

> who should on either hand
> In chief escort her; one, seraphic all
> In fervency; for wisdom upon earth
> The other, splendour of cherubic light.

Higher encomium than that it was impossible in that age to pronounce.

Those two simple Friars, those two Beggars, such by solemn vow and religious profession, were to escort the church *in chief.* Of them one, Francis, was *seraphical,* afire with love of God; the other, Dominic, shone with the "splendour of cherubic light," which in the language of mystics means the inner light of divine faith. The life of St. Francis was to be a romance of love, at once divinely tender and divinely austere. His elect Bride was

> A dame to whom none openeth pleasure's gate
> More than to death.

This is the Lady Poverty, to whom Francis was espoused by solemn vows before the spiritual court and in his father's presence; and thereafter he loved this Lady more devoutly as the days passed—her and her train, the lepers, the outcasts of society, the moral and physical wrecks of humanity. It was at the age of about twenty-five years that Francis, after passing through a severe illness, resolved to give up worldly vanities and delights, and to walk in Christ's footsteps, to follow the example of Him, who "went about doing good." In the letter and in the spirit he fulfilled the injunction of Christ when He sent His apostles forth, "Get you no gold nor silver nor brass in your purses; no wallet for your journey; neither two coats nor shoes nor staff." So he went on his errands of mercy, clad in coarsest and poorest attire, moneyless, provisionless, unshod, girt with a cord, like shepherds in his country. To lepers and those stricken with the plague he ministered with the tenderest affection of divine charity, performing for them with joy the most distasteful services. Dante celebrates high above all the virtues of Francis, his devotion to the Lady Poverty, long desolate after the departure of Christ, her first lover:

> She, bereaved
> Of her first husband, slighted and obscure,
> Thousand and hundred years and more, remain'd
> Without a single suitor, till he came.

The sanction of the Church was necessary to give the brotherhood legitimate standing before the people, so he visited Rome and there

> royally
> His hard intention he to Innocent
> Set forth; and from him first received the seal
> On his religion.

Royally set forth, in beggar's garb attired! Truly so, for here was, to use the words of Forsyth, "a genuine hero, original, independent, magnanimous, incorruptible"; in whatever guise, or disguise, such a man could not fail to be recognized for what he was in the soul of him by so great-hearted a pontiff and statesman as Innocent Third. So the pope approved the design of Francis to found a religious order whose mission, as defined in its Constitution, was "to promote peace and patience, tend the wounded, relieve the distressed, reclaim the erring." Dante singles out from among the exploits of this hero of divine charity, for special commemoration, the saint's voyage to Egypt, there to preach to the Soldan the gospel of Christ. Francis

> through thirst for martyrdom, stood up
> In the proud Soldan's presence, and there preached
> Christ and his followers; but found the race
> Unripen'd for conversion.

He preached Poverty to the Soldan: small cause for
wonder that he found the Soldan a listless hearer of
his word.

Dante's life was full of bitter experiences; his temper was soured, and while he could admire and duly
value the saint's heroic contempt for worldly riches
and distinctions, he was perhaps less in sympathy with
him in his artless affection for all of God's creatures.
Of this trait of St. Francis's character Principal
Tulloch well says: "His love for animals of all kinds
was one of his most remarkable and winning features.
Of the birds in the woods, the sheep in the fields, the
ass on which he rode, the bees, the hares, the rabbits,
he always spoke as his brothers and sisters. When
the birds sang, he said, 'Our sisters, the birds, are
praising God.' The very wolves were tamed by him,
and came like lambs and crouched at his feet."

Two years before the close of his earthly labours,
St. Francis received, according to the records of contemporary annalists, the stigmata or marks of the
five wounds of Jesus Christ upon his hands and feet
and side:

'Twixt Arno and the Tiber, on the hard rock, he from Christ
Took the last signet, which his limbs two years did carry.

It will not be superfluous to quote here Alban Butler's description of the stigmatization of the saint of
Assisi. Butler writes in his *Lives of the Saints:* "The
marks of nails began to appear on his hands and
feet, resembling those he had seen in the vision of

the man crucified. His hands and feet seemed bored through in the middle with four wounds, and these holes appeared to be pierced with nails of hard flesh: the heads were round and black, and were seen in the palms of his hands, and in his feet in the upper part of the instep. The points were long, and appeared beyond the skin on the other side, and were turned back as if they had been clenched with a hammer. There was also in his right side a red wound, as if made by the piercing of a lance; and this often threw out blood, which stained the tunic and drawers of the saint" (*Apud* Longfellow, Par. 246).

The closing scene of the saint's life needed no poetic embellishment, and it is described with fitting simplicity by Dante in the person of Aquinas:

> Then, the season come that he,
> Who to such good had destined him, was pleased
> To advance him to the meed which he had earn'd
> By his self-humbling; to his brotherhood
> As their just heritage, he gave in charge
> His dearest Lady; and enjoined their love
> And faith to her; and, from her bosom, will'd
> His goodly spirit should move forth, returning
> To its appointed kingdom; nor would have
> His body laid upon another bier.

The last words of St. Francis were: "Welcome, Sister Death."

The date of Dante's Vision is the year 1300; Francis had died some seventy years before: how is it with the disciples of Francis in this year 1300? Does his spirit still live in his myriads of disciples; or have they grown lax in their faith, and become themselves worldly and corrupt? Dante deftly parries the question for the moment, but he will answer it with all candour later. It were an ungracious thing to make of the Light of the Dominican Schools a censurer of a sister order, and rival of the Order of St. Dominic. Let that disagreeable duty be discharged by a disciple of St. Francis, Bonaventura. So instead of noting the vices of the sons of St. Francis, Aquinas laments the shortcomings of his own brethren the Dominicans.

The two orders received the Papal sanction about the same date. They constituted as it were the right and left wings of the Church's auxiliary militia; and so alike were their purposes, that Dominic earnestly desired a combination of the two brotherhoods in one body, and more than once made overtures for union. The special mission of the Dominicans was that of preaching and teaching; while that of the Franciscans was primarily that of ministering to the bodily ills of the poor, though spiritual solacement was their function in an almost equal degree.

The discourse of Aquinas prompts Bonaventura to tell of the other guide, the other guide being St. Dominic; the two orders are one in soul, one in aim:

> Where one is
> The other worthily should also be;
> That as their warfare was alike, alike
> Should be their glory.

Cary,[1] in a note upon this passage, quotes Machiavelli as attributing to Francis and Dominic the revival of Christianity in their age: "If our religion had not been drawn back to its principle by St. Francis and St. Dominic, it would be entirely extinguished." Machiavelli, as Cary remarks, was no great friend to the Church, and Dante was a declared enemy of the popes in their secular ambitions: but they both give to the friars the credit of having upheld the banner of the Cross in an evil time.   These new orders were, says Bonaventura, commissioned by Christ Himself to reform Christendom:

> As thou heard'st,
> Two champions to the succour of his spouse
> He sent, who by their deeds and words might join
> Again his scatter'd people.

Using a word (minion) which like many another good word has fallen into discredit through vulgar use, he styles Dominic

> The loving minion of the Christian faith,
> The hallow'd wrestler, gentle to his own,
> And to his enemies terrible.

This last line for us moderns suggests the Inquisition.   Principal Tulloch quotes the following as a passage in an address made by Dominic to the Albigeois of Provence: "For many years have I spoken to you with tenderness, with prayers and tears; but according to the proverb of my country, where the

---

[1] Whose translation is used, except when otherwise stated.

benediction has no effect, the rod may have much. Behold now we rouse up against you princes and prelates, nations and kingdoms, and many shall preach by the sword." On the other hand, St. Francis is credited with the saying: "If I cannot convert men by preaching, it is not for me to act the executioner, like the secular power."

Bonaventura recalls signs and wonders alleged to have attended Dominic from before his birth:

> So replete
> His soul with lively virtue, that when first
> Created, even in the mother's womb,
> It prophesied.

His very name was God-given: his godmother

> in her sleep
> Beheld the wondrous fruit, that was from him
> And from his heirs to issue. And that such
> He might be construed, as indeed he was,
> She was inspired to name him of his owner,
> Whose he was wholly; and so called him Dominic;
> (*Dominicus,* belonging to *Dominus,* the Lord)

> And I speak of him as the labourer,
> Whom Christ in his own garden chose to be
> His helpmate. Messenger he seem'd, and friend
> Fast-knit to Christ; and the first love he showed,
> Was after the first counsel that Christ gave—

that first counsel being that of total renunciation of worldly goods: "If thou wilt be perfect, go sell that thou hast," etc. Herein he is in accord with Francis: like Francis, Dominic sold his clothes to feed the poor:

he once even offered to sell himself to the Moors to
ransom the brother of a poor woman who sought his
aid. It is the part of Bonaventura, in this discourse,
to praise the Father of the Preaching Friars and to
reserve his censure for the brethren of his own order,
the Cordeliers. But Bonaventura obliquely scores the
degenerate sons of Dominic by lauding the Founder
of their order for that, unlike certain others, and
among them perhaps here and there a Dominican,

>   he besought
> No dispensation for commuted wrong,
> Nor the first vacant fortune [1]
>   nor the tenths
> That to God's paupers rightly appertain,
> But, 'gainst an erring and degenerate world,
> License to fight.

It is a very spirited account of the battles of Dominic for the faith that Dante now gives:

> Forth on his great apostleship he fared,
> Like torrent bursting from a lofty vein;
> And, dashing 'gainst the stocks of heresy,
> Smote fiercest, where resistance was most stout.

Bonaventura turns now to his own order, upon
which his judgment is as unsparing as the judgment
of Aquinas on his Dominican brethren. He likens
the founders of the two orders to the two wheels of a
chariot, a war chariot, one of the wheels being
Dominic, the other Francis. Now if the Dominican
wheel is such as I have shown it to be, says Bonaven-

[1] Church benefice.

tura; and if in the chariot sustained by those two the
Holy Church

> rode triumphant through the civil broil;
> Thou canst not doubt its fellow's excellence,
>   Which Thomas, ere my coming, hath declared
> So courteously unto thee.

Oh, if the two wheels had been kept in the track
traced by the Founders! Alas for the Franciscan
wheel:

> The track,
> Which its smooth felloes made, is now deserted.

The Franciscan family that were wont to follow
their founder's steps, now

> Turn backward, and invert their steps; ere long
> To rue the gathering-in of their ill crop,
> When the rejected tares in vain shall ask
> Admittance to the barn—

and we know what follows denial of admittance to
the barn: "I will say to the reapers, Gather up the
tares and bind them in bundles to burn them." The
order is broken up into warring factions: only a few
true Cordeliers are found anywhere. There is little
to cheer the loyal son of Francis as he considers the
state of his order; though

> I question not
> But he, who search'd our volume, leaf by leaf,
> Might still find page with this inscription on't,
> "I am as I was wont."

In Heaven, too, with Bonaventura are many of the
first brethren: among the twelve in the second wreath
of glorified spirits are two friars of the order besides
himself: of the other nine in this company, two, at
least, are greater figures in the history of the Church
than any of St. Thomas's company except himself.
With Bonaventura are Chrysostom, the greatest light
of the Greek Church, and Anselm, an eminent theologian, archbishop of Canterbury in the Eleventh Century. The rest are a miscellaneous lot, whose names
signify nothing for the world of to-day.

In Canto XIII St. Thomas resumes his discourse
to Dante, and explains certain points of the divine
science of Theology: but without a pretty voluminous
commentary his teaching would be quite unintelligible to any one unacquainted with scholastic divinity.
What place and rank the friar holds in the *Paradiso*
we have seen; and from the discourse of the Angel of
the Schools and of the Seraphic Doctor, we can infer
that the friars must have a large representation in
the other Kingdoms: indeed it had been no surprise
had Dante seen a vast circle of Hell paved with the
shorn pates of Cordeliers and Dominicans, White
Friars and Augustines—of those faithless ones, who
vowed to walk in the steps of the Founders and to live
by their holy Rule.

Yet Dante descried in Purgatory none of the liveries
of the mendicant orders; and in Hell, though he rec-
ognizes a few friars so called, not one of these is identified by him, or is identifiable, as of the family of

Dominic or Francis, or of the Carmelite or of the Augustinian rule. Four friars or *frate* in all are found among the thronging multitudes in the infernal kingdom: and indeed so many of the poet's personal enemies and persecutors, or of the enemies of his party in Church and State, arrested his attention as he journeyed from circle to circle, gulf to gulf, that he must needs pass unnoticed mere rebels against monastic rule and contemners of religious vows.

Among the *frate* encountered by him in the dismal realm were two of the *Frati Gaudenti* or Jovial Friars, as they were commonly named, but originally styled Knights of Saint Mary; and one of these two was the very founder of this Order, Loderingo di Liandolo. The pair were of opposite politics, Loderingo of the Guelf party, his companion Catalano di Malavolti of the Ghibelline. In a crisis of the State of Florence they were chosen to exercise conjointly the supreme authority of the Podestà; it being supposed that as they were of opposite political parties they would serve each as a check upon the other. But, like true politicians, they forgot partisanship and worked with an eye single to their joint interest in the profits of office-holding: to their peculation and hypocrisy are they indebted for the infernal honours with which Dante crowns them. In Hell their place is among the Hypocrites, "the painted people," and like their fellows there, they wear leaden cloaks gilded outwardly.

To Dante's question who they are and why thus laden, Catalano makes answer:

> Frate gaudenti were we, and Bolognese,
> I Catalano and he Loderingo
> Named, and together taken by thy city,
> For maintenance of its peace; and we were such
> That still it is apparent round Gardingo.

Another member of the same merry order is Friar Alberigo, who figures in the Ninth Circle of Inferno among the Traitors: He invited to supper certain hostile fellow-citizens and when they were at board, had them all assassinated: at the pretended date of Dante's Vision, the year 1300, this Fra Alberigo was still living: he

> for his deeds
> In soul already in Cocytus bathes,
> And still in body seems to be alive.

Dante, while surveying that same Ninth Gulf, is entrusted by Mahomet, chief among the founders of false religions and contrivers of schisms, with a message to Fra Dolcino, still on earth and battling with the powers of Church and State in northern Italy. Fra Dolcino, who in early life seems to have been a Franciscan friar, was, about the time of the vision of Dante, at the head of a very zealous sect of religious reformers calling themselves Apostolic Brethren, and in 1305, five years after the pretended date of the Vision, was compelled by persecution to seek refuge with a multitude of his disciples in the mountains of Piedmont. There, hemmed in by an army of crusaders, he withstood for two years the assaults of his enemies, but at last was compelled by famine and

stress of wintry storms to surrender with all his host.
The message sent by Mahomet to Fra Dolcino bade
him

> to arm him,
> If soon he wish not here to follow me,
> So with provisions that no stress of snow
> May give the victory to the Novarese.

The prophecy of capture,—a safe prophecy of the
kind that are made after the event,—was of course
fulfilled, and in June, 1307, Fra Dolcino and his fair
and heroic companion, Margherita of Trent, were
tortured and burnt alive at Vercelli.

There remains one friar more of those who figure
in the vision of the Inferno, Fra Gomita, the faithless
lieutenant of "the gentle judge Nino de 'Visconti."
Of what religious order this Gomita was a member
does not appear: in Hell he has a place in the lake
of burning pitch of the Eighth Circle, among the
Barratores, those who in the administration of justice
take bribes. Gallure, in Sardinia, was the theatre of
Gomita's iniquities, as appears from the account of
the captive of the ten devils:

> Fu frate Gomita,
> Quel di Gallura, vasel d'ogni froda,
> Ch'ebbe i nimica di suo donno in mano,
> E fe si lor che ciascum se ne loda.
> Denai si tolse, e lasciolli di piano,
> Si com'ei dice. E negli altri uffici anche
> Barattier fu non picciol ma sovrano.

His earthly life was ended on the gallows.

Because Dante Alighieri is the supreme poet of Italy, and his *Divina Commedia* a literary monument for all the ages, we have considered at some length the friars mentioned in that great poem. It must, however, be remembered that Dante never undertook to create a friar character, as such, as did Manzoni and Boccaccio among Italian writers, Rabelais among the French, or Chaucer among the English, and as are some of the other fictional friars considered in these pages. Dante attempts no analysis of the friar character. You cannot select any friar from the pages of the *Commedia,* and say, "there is the typical friar, according to Dante." For Dante the friar was as much a part of the established order of every day life as were shoemakers; St. Francis, St. Dominic, St. Bonaventura, St. Thomas Aquinas, are in Heaven because they were holy men, not because they happened to be friars: Loderingo and Catalano, Alberigo and Dolcino are in Hell not because they were friars, but because they were traitors, simoniacs, evil rulers. That the individual happened to be a friar is to Dante an accidental circumstance; no part of the Inferno is given over to the punishment of the friar as such. It is, however, undoubtedly true that Dante was keenly aware of the degeneracy of the friar-orders in his time, and the first formal attacks which were directed against the poet's orthodoxy seem to have been based upon his attitude toward the mendicants and other religious orders.

Among the many hundreds of Italian *novelle* that
were written during the Fourteenth, Fifteenth and
Sixteenth centuries, no character is more common than
that of the friar. Boccaccio, Sacchetti, Bandello and
all the other *novellièri* find him a friend indeed when
in search for a stock character for their tales. And
when you have read one you have the psychology of
them all. The same glib tongue, the same shameless
front, the same impudent mendacity, lazy beggars,
lovers of women and lovers of gold; Chaucer may well
have borrowed his friars from the Italian *novelle,* if
he had not taken them from the life of his own England as he saw it.

Boccaccio's story of Fra Cippola (Friar Onion) may
be accepted as a fair representative of these friars.
He suggests the friars of the *Canterbury Tales* and is
the counterpart of the Pardonere. He is a little red-
haired man of jolly countenance, and "as artful a
knave as any in the world." Like all successful prac-
ticers of his branch of knavery, he had the trick of
plausible speech and the grand manner of oratory.
Visiting the town of Certaldo in the Florentine ter-
ritory, in the course of questing throughout his begging
district he entered the church on a Sunday morning
and from the pulpit appealed to the people for the customary alms of corn and provisions for *i poveri frati,*
the poor friars. To stimulate them to liberality, he
announced that at the hour of nones, or the third hour
of the afternoon, he would as a most special favour exhibit to them a feather dropped from the wing of the

angel Gabriel, on the occasion of his visitation to the Virgin Mary.

While his reverence the Friar was dining at his inn, two merry blades got access to his chamber and abstracted the feather, and substituted for it lumps of charcoal, then replaced the casket in the friar's wallet. Fra Cippola appears in the pulpit, and has two lighted candles placed beside the precious relic, and then invoking the intercession of the great archangel, lifts the lid of the casket. What he saw gave him a momentary shock, but without the least show of embarrassment he exclaims, "O God, praised for ever be thy power and might," and shutting the casket he proceeds to tell of his travels to earth's uttermost bounds, east and west, north and south, visiting the kingdom of Truffia and Buffia, and India Pastinaca, where he saw serpents fly. He tells of the holy relics shown him by the patriarch at Jerusalem,—a finger of the Holy Ghost, etc. The patriarch made him a present of the feather of the angel Gabriel, which he proposed to show them to-day. Instead he has decided to show them some coals from the fire over which St. Laurence was grilled, since to-day is the festival of St. Laurence, and God desires to kindle your devotion to that martyr. So let all kneel with reverence, while the holy coals are exposed to view.

Without doubt the most important comedy written in Italy in the Sixteenth Century is the *Mandragola* of Niccolo Machiavelli, and equally without doubt no

Italian previous to Machiavelli produced so effectual
a picture of the false and evil clergy, and has penetrated so deeply into a human soul as did he in the
character of Fra Timoteo. His soul is a livid and stagnant pool.

The *Mandragola* of Niccolo Machiavelli drew its
title and story from two popular legends, the first regarding the virtues of a medicinal herb, which was
called mandragola or mandragora, and the second regarding a poisoned or poisoning maiden. This latter
legend reputed that a certain maiden had been nourished from her first years on the poisons of venomous
serpents, and that, having grown up, she could poison
and kill men in various ways, especially in the act of
sexual union. As for the mandragola, for centuries
there had been current the most fantastic stories.

One of its supposed powers was that of rendering
women pregnant.

Savonarola, who belongs to the Fifteenth Century,
in his *Practicade aegritudinibus a capite usque ad
pedes* published at Venice in 1486, numbered the
mandragola among the means most apt to produce
fecundity.

From these two popular superstitions, Machiavelli
constructed his play, which centres round a presumptuous fool, Nicia, convinced of his own astuteness, but
so credulous as to believe the most absurd tales, provided they are told with big words. He wants to have
children, and the doctors have advised him to take
madonna Lucrezia to the baths.

From the first entry upon the scene messer Nicia

appears as one of the most comical characters known to the theatre. When Callimaco, having heard his vain desire, says that, before deciding which is the most convenient bathing station, he would have to know the true reason of the woman's sterility "because there can be various reasons. *Nam cause sterilitatis sunt aut in semine, aut in matrice, aut in instrumentis seminariis, aut in verga, aut in causa extrinsecus;"* in his enthusiasm for the learned doctor he cries: "This is the most worthy man that can be found" (Act II, sc. 2). Callimaco promises that he will give Lucrezia a potion of mandragola to drink; he will introduce into her bed a youth invited in from the street so that he may absorb the poison of that potion and render it possible for Nicia subsequently to approach the woman without dying of it; he will even assist in the capture of the unknown youth who is destined to a brief pleasure and a certain death. When to Nicia's objections—"I do not want to make my wife a whore," Callimaco answers, "What say you, doctor? I do not hold you for as wise as I believed. What! You are doubtful of doing that which the king of France has done, and so many *signori*," he is immediately persuaded (Act II, sc. 6). If messer Nicia is a caricature, Callimaco, madonna Lucrezia and Fra Timoteo are reality itself.

Callimaco is a true lover, who desires ardently, acts resolutely. He has heard of the marvellous beauty of Lucrezia Calfucci; he has come to Florence; he has found the woman more beautiful than reported; he loves her violently; at any cost he will have her. The

violence of his passion is expressed when he declares
to Ligurio—"I know that thou tell'st the truth. But
what am I to do? What part am I to play? Where
am I to turn? I must attempt something, be it great,
be it perilous, be it harmful, be it infamous: better to
die than live thus" (Act I, sc. 3).

Sostrata, a woman of few scruples, tells Lucrezia
that it is impossible that she, her mother, should counsel her "to a thing that was not right," while Fra Timoteo himself assures her that there is no "burden of
conscience" in what it is proposed for her to do.

Fra Timoteo weaves around her his subtle argu-
ments, and says that he has "been over his books more
than two hours studying this matter," and declares
"that where there is a certain good and an uncertain
evil, one should never let go that good for fear of
that evil," and demonstrates that there is here the
certain good of winning "a soul for messer Domeni-
dio" (for the Lord God) and an uncertain evil, which
is the possible but not inevitable death of the young
man put to lie with her, and assures her that there is
no sin where the will does not concur "because the will
is that which sins, not the body," and he sustains that
"the end has to be looked to in all things," and that
when that is good the means employed to attain it are
good. The pure and virtuous Lucrezia debates and
resists; and, in the end, conquered by the persuasions
of the friar and the exhortations of her mother Sostrata, she resigns herself to her destiny with a gloomy
repugnance. "I am content; but I believe I shall never

be alive to-morrow morning. . . . God help me and Our Lody, that ill befall me not."

It is a chaste and noble figure of a woman that Machiavelli has vigorously shaped with a few touches. Afterwards, when it is an accomplished fact, the power of love accomplishes a transformation in her conscience. She says to Callimaco: "Since thy cunning and the foolishness of my husband, the simplicity of my mother and the roguery of my confessor have led me to do that which of myself I would never have done, I am not able now to refuse that which Heaven wishes that I accept. Hence I take thee for lord, master and guide. Thou my father, thou my defender, and I will that thou be my every good; and that which my husband has willed for one evening, I will that he shall have always." All those whom she held dearest conspired to make her fall into sin: she now knows the stupidity and iniquity of men and has experienced undreamed felicity. Should she renounce love, beauty, youth, joy, should she keep faith with her husband, bear respect to her mother, show herself reverent to the friar?

Fra Timoteo is the chief corrupter of madonna Lucrezia. As we have said, his soul is a livid and stagnant pool. And when he is offered a rich bribe, he lends himself easily to crime.

No Italian writer previous to Machiavelli, neither Dante nor Boccaccio, had produced so effectual a picture of the false and evil clergy and had cast so acute a glance into the interior of their conscience.

TWO FICTIONAL
FRIARS

TWO FICTIONAL FRIARS

FRIAR LAURENCE, FRA CRISTOFERO

FRIARS have disappeared from the stage of life. Their day has passed.

In Italy the *frate* are still to be seen, lurking in the background. In by-streets their faces sometimes appear emerging from their cowls; and as they cross the gay avenues of the cities their sandaled feet are in danger from prancing horses and swift automobiles. Unobserved they pass, neither loved nor hated by the hurrying crowd. No one could now describe them as Manzoni did in the first pages of *I Promesi Sposi*.

In Manzoni's day no station was too high, none too lowly for a Capuchin. He served the most miserable wretches, and was served by the most powerful lords. With fearless yet humble mien he crossed the threshold of a palace; yet the dweller in the sordid hovel was his brother. In the same house he might be the amusement of the menials, and yet the counsellor and guide of the master. He took alms from all, and gave to all who came to his convent door; a Capuchin was prepared for all things.

Even more thoroughly than from the stage of real life, have the friars been evicted from that world of romance, in which, for centuries, they played so important a part.

This *Deus ex machina* of ancient plots, this solver of puzzling intrigues, intermediary in bringing about the marriage of desponding lovers, and the penitence of condemned malefactors, is dead and gone in his turn. Be the *Requiescat in pace* which he so often pronounced over the remains of poor humanity the inscription on his own tomb.   His place is filled in fiction as in real life.   In the modern story, or play, a sober professor, a learned physician, appears to speak the word or to produce the paper that turns the tide of events.

Since the friar is a figure of the past, and not likely to rise from his sepulchre, it will be interesting to catch one of the vanishing aspects of this shadow of eld, as it was apprehended by a great and sympathetic writer of modern Italy.

It were an easy task but useless to seek among French *fabliaux* and Italian *novelle* for the original type of the friar of fiction, for the characteristic of all those figures is their incompleteness.   In them the friar is never a whole personality.   Even as portrayed by the masters, he remains an unfinished figure, a silhouette, an outline seen from one side, a *profil perdu*.   The *fabliaux* show us a burlesque manikin, a butt of broad humour and obscene jests; and the *novellatori* accept this model, never troubling their minds to put a real man under the cowl of their jolly masks.

Chaucer, Boccaccio and Rabelais have given us

masterful portraits of friars; but if we compare these
with the same authors' portraitures of other characters, we must acknowledge that even these men of
might ofttimes failed to impart lifelikeness to their
hooded offspring.

Very different is Shakspeare's Friar Laurence; and
Manzoni's Fra Cristofero is perhaps one of the best
examples of the friar that is to be found in literature.

The two figures have traits in common; both are
Italian; both are connected with a love affair; but
there the similarity ends.   And in these two authors'
widely divergent views of the friar type, we have perhaps a measure of the distance between two quite
different epochs of literature; for Manzoni, writing
in the first quarter of the nineteenth century, describes
a scene from the seventeenth century, while Shakspeare, writing at the close of the sixteenth century,
presents a picture of fourteenth century life.   Since
every just comparison achieves for the mind that it
may see two truths at once, and since great general
power is inconsistent with novelty, and, the real poet
creates more when he finds his work half done for
him; without borrowing trouble as to their origin, but
rather as if they were new creatures of poetic imagination, let us consider Friar Laurence and Fra Cristofero
as they are depicted, the one by Shakspeare, the other
by Manzoni.

In the Shakspearian fresco the friar stands second
only in importance to the immortal lovers; though he
is not meant to be fully seen; the light falls on one side

of the figure, while some parts are purposely left in shadow. Manzoni's friar, on the contrary, is accurately pencilled, nicely finished and set in full sunshine; yet, of the two, the more fully outlined figure is the less complete.

The first words uttered by the friar of Romeo and Juliet give an idea of the man; of his kindliness, his admiration for nature, his sympathy with all that surrounds him. The gray-eyed morn smiling on the frowning night; the winsome grace that lies in herbs, plants, stones; all these he studies and loves; but neither his mind nor his heart is indifferent to the wants and the frailties of his fellow men. He knows that virtue itself changes to vice being misapplied, and that sometimes even crime is dignified by heroic action. He knows, too, that a young man's love lies not in his heart but in his eyes. He perceives the inconstancy of Romeo's change of sweethearts in a single night. Still, he does not despair of human nature; and with this young love as his lever, he hopes to turn rancour into sweetness and that ultimately he may bring peace to the warring houses of Montague and Capulet.

Manzoni has not found for his friar so effective an *entrée;* but with care and exactitude he describes this friar who so readily obeys the summons of the afflicted mother and daughter. Fra Cristofero's father is depicted as a vain, self-made man, anxious to have his earlier life as a tradesman forgotten by others and by himself also. Ludovico, Fra Cristofero that is to be, was a young man of brilliant talent, but sowing his wild oats and reaping a plentiful harvest of bitter experience. The tragical ending of a street broil, which leads to the young man's taking refuge in a convent, is a finished picture of the times, and shows with what care Manzoni worked; but this scene gives us no insight into the young man's feelings. Any other Christian soul in like circumstances must have had the same suffering. We do not see an individual tortured by the pains of his guilty conscience; we have only a noble portraiture of remorse.

"Ludovico had never before that day shed blood, though in that age homicide was a thing so common that all eyes had become inured to such sights and all ears deaf to such tales; yet the shock given him by the sight of one man slain by his hand and another slain on his account, was in its newness awful, appalling. Emotions as yet unwonted were suddenly stirred by the fall of his enemy. The rapid change in that countenance, passing in an instant from rage and menace to the calm and stillness of death, made such a spectacle as produced a revulsion in the mind of the slayer."

He escapes from arrest by fleeing to a neighbouring convent, and there resolves to make amends for his crime. Summoning a notary he conveys his property to the widow and children of Cristofero, whom he has slain; and convinced that the hand of God has led him to the convent, thus saving him from his pursuers, he resolves to enter religion and become a friar. "Thus at the age of thirty Ludovico took the religious habit, and, being required, as customary, to change his name, he chose one that would continually remind him of the sin he had to expiate—the name of Cristofero."

To the mind of a devout Catholic, as was Manzoni, this action needed almost no explanation, and on it he makes little reflection. The feeling of the victim's brother, a proud nobleman, and his clever management by the father guardian of the convent, is a delightful bit of description. Before he departs for a distant cloister, the newly-made friar wishes to supplicate the pardon of the murdered man's brother. The latter desires the interview to be as formal and solemn as it can be made; for he perceives that in this way his importance as head of the family will be enhanced. And besides, the incident will make a good figure in the family history.

On the appointed day the friends and dependants assemble in the palace, while the *Seigneur*, surrounded by his nearest relatives, stands in the centre of the room, his looks downcast; his right hand crossed over his breast, his left hand grasping the hilt of his sword. Although there is no evidence that he had ever entertained the slightest affection for his brother when living, and had certainly profited by his death, yet he has the true Italian instinct for the value of *pose*, and enjoys his *rôle* as chief actor in this drama of forgiveness and reconciliation.

The pardon having been duly asked and granted, and the proffered refreshments declined, Fra Cristofero begs a loaf of bread, "That I may partake of your charity and eat of your bread after being blessed

with your forgiveness." Apart from its environment
of place and time, this sounds rather theatrical; but
considered as a whole, the scene is effective, though it
fails to reveal the soul of this particular friar. For
Cristofero has only acted as every other humble Franciscan would have acted in his place. Vainly we listen
to catch "the very pulse of the machine" beneath the
cowl; its throbs are not to be heard.

Turning to the other picture. When called by those
lovers, Friar Laurence does not stop to reflect. He
rushes onward and assists as he may to forward the
object of their desire. He wastes no precious moments in vain words, like Fra Cristofero, who very
bravely but very unprofitably beards the lion in his
den. Friar Laurence is worldly-wise enough to feel
the uselessness of such a proceeding.

The words Cristofero addresses to his angry adversary are both brave and inspired by a Christian
spirit; but are they likely to produce any good result?
The friar dimly feels that he is rather spoiling than
mending matters, yet is he impelled to action rather
by his desire to triumph over his own proud spirit, than
to overcome the wickedness of others. He aspires to
holiness, and on that are his thoughts fixed, not on his
protégé's welfare.

This outburst, however, will not be fruitless. Like
every other generous effort, it must bring some good,
and when Roderigo falls a prey to the plague, in his
fevered brain this warning figure of the friar calling
him to repentance will be forever rising and repeating

the brave words. No wonder that same cowled visage, later on, bending over the young profligate's death-bed, has power to recall the guilty soul to repentance.

Friar Laurence is prompted by quite different motives. Of course, he will devoutly say:

> So smile the heavens upon this holy act,
> That after hours with sorrow chide us not.

But he is wondering, not so much if this hasty marriage be right or wrong, but if it will bring good or bad consequences. He allows the lovers' impatience to urge him on; and though he knows that "violent delights have violent ends," and that "too swift arrives as tardy as too slow," still, out of the generous impulses of his heart, he cannot rest a moment while they are unmarried, and so he makes short work of it, and holy church incorporates these two in one.

Many are the examples of this inconsistency in everyday life. Our short-sighted human wisdom speaks soberly and acts foolishly. And because Friar Laurence is not a saint, but just a man like our next-door neighbour, with all the weakness and warm feelings of real life, do we love him dearly, and do we admire the creative power of his many-souled author.

When Romeo is raving in despair after his banishment, who could soothe him with gentle words, with human sympathy? Who but the friar? How clearly he points to the "dear mercy" which the unlucky youth cannot as yet see? When Romeo would kill himself "to sack the hateful mansion," with what authority does the friar chide this unmanly sorrow. He reminds Romeo that Tybalt, who would have killed him, is disposed of; that his sentence of death has been changed to that of banishment, and that this will soon be annulled; that meanwhile his Juliet lives; and out of his heart, big with compassion, he bids this forlorn husband hasten to his expectant bride.

> Go, get thee to thy love, as was decreed,
> Ascend her chamber, hence and comfort her.

And this, considering the circumstances, is real human charity; but is it a friar that acts and speaks so?

If Manzoni forgets to put a man in the monastic robe, here Shakspeare has forgotten to put the cowl and hood over his figure of a man. Whilst Friar Laurence marries these lovers and sends Romeo to his lady's bedroom, Cristofero, for some unknown reason, has not even tried to marry the two lovers he is endeavouring to assist; but on the contrary gives to Renzo the unexpected advice that in this moment of danger he should part from his betrothed, and that they should go each a different way.

The inner soul of our saintly friar stands better revealed in the few words of prayer and forgiveness which he wants his *protégés* to pronounce with him, before they part on their several ways. His saintly soul strives to submit; he prays for the tyrant and calls God's blessing on the heads of the innocent and the wicked alike. Such a prayer is the greatest effort of human nature toward perfection; let us be thankful to Manzoni for showing us the way, even though we are conscious of our inability to follow it. Rising from his knees the good *frate* exclaims: "Come, my children, you have no time to lose; God guard you, may his angels go with you; fare ye well! My heart tells me we shall meet soon again"; and without waiting for reply, Fra Cristofero hastily withdraws. Certainly the heart, to those who listen to its still small voice, often tells us what will happen; yet how often do we think we hear its voice in prophecy, when it is only our desire that prompts the thought! And so it was with Fra Cristofero.

From this point, which is in effect the opening of the story, the plot unfolds itself and continues almost to the end without the assistance, or even the presence of the good friar; whereas when once Shakspeare has brought Friar Laurence on the stage he keeps him constantly before us. We feel that Manzoni's story could have been told even if he had not thought of the character of Cristofero. Friar Laurence, on the contrary, is as essential to the story of Shakspeare's play as is Romeo himself. In this also is revealed the supreme genius of the English master; none of his characters are ever superfluous; and when he presents them to us, he keeps them before us, and through them binds all the story into one homogeneous whole until their parts are played out, and usually until the close of the play.

> I'll give thee armor to keep off that word;
> Adversity's sweet milk, philosophy,
> To comfort thee, though thou art banished.

These words of cheer could avail little for Romeo, if there were words only, and had not Friar Laurence provided that "good counsel" which the nurse would stay all night to hear, and which sends Romeo to "a joy past joy."

The rest is familiar to us. Paris and Juliet both turn to the friar for advice, because they know how well he is able to help and protect. His sympathy for Juliet prompts him to give a desperate counsel which none but a woman in despair would accept. He spies

> A kind of hope
> Which craves as desperate an execution
> As that is desperate which we would prevent.

Friar Laurence has quite forgotten that he is a friar, and we, too, are quite ready to forget it, and to see only the man fighting, not wisely, but with all his might against cruel misfortune.

In considering an individual, that which must ever most appeal to us is the stuff of which he is made. The humanity within him, "that touch of nature which makes the whole world kin," must ever come home to us as could no characteristic or habit of mind or body peculiar to the individual's special calling. Not being ourselves friars, we may not understand the friar nor be specially interested in what a friar might do or say in a given situation; but what a man would do and feel in such circumstances does interest both the heart and the mind.

In Friar Laurence it is the Man that interests us, not the Friar; in Fra Cristofero it is the Friar. Cristofero is not made for action; he is discreetly set aside while the action of the story proceeds. The most important things happen while he is away somewhere in the South, sent there to please the lordling, who wants to be rid of the officious friar. Here we feel the weakness of Manzoni; it is as if in these stirring events he did not know what to do with the saintly Cristofero; so he locks him up in a closet, or, what is the same thing, in a convent; and there keeps him till the time comes for him to reappear, when he is brought forward again. Toward the end, we find him attending the sick with characteristic devotion and the love for his fellow men.

Here, surrounded by distress and pain and amid the saddest spectacle that human misery can present—scenes which Manzoni describes with a power unequalled perhaps by any of his younger rivals—Cristofero looms grand as the spirit of compassion over this ocean of suffering.

Renzo has been wandering through the lazaretto in search of Lucia, dreading yet longing to find her there, when he espies Fra Cristofero, and hastens to address him. The friar is partaking of such frugal repast as the place affords, still peering about and listening for the first call from one of the many sufferers around him. He is here, not by order of his superiors, but at his own entreaty, to be permitted to serve the sore stricken Milanese. He is now exhausted by his heavy task; death's seal is stamped on his pallid features; but his heart is unchanged, his holy zeal unquenched. After the first inquiries Renzo mutters curses against the author of all his misery.

"Miserable man," exclaims Fra Cristofero, in a voice full and sonorous as in former days; and the drooping head is raised erect while the eyes flash fire and his breast heaves with emotion long unwonted; "Look, miserable man! Behold all around us who punishes! Who judges? What do you know of vengeance, what of justice? Begone! You have betrayed all my hopes."

Renzo is a good fellow, and it is not very difficult to persuade him that he must forgive his enemy; but Cristofero is bent on obtaining a complete triumph over Renzo's rancour, as well as over his own; and suddenly bending his head very low, in slow deep tones he adds: "Do you know why I wear this garb?" Renzo hesitates.

"You know it well," repeated the old man. "I do," answered Renzo. "I too have hated. I who resented a hasty word of yours. I killed the man I hated. I too have hated with all my soul; and the man I hated, that man I slew."

"Yes, a tyrant; one of those—"

"Hush!" interrupted the friar; "Think you that if there were any good reason for it, I should not have found it in thirty years? Ah, if I could but instil into your heart the sentiment I have ever since had and still have, for the man I hated! If I could! I? But God can! Listen, Renzo." . . .

The sequel is beautifully worked out, but it must be read in its entirety if we would appreciate the character of the saintly friar.

Cristofero rises to heights that human frailty dares not essay. His soul has gone forward toward full-orbed splendour, and radiates a charm so exquisite, a sweetness so winning, an energy so puissant, an essence intangible, evanescent, spiritual, that he seems to breathe a more ethereal atmosphere than this of earth. The friar rises even above the petty rules of religious scruples, when, with the authority given him by his order, he declares Lucia released from her vow.

In Friar Laurence we feel the touch of our common humanity, in him it is the man, the human-hearted man that we love; but in Fra Cristofero we recognise sainthood. We understand and sympathise with Friar Laurence; we look up to and strive to imitate Fra Cristofero.

Both Shakspeare and Manzoni have given each to his friar an appropriate exit. As the story permits Friar Laurence to go in peace and the Prince is justified in saying, "We still have known thee for a holy man"; so too with Lucia we learn "with more sorrow than surprise that he died of the plague."

This is the beauty and also the weakness of such a character; it is above nature. But yet, if a human soul has been able to think it; if other human souls have understood and for one moment at least comprehended the beauty and purity of this splendid unreality; can we not hope that some hidden flame of pure love is still living unseen, unfelt, in our hearts, ready to leap and flash forth at the call of some kindred spirit above? Our modern romanciers are always ready to show us what demons or hellish passion lurk in the best of us; let us be thankful to those, like Manzoni, who show us the possibilities of our *ardoyante et diverse* human nature.

SAVONAROLA

SAVONAROLA

W ITH the dolorous wailing of a loving mother for her missing son begins Lenau's *Savonarola*. At close of a sultry day a thunderstorm threatens to burst upon Ferrara and Elena is anxious for the safety of Girolamo whom she fancies in some recess of the forest rapt in prayer and contemplation as was his wont, and insensible of the storm's menace. Such is the chord of deep human affection, of anxious mother-love, struck in the opening lines of the first canto: like the overture of Rossini's *Les Huguenots,* it seizes and subdues to its own melancholy the soul of the reader and induces the sombre mood of compassion joined with admiration, in which we contemplate the heroic figure of the Dominican friar Girolamo Savonarola as he advances on his *Via Triumphalis* and his *Via Dolorosa* to martyrdom: for this fine lyric epic of Lenau's, though it celebrates a life supremely heroic which scorned dangers and pains and death in the cause of righteousness, is nevertheless dominated throughout by the poet's own mood of melancholy, expressed in his sonnet on Solitude.

Die ganze Welt ist zum Verzweifeln traurig (The whole world is to despondency sad). Even where the poet sings of victories the poem is not joyous, for the ignominious ending of the heroic friar's career casts its shadow back, dimming the glory of his triumphs and his momentary successes. Lenau of course does not wear the trammels of history: he is in soul communion with the spirit of the reformer Friar, and he moulds history to more apt expression of the teaching of Savonarola's life and labours. The life of Savonarola, as portrayed in Lenau's poem, is fiction: but it is for all that, truth as genuine as is found in what we call history. Lenau has gone deeper than history. He has found the very soul and spirit that lived in Girolamo Savonarola. And this is why this work of Lenau's is to be reckoned among the great poems, and why we regard his friar Savonarola, an historical character, as a Friar in Fiction.

Lenau was a man of the highest sensibility and as a poet so identified himself with whatever character he designed to portray in verse, that while the work was on the anvil he verily lived the life and thought the thoughts, as the case might be, of his *Faust,* of his *Don Juan,* and of his *Savonarola;* his poems were therefore in the highest degree subjective, so to speak, of himself imagined as a human soul set in the same environment as the characters he was describing. And this union of his own personality with that of his subject was neither momentary nor superficial: not only was he his own Faust or Don Juan or Savonarola or Albigensian Puritan while the work was under his hand; each of his great compositions left on his soul its distinctive impression not to be easily effaced. In the *Faust* Lenau is in heart and soul a pronounced sceptic with a strong leaning to pantheism: in *The Albigenses* he is an apostle of freedom of thought: in *Don Juan* he is still the sceptic and liberal but with a tendency to Epicurism: but in *Savonarola* he is a firm believer in the Christian religion. Hence he could most truly say, *Mein sammtlichen Schriften sind mein sammtliches Leben* (My complete works are my complete life).

His *Savonarola* was designed to be the second member of a trilogy: the other two were to be *John Huss* and *Ulrich von Hutten*. He chose to write the *Savonarola* first, but the influence of the great Dominican friar upon his views of human life and its mysteries was so profound and so far reaching as to change his whole mental attitude toward those problems. Hence when he set about the work of writing the *Huss* he was discouraged by the seeming poverty of that subject and gave up the projected trilogy: of the third member of the trilogy we hear nothing more: and in truth the man who could be in communion of soul with Savonarola could never have sympathy of thought with such a character as Ulrich von Hutten. The *Savonarola,* precisely because it is eminently sincere and sympathetic, practically wrecked Lenau's career as a poet: it alienated all those who had admired his sceptical, liberalistic, epicurean *Faust* and *Don Juan,* and instead of placating the enmity of Orthodox Catholic and Protestant public opinion in Austria and Germany, made it only more fierce.

The opening scene of the poem is Ferrara, birthplace

of Savonarola and home of his early years: it was in his time the seat of a ducal court, a strongplace fortified, as it still is, with walls, bastions, citadel and ditches, defences against human foes and against the invading floods of the Po di Volano, which often overflow the surrounding country and drive the inhabitants into the city as a refuge. For all its clear Italian skies of deepest azure and golden light, and for all the life and bustle of its streets, thronged with a population of a hundred thousand souls and the gaiety of the court of that magnificent prince, the Duke Borso d'Este, Ferrara was a sombrous place as Savonarola knew it in the latter half of the Fifteenth Century, or as Tasso knew it a century later when he resided at the courts of the no less magnificent princes, the Cardinal d'Este and the Duke Alfonso II.

There is a constitutional sombreness of mood peculiar to the Italians as deep as that which characterizes the Scandinavian populations, but different: of this the Ferrarese possesses full measure. And the situation of the town, at the confluence of many of the streams which drain Lombardy, is not without effect upon the mood and temperament of the inhabitants. The vast expanse of surrounding lagoons produces a miasma that poisons the blood and gives a dreamy brooding habit of thought and a disposition to indulge fantasies and visions: as pre-eminently illustrated in Savonarola and Torquato Tasso. This sombre mood was congenital in the prophet-reformer Savonarola, from boyhood and to his last day a dreamer of dreams and seer of visions: it was doubtless congenital also in Tasso, but a long residence amid the *miasmata* of the Po di Volano, where he was frequently stricken by the endemic fevers, fostered his malsain mental constitution, till after long years of sorrow and misfortune the poet "the Odysseus of many wanderings and miseries, singer of sweetest strains still vocal," found refuge in the convent of St. Onofrio on the Trasteverine Hill.

Girolamo bears the stamp of the mystic and the spiritual seer even in boyhood. While the stormclouds are gathering fast Elena thinks of her boy, not as roaming the forest for a summer day's play, but as recluse in one of his favourite haunts for prayer: "He is surely praying at his tree." But the father, Niccolò, has faith that no harm can befall Girolamo. "He will soon return from his forest reverie," says Niccolò, "and recount to us the secret things he has heard: how often has he come back out of the forest solitudes to guide us into another and deeper forest: how often have we heard from his lips the word that is life!" But Elena would not be comforted: before the dawn she was searching the woods for her boy and calling him by name: and on returning home at nightfall, weary and disconsolate, a letter from Girolamo was put in her hand, in which he bids farewell to his parents and announces to them his call to the religious life: that call had come to him during the storm of the night before while he was praying at "his tree." The storm was at its height when he prayed for a sign which should determine his vocation: and straightway the tree was struck with lightning and riven: but the youth, unhurt, rose to his feet "God's Knight" henceforth for ever. The day was the festival of the martyr St. George and it awakened in Elena's breast disquieting forebodings.

Girolamo meanwhile is on the road to Bologna and at evening knocks at the garden gate of the convent of St. Dominic. He is admitted by the Prior, a venerable man of noble aspect, who is himself tending the flower beds. It is a pleasant scene, and it recalls the early and best days of these mendicant orders. The venerable Prior and the youth tread the garden paths, Girolamo unfolding the story of his life and of his vocation to the religious state; the Prior listens with sympathy to the narrative and quaintly expounds the mystic symbolism of the flowers. Are not they too under religious vows? Are they not chaste and pure? Faithful lovers of poverty, content with heaven's dews and the blessed sunshine, how obedient they to rise when the Springtide summons them, and at the matin hour to make their offering of sweet perfume?

Girolamo is taken into the brotherhood and the novice Domenico is assigned to be his cell-mate: straightway this pair are brothers, bound by firmer ties than those of Dominic's rule—brothers unto death: for the novice Domenico is the friar Domenico who in the death by fire will not be separated from his fellow knight of God, Girolamo. In their cell their conversation is of the state of Christendom and the Church and of the glorious martyrdom of those apostles of reform, Jerome of Prague and John Huss. Henceforth these two novices are vowed to each other to walk in the footsteps of Jerome and Huss, even though their path leads to the death by fire.

History tells us nothing of the thunderstorm with its "sign" determining Savonarola's vocation. It only relates how three years before his entry into the order of St. Dominic, and when he was nineteen years of age, he was in love with the daughter of a noble Florentine exile, of the Strozzi family, but was contemptuously rejected by the girl's father. It tells of his grief and mortification and of his determination no more to aim at worldly goods or worldly joys, but to devote himself wholly to the religious life. He left behind, when he set out for Bologna, a well considered treatise on "Contempt of the World," in which he laments the universal corruption of the times and foretells speedy chastisement from Heaven. The story of the "sign from Heaven" Lenau borrows from the life of Martin Luther who, half a century later, and when about twenty-two years old, was overtaken by a thunderstorm while walking with a fellow-student at Erfurt, and his companion was killed. Luther fell upon his knees, confessed his sins and, the terror of death upon him, vowed to devote his life to religion, and immediately resigning his chair in the Erfurt university, entered as a novice the Augustinian convent in that town.

There was justice and propriety in Lenau's incorporation of this scene in his *Savonarola:* both of these men were Church reformers, and it was eminently congruous that, like Luther and like St. Paul, the great reformer of the Fifteenth Century should also have the signet of Heaven's approval of his work.

At the age of about forty years he is elected Prior of the convent of San Marco in Florence. He is to preach in the Cathedral on a Christmas day and the great duomo is thronged to its full capacity with citizens and country people eager to hear the words of the already famous evangelist. The poet before he essays a rendering of Savonarola's discourse upon the mystery of the Incarnation and its lessons of peace and goodwill, as also its denunciation of Godlessness in the high places, makes a beautiful invocation of the Spirit of Girolamo, asking him to bless his verse, lest it should, instead of glorifying his memory, do it dishonour:

> O dass der Strahl, der gottesklare
> Erlischt und flicht, der Zeitem Raub!
> Girolamo! dreihundert Jahre
> Sind nachgeflogen deinem Staub!
>
> Komm, segbe nich mit deiner Nahe,
> Und segne meines Liedes Klang,
> Dass ich dein grosses Herz verstehe,
> Und nicht verletze im Gesang!

Lass weihend in die Seele fallen
Von jenem Strahl mir einen Schein,
Und lass ein leises Wiederhallen
Main Lied von deinem Worte sein!

That is a bold and original figure of speech—albeit indeed it is a "conceit"—by which he fancies a new genealogy of Mary the Virgin: the longings of the generations of mankind for reconciliation with Heaven and for a redeemer become embodied: they become Mary, and conceive!

Die schnsucht, die so lange Tage
Nach Gotte hier aud Erden gieng
Als Thrane, Lied, Gebet und Klage
Sie ward Maria—und empfieng.

Another ingenious conceit—this too, like that quite in consonance with the mediæval forms of thought— has reference to the Saviour's crown of thorns: fain would the bush that bore those thorns perish out of the earth: but its seeds are fated to be wafted by the winds every whither. Under that briar can no flower bloom, no bird will sing, the wayfarer as he passes feels its malign power. The thorn-bush is nature's dark chill (*das Finsterkalke*); and Ahasuerus, the Undying Jew, is Unbelief: yearly in his wanderings he cuts from that thorn-bush a new staff: the stage on which he practises his juggling acts is the Church's sanctuary, whence God is shut out.

In the highest places of Florence the preacher sees the religion of Christ banished and in its stead enthroned the ancient paganism and pantheism, the worship of "ravin nature red in tooth and claw" as one of our own poets has it. Fittest tabernacle for their altars would be a tiger's head full of its own pearls and rubies and in the midst the Sacrament! Their Ark of the Covenant should be the jaws of a shark enclosing with its murderous rows of teeth the holy law; their Gabriel summoning the dead to rise, an hyena:

Als Tabernakel, voll Rubinen
Und Perlen, mit dem Sakrament,
Mag euch des Tigers Rachen dienen,
Der brullend durch die Wuste rennt.

Und die Kinnlade eines Haien
Fur euch als Bundeslade passt
Das Mordgebiss, in Stachelreihen
Das heilige Gesetz umdasst.

From Florence the preacher turns to Rome, and there on this Christmas morn sees the same brazen irreligion and impiety in the ministers of the ceremonies and the same profound spiritual torpor in the people which so impressed the mind of Martin Luther when he visited the papal city twenty years after Savonarola's death. Luther reports many anecdotes of the amazing impieties of Roman ecclesiastics. Once he was in the company of a number of prelates, one of whom, to add to the feast of reason and the flow of soul, enlivened the conversation by telling how he was wont, instead of pronouncing the ritual formula

of consecration in the mass, to employ these words—
panis es et panis manebis (bread thou art and bread
shalt remain) then he would hold the wafer up for
adoration by the people. Lenau's Savonarola matches
Luther's narrative with a comparison between the
officiating priest at the altar and a gambler at the card
table: the priest while performing the mass, and at
its most critical moment, is thinking only of a game of
cards: he waves the sacred cup like a dice box and
fingers the Host like a playing card:

> Ein andrer traumt in Spielgemacher
> Sich an den Goldtisch, nummersatt,
> Er schivingt den Kelch wie Wurfelbecher,
> Die Hostie wie ein Kartenblatt.

And Savonarola asks, Is this the natal day of him who
won heaven back for us? Or is Christ then a fond
dream? Not so: the Saviour's word shall never pass
away, nor will God suffer Himself to be robbed of the
world He created: the Church will rise out of this mire
and will be renewed: priests faithful and pure will
serve her altars, and peace shall reign on earth, goodwill among men.

Such speeches were not to be tolerated either by
Lorenzo or Pope Alexander, and the Pope commissioned Mariano da Ghenezzano, an Austin friar of
great fame for learning and eloquence, to be the
Church's defender against the disturber of the peace
of Holy Church. On Ascension day Mariano had for
his auditory Lorenzo, all the highest magistrates and

the nobility of Florence; the common people were there too, and it is to them that Mariano's harangue is chiefly addressed—why should they put faith in that deceiver and follow him in his impious courses? That prophet of evil, that sour-visaged ascetic who grudges them all the innocent joys of life? Girolamo is sowing discord between prince and people and inciting to bloody war. God's blessings are now poured out abundantly on Florence: may they never cease! Lorenzo is God's instrument to lift the state of Florence to the most eminent place among the nations of Christendom. He is the patron of science, philosophy and art. All the kingdoms of the earth acknowledge his wisdom, do him honour and seek his counsel—the Emperor, the King of France, the Kings of Aragon and of Portugal: nay infidel princes—the Sultan and the Kings of Barbary—seek to conciliate his favour by gifts of priceless value—costly fabrics, jewels, rare animals from the African wilds. Monuments of Grecian antiquity are rescued from oblivion; the wisdom of the ancients is revived, and the dark cloud of ignorance is dispelled. O happy Florentines in having such a prince! Woe to him who would disturb so auspicious a reign.

The next morning the bells of San Marco are ringing and the whole population, gentle and simple, are thronging the church. Savonarola will expose the hypocrisies of the rulers in Church and State and summon the people of Florence and Christendom to make an end of the reign of Satan in the Church of God. The Church has lost faith: the people, leaderless, guideless, are nearing the brink of the abyss. The clergy, suppressing God's word and ignoring His gracious promises, have put themselves in His place and are exacting faith and trust in themselves. The Church — Savonarola honours the Church — his mother! but the Church is no longer herself: he would but stay the hand with which she would do herself mortal hurt. He would not call men to a life of our austerity, but would warn them of the dangers of worldliness and godlessness. War and discord? Yes, he will till his last breath incite to war on lies and scandalous living.

Mariano, smooth-speaking corrupter of the people, does he know what the Gospel means? Can he bring to the sorely troubled soul no other solace but a message from the tombs of ancient heathen philosophers and poets? Cunning pulpit juggler that he is, he cannot make the sinner blush, he cannot stir the souls of men. Away with your pagan philosophy, your pagan art, your pagan poetry: in Faith and Prayer alone is safety! God will visit Italy in His wrath: God will bring to naught the Medici and all their glory. The Church must be reformed, else will she be taught by the lessons of Pestilence and War that the Lord God Omnipotent reigneth!

The next scene is the deathbed of Lorenzo. Here the bare historical record, even when reduced to its lowest terms and presented with the utmost brevity possible, leaves little room for poetical adornment. In fact it is weakened by any attempt at adornment.

When Death with its unfathomable mystery and above all with its traditional terrors faced Lorenzo, the whole structure of his artificial platonism and paganism crumpled away and there was nothing left but such images of the other world as exist in the popular mind—images made almost palpable realities, or at least haunting visions, by the genius of Dante.

And Lorenzo was above all things a scholar and deeply versed in his Dante. His Plato was now for him an untrustworthy guide, no pilgrim's staff for that last journey. Whatever was most terrible in his childhood's religious beliefs was revived, and he must make no mistakes in this supreme moment of his existence. Therefore he calls to his deathbed, as minister of reconciliation, not the fawning priests and friars who had flattered him in his sinful life, but Fra Girolamo, who, like another John the Baptist, had never failed to rebuke his infidelities, his licentiousness, his sins against God and the people of Florence. Savonarola obeyed the call and that reluctantly. He would not, could not exercise his ministrations save on conditions that it was hardly possible, perhaps even entirely impossible for Lorenzo to fulfil. No doubt he also knew that whatever Lorenzo might do or promise while the terrors of death were before his eyes, his repentance would be in effect a bargain which Heaven would not ratify, and Savonarola's ministration a mockery of God.

Yet the friar obeyed the summons to come to the dying prince and offered to him the sacramental absolution upon three conditions: First: You must repent and have true faith in God's mercy; Lorenzo assented. Secondly, You must give up your illgotten wealth; this too Lorenzo promised. On hearing the third condition, You must restore the liberties of Florence, Lorenzo turned his face to the wall and made no reply. Savonarola waited a few moments and then went away. Shortly after Lorenzo died unabsolved.

Lenau elaborates this deathbed scene to an extraordinary length. He will have the medical men prescribe curious medicaments—compounds of powdered pearls and precious stones with strange and costly drugs. He has the figures of Grecian gods that are ranged round the chamber veiled lest they should seem to rebuke the dying man for his weakness. His ravings in delirium are recounted—how he with might and main urges on his span of ill-matched steeds—his lower and higher nature—to bear him to Olympus's heights, and how he is discomfited and left naked and shivering on a wintry moor, soon to awake and find Savonarola kneeling in prayer at his bedside. The catechising of the dying man and the too long drawn exhortation to repentance are consistent neither with the characters of the two actors nor with the situation in that death chamber, but the outcome of it all is, as in the history of that scene, that Lorenzo dies unshriven.

Before leaving Lorenzo to his own devices, however, and to his fate, the friar holds up before the face of the dying man in one hand a Gospel—in the other a rose. Lenau had learned from Roscoe that Lorenzo was insensible to odours; and his Savonarola takes occasion from that in his parting words to declare to Lorenzo that his soul had ever been closed against the Gospel, even as his sense had been closed against the perfume of flowers. Lenau, before *Savonarola* was published, wrote thus to his friend Johannes Martensen: "Lorenzo de Medicis had no sense of smell—a fact of much importance for me—and yet roses grew in his garden. When he was upon his deathbed Savonarola, who was there to absolve him from his sins, held up before his face a rose and a Gospel, saying: 'As the perfume of this flower is inhaled and exhaled by you, without your being sensible of it, so is it with the odour of these holy pages.' Lorenzo's apologist, that poor creature Roscoe, has done me a good turn in acquainting me with Lorenzo's insensibility to odours." The pretty, and petty, conceit has thus a ground in history, as has also the speech which Lenau puts in the mouth of Savonarola: nevertheless it was a trick unworthy of a great mind or a great soul or a generous heart.

The invasion of Italy by Charles VIII is for the poet as it was for his hero the fulfilment of one of the prophecies of Savonarola when he denounced God's vengeance upon the land because of the infidelities of princes and people, popes and priests. Lorenzo's son and successor, Piero de Medicis, has neither courage nor wisdom, yet he must needs make a feint of armed resistance to the invading French army: but instead

of doing anything to withstand the invader, he gained
access to the French King, and prostrate at his feet,
sought to safeguard his own and his family's fortunes,
private and political, by the offer of an enormous ransom to be paid by the Florentines. His report of the
embassage—for such it was and not a military oper-
ation—was received with indignation by all Florence,
and straightway the fall of the house of Medici as
foretold by Savonarola is accomplished. Piero and all
his house go into exile. The vast treasures of ancient
art, philosophy and literature are looted and wrecked
by the populace.

But Charles appears at the gates and forces an
entrance with his host. There is but one man that
dare hope to save the city from sack and its inhabitants
from slaughter; Girolamo the friar prevails on the
conqueror—in whose eyes he was indeed a prophet,
having foretold this very invasion—to retire, even as
Leo the pope turned Attila back when he was at the
gates of Rome. And now arises the question of the
reconstitution of civil government: it was determined
with the same supernatural dispatch in favour of the
Republic—the theocratic republic. For a season
Savonarola is the Calvin, the John Knox of Florence.

A tempter visits him from Rome who offers not
indeed all the kingdoms of earth and the glory thereof
but the sufficiently splendid decoration of a Cardinal's
red hat if he will but be silent regarding scandals in
the Church. But Girolamo is not to be bribed: the only
red hat he will wear is one dyed in his own blood. Let

not the Pope cherish the vain hope of peace: between him and Savonarola is war to the death. He recounts the genesis of the reigning pope, Alexander the Sixth, in terms that might excite the envy of Martin Luther, Ulrich von Hutten or the authors of the *Epistolae Obscurorum Virorum.* The Devil took of Treachery, Mendacity, Incest and Assassination q. s.; wrought these into one homogeneous mass and stamped it with some human feature; there's your pope!

> Der Teufel hat Verrath und Lugen,
> Blutschande, Meuchelmord gebracht,
> Und sie gebalt zu Menschenzugen
> Und einen Pabst daraus gemacht!

Satan has a free hand in the pillage of the Church. But hold! Savonarola will rehearse you an apologue that may be of interest for people at the centre of Christendom.

It happened on a time, there lay upon her bier a wealthy dame, seeming-dead. False friends haste to make away with her possessions: they rummage chests and lockers and divide among themselves her pearls and diamonds and jewellery. At last they come to blows over the division of the bridal parure. Meanwhile her members are held fast in bonds as by death and everlasting night has settled on her eyelids. But she heard and was conscious, and they had now in their hands her dearest treasure, the Gospels. The thought set her heart beating, colour came back to her cheeks; she raised herself up on the bier, and the plunderers fled affrighted. The shock saved the lady's life and from that moment she grew steadily better. Hence your faith must not falter. You see in this story the Church's state. God will not suffer His Church to go down to the grave. Lenau then gratuitously brings in the episode of the banquet (and its sequels) given by Vanozza, Alexander's concubine to her two sons and her daughter Lucrezia, her children by his Holiness: but as it has really nothing to do with the life and career of Savonarola, it may be passed without further notice here.

After war came pestilence, as Girolamo has foretold. The five quatrains with which Lenau's account of this visitation opens are grand in their simplicity, touchingly melodious, and true to nature in every note. Two lovers exchange rings in token of undying love: yet a little and the Plague has them both.

"Nimm du mein Ringlein, gib mir deines!
Komm Taubchen, bau'n wir unser Nest!"
Das Nest Bleibt leer, denn ach! ein Kleines,
So sterbt ihr beide an der Pest!

In a jovial party, one, as the wine goes round, alludes playfully to the pestilence: he is already stricken.

Spielt auf! schenkt ein! und dann willkommen!
Hinunter noch den sessen Rest!
Ja wohl, du wirst am Wort genommen,
Schon hat ergriffen dich die Pest!

A prisoner is groaning under the weight of his chains: the Plague will set him free:

> O kerkernacht, o bittres Harmen!
> Wie qualend mich die kette presst.
> Wirt nicht mehr lang das Eisen warmen,
> Noch hente stirbst du an der Pest!

A penitent is confessing; the multitude of his sin confuses him; he halts; he is dead: does the Plague absolve?

> "Viel Sunden noch. . . . doch sprintdie Heerde
> Mir durcheinander . . . haltet fest."
> Am Beichtstuhl fallter todt zur Erde,
> Und hat ihn absolvirt die Pest?

An artist cries, *"Io triumphe!"* as he gives the last touch to an *Ecce Homo*. Plague snatches the pencil out of his hand:

> "Triumph! wie schon das Blutgerinnoel
> Dem bleichen Ecce Homo lasst!"
> Da reisst ihm aus der Hand den Pinsel
> Und malt ihnselber bleich die Pest.

Meanwhile Savonarola is the one man in Florence who amid the Plague panic stands unappalled: he ministers to the plague-stricken, comforts the sorrowing, buries the dead: the convent of San Marco is open to the destitute. His nights are spent in prayer and in composing appeals to the Emperor, the King of France, the Spanish sovereigns, the Kings of Hungary and England, that they would write to call a general council of the church for correction of the prevailing disorders *in capite et in membris*. He will himself in that council raise his voice against the false head of the church, the infamous Borgia, the Antichrist.

Then follows the Pope's brief of excommunication, and in the cathedral the Bishop of Florence, with all the canonical solemnities, cuts Savonarola off from fellowship with the faithful. Whoever attends a sermon by the contumacious friar is stricken with the same anathema. The streets of Florence resound with the shouts of victory raised by the enemies of Savonarola; the convent-house of San Marco is assailed with showers of stones and other missiles by a mob. Fra Domenico, Girolamo's cell-mate in the early days, is by his side, a trusted supporter in this time of trial, and is with him to the end. To the insults of the rabble Domenico replies with words of defiance: the anathemas of the Devil's ministers are God's blessings: the Church must and shall be reformed: Girolamo is God's prophet and speaks truth. And Girolamo himself, in contempt of the Church's solemn ban, ascends the pulpit of San Marco and with increased emphasis and passion voices his denunciation of the Pope: thus is the hand of the Church challenged to battle. Henceforth Alexander will be fast set against all pleas for mercy or tolerance toward the insolent friar.

The Signory of Florence now intervenes, compelled by threats from Rome, and Savonarola and Domenico are arrested and put in prison. The pair have been through life faithful to the vows they mutually pledged in the convent of San Dominico in Bologna, that they would walk in the footsteps of Jerome of Prague and John Huss: they are now in sight of the sacrificial fires, and they are still constant and true. Lenau reproduces the scene of the torture chamber where a recantation is demanded of Girolamo by the rack, the boot, the thumbscrews and the other enginery of the law. Savonarola's answer ever is: "I will not recant." History tells of moments when this victim, tortured beyond endurance, expressed a willingness—or a willingness was expressed from him—to recant: but when his pains were lessened he was again uncompliant as ever. Lenau's Savonarola has no other reply to the pressing questions of his judges but only that, "I will not recant." The circumstance of the death of Savonarola, of his heroic friend Domenico, and of his loving but not so heroic Silvestro, are sufficiently poetical, tragical, without addition from the poet's fancy.

JOSEPH
THE DREAMER

JOSEPH THE DREAMER

"The people that is heir to the Kingdom of Heaven has no intercourse with those who are disinherited."

SUCH was the inscription over the portal of the Ghetto of Padua. The same inscription might appropriately have been written over every mediæval ghetto gate.

The "disinherited" are no longer separated from the "heirs of the Kingdom" by ghetto gates and brick and mortar walls. More absolute though intangible were those dividing barriers of race and religion. Raised by both Jew and Christian, they endure even until now.

At times a note from without the barrier penetrated the ghetto stillness. Sometimes this note found an answering echo in some single soul of the outcast people. Then from within the ghetto was born an irresistible desire for the grand, the beautiful, the admirable, the satisfying, out there in the Christian world. In every generation from behind every ghetto barrier throughout Europe was to be found some high-souled dreamer, some heart parched with eternal thirst; a thirst which neither Talmudic lore nor Jewish ceremonial could quench. Oblivion spread its sable wings over the greater number of such aspiring souls. A few were touched by History's eternal rays.

137

Some of these were Jewish apostates, stepping out of dreary ghetto doors joyous and hopeful, never to re-enter or even to cast a backward glance: of such was Spinoza. Others raged with bleeding foreheads against the iron walls of Jewry, alternately accepting and then rejecting the intolerable yoke of the rabbis. Tragic is the pregnancy and pitiful in the telling, that autobiography of one of these—Uriel Acosta, *An Example of Human Life,* he called it.

Still others loving their fellow men and free from prejudice, essayed brick by brick to bring down the old ghetto walls and establish a common brotherhood of man; of such was Moses Mendelssohn. And there were others in those Seventeenth Century days of Messianic dreams, as David Reubeni who came from the far East, and Solomon Malcho and, most noted of all, the Turkish Messiah Sabbatai Levi, who tried to renew and regenerate the ghetto life while remaining within. "I believe with a perfect faith that the Messiah will come, and though His coming be delayed, nevertheless will I daily expect Him." This was the morning prayer of all Jewry; for they felt that their cup was full and their redemption was nigh. What wonder if in response to Israel's dream of the near Messiah there were those who exclaimed: "Behold! I am he." Differing as wide as the world were the ideas of these, yet all strove for that one ideal. The ways were many but the end sought was ever the same; to bring the microcosm of the ghetto into accord with the great world without. Heroes, martyrs, fanatics, history calls them. As *Dreamers* they are known in fiction.

Isidore Zangwill in his story of *Joseph the Dreamer*
tells us of one of these heroes of the ghetto; of one
who was at once both a Jew and a friar. Mr. Zangwill freely admits that there is no historical basis for
this fictional character. As he says, it is merely "the
artistic typification of one of the many souls through
which the great ghetto dream has passed." The time
is about the middle of the Sixteenth Century, and the
place is the Ghetto of Rome. It is the night of the
Jewish Feast of Dedication which by some sinister
chronological coincidence is also the night when the
Christian persecutor celebrates the birth of his
Saviour. The old father Manasseh and Rachel his
wife are filled with anxiety, for their son Joseph is
outside the ghetto gates and on such a night that means
dire peril.

The next morning Miriam appeared at the house
of Manasseh. Miriam to whom the word love and
the word Joseph sound the same. Her fair young face
is such as painters give to the Madonna when they
remember that the mother of Jesus was only just
budding into womanhood and that she was a Jewess.
Soon Joseph appeared, a curious poetic figure in his
reddish-brown mantle and dark yellow cap. *"Pax
vobiscum,"* he cried in jubilant accents. He tells them
that these anxious hours of his absence were passed in
the Christian church of St. Peter: how at the Midnight
Mass, at the adoration of the Christ, overwhelmed by
the mighty wave of organ music and the yearning

prayers of a thousand hearts, he had found that for which his soul craved, he had learned the secret of peace; all was comprised in the word "sacrifice." The despair of mother and sweetheart at the news of this apostasy was extreme. On the return of Manasseh, who has learned all, the mother ventures to remark, "Our son is back." "Son," replies the old man, "What son? We have no son." The renegade suffers the great excommunication from Jewry; Manasseh totters home to bewail the death of his son; Miriam, bitterly weeping, burns the praying-shawl she was weaving in secret love for the man who might one day have loved her; and Rachel wept for her child and would not be comforted.

The succeeding pages tell of his preparation for admission as a Dominican friar; of his interview with Helena de' Franchi, who had learned to love him in the many hours they had spent together in her father's library. Plainly he tells her he can wed no Christian maiden. That so to do would defeat his purpose to bring his brethren to the light. It was not for her he gave up home and father and mother. Henceforth his life will be devoted to the reconciliation of Jew and Christian. He will bring his own race to acknowledge and love the Crucified.

Then comes the scene of his meeting with Miriam in the streets of Rome. "An angry sulphur sunset streaked with green, hung over the ruined temples of the ancient gods and the grass-grown fora of the Romans. It touched with a glow as of blood the

brightest fragment of the Coliseum wall . . . the rest
of the Titanic ruin seemed in shadow." "Is it well
with my parents?" said Joseph at last. "Hast thou
the face to ask? But how canst thou become a
priest; thou lovest Helena de' Franchi." "How know-
est thou that?" "I am a woman." "Thou thinkest we
Jews will point the finger of scorn at thee; that we will
say it was Helena thou didst love, not the Crucified
One; that we will not lisen to thy gospel." "But is it
not so?" "It is so." "Then——" "But it will be so,
do what you wilt. Cut thyself into little pieces and
we would not believe thee or thy gospel. . . . Joseph,
thy dream is vain. . . . Thou wilt no more move them
than the seven hills of Rome. They have stood too
long." "Ay, they have stood like stones. I will melt
them. I will have them." "Thou wilt destroy them.
The Jews hate thee; save rather this woman and be
happy . . . as for me, were I a mother in Israel
my children should be taught to hate thee even as I
do." He called after her, "But why didst thou risk
thy good name to tell me thou hatest me?" "Because
I love thee. Farewell." He stretched out his hands
after her and "a drunken Dominican lurched into his
arms."

Though the pope granted the request of Fra
Giuseppi that the Jews might be compelled to come to
church to be converted, he respected their hatred of
the apostate and their protest that they would more
willingly listen to any other preacher. Rejected by
his race, yet the new friar gained great fame in other

pulpits. He absolved the dying, he exorcised demons.
But there was one sinner he could not absolve—himself. Now he was grieved by the shortcomings of
Christendom as formerly by those of the ghetto. In
all his efforts he sees but failure. The Jews reject
him with scorn, the Christians remain as intolerant
and worldly as ever.

The last three chapters of the story concern the Carnival week—the mad blaspheming week of revelry
and devilry. We all know what a modern Roman
carnival signifies; we have all read of what a mediæval
Roman carnival meant. The masqueraders, the bloody
tumults, the popular license, the rush and the roar,
the race of asses and buffaloes through the length of
the Corso. The rare spice of baiting the Jews, concluding with that extreme of indignity, the Jew races.

A mounted officer gave the word, the half-naked
desperate creatures pell-mell started on their wild run
down the Corso of St. Angelo, soldiers galloping at
their heels, even threatening to run them down as they
ran puffing, panting, apoplectic. Determined to be one
with his brethren of the ghetto, determined if possible
thus to shame their Christian persecutors who affect
to venerate him, and thus to end the Jew-baiting, Fra
Giuseppi becomes one of the racers. At the end of
the race he draws the crucifix from under his cloak,
reveals his personality with flashing eye and voice of
thunder; in the name of Christ denounces this devil's
mockery of the Lord's chosen people. Then stirred
to frenzy he proceeds to denounce the pope and his

bastard son, Baccio Valori, and all the corruptions of
pope, cardinals and priests. For a moment the crowd
swayed by his eloquence are with him, and shouting
"Down with Antichrist! Down with the Pope!
Down with Baccio Valori!" They rush toward a
statue of the pope with purpose to destroy it.

But Fra Giuseppi, this dreamer of the ghetto, was
not a man to lead a mob to victory. Nor was the mob
stirred by any higher emotion than the desire of re-
venge and the hope of pillage. At the first charge of
the soldiery they desert their leader and he soon lies
bleeding, exhausted in a prison's deepest dungeon. His
execution follows. Not a face shows sympathy. He
was an outcast from both worlds and both Jew and
Christian rejoiced in the heavenly vengeance which
had overtaken the renegade.

This story of Joseph the Dreamer is in no sense
a great work of fiction. Nor will the delineation of the
character of Fra Giuseppi at all compare with the great
friar characters of fiction, either in what is attempted
or in what is achieved. We feel that there is an anti-
climax to the story; or rather that there is failure
in what seems to be an ambitious attempt at a climax.
There is unreality and weakness in what is meant to
be the crowning scene of the Jew race. We do not
feel that there is a personality behind the declamation
of the friar, and the mob is rather a tame rabble of
stage supernumeraries, not a raging, revenging city
populace.

The scene of the execution of the friar is not

effective, it fails to rouse us. The miraculous shower of rain which extinguishes the blazing fagots is melodramatic, spectacular and weakening. The concluding lines of the story are stronger. The rejoicings at the house of Manasseh over the death of the outcast are more than picturesque; there is genuine truth and pathos in the picture of the tragic white-haired wreck of a father gravely handing fruits and wine to his guests and the old mother dancing with set smile, while the musicians render sweet music, and all rejoice as tradition demanded over the death of the renegade. So too, in conclusion, in the meeting of Miriam and Helena de' Franchi at the grave of the friar, there is tenderness and truth, apt contrast, simplicity and restraint. Helena's tears flowed unrestrainedly. "Alas! Alas! the Dreamer! He should have been happy—happy with me, happy in the fulness of human love, in the light of the sun, in the beauty of this fair world, in the joy of art, in the sweetness of music."

"Nay, signora," replies Miriam, "he was a Jew. He should have been happy with me, in the light of the Law, in the calm household life of prayer and study, of charity, and pity, and all good offices. I would have lit the Sabbath candles for him and set our children on his knee that he might bless them. Alas! Alas! the Dreamer!" But no! Neither of these fates was to be his. The dream of the ghetto has once more been dreamed in vain.

The story presents some scenes of true beauty, of

power, of human interest and successful portrayal of
character. That between Joseph and Helena is such;
it is however marred by being too reminiscent of a
somewhat similar and much more powerful incident in
Charles Reade's *The Cloister and the Hearth*. The
short interview between Joseph and Miriam is effective
and true to nature. Its close, at the lurching of the
drunken Dominican friar into Joseph's arms, is pathetic, suggestive and dramatic. On the morrow poor
Joseph the idealist is to become a member of this very
Dominican order and a brother of this drunken friar.
The character of Joseph's father Manasseh is drawn in
a few lines, but those lines are masterly: the stern
ritual-keeping master of the house, joining in the excommunication of his renegade but undoubtedly loved
son, and later presiding over the feast of rejoicing at
his death: it is a portrait.

Judged as a writer Mr. Zangwill is temperamentally
mournful and pessimistic. In this story his apparent
purpose is to indicate the hopelessness of war against
the overwhelming actuality of Church and State. He
sympathizes with revolt, but he assures us that it is
vain.

Though perhaps beyond his intent, he has in this
story done more than this. Though he has said nothing more harsh against the Roman Church of the Sixteenth Century than has been before said by both
Protestant and Romanist, nevertheless we feel that
it is a Jew who is speaking, and a Jew who is not sorry
to put his finger on the festering sore. His wounds,

though deserved, are not the wounds of a friend. None but a Jew could have written the story just as it has been written. No Jew has given us so profound an insight into Jewish character as has Mr. Zangwill. Fra Giuseppi is unique among the friars of fiction: he is at once both Jew and friar; more than that he is manifestly the product of a Jewish intellect. The friar is viewed from an unwonted but legitimate standpoint, the standpoint of the Sixteenth Century Jew. We feel that Mr. Zangwill has given us this, and has therefore attained to that "artistic truth" which he himself says is "literally the highest truth." For this reason the story of Fra Giuseppi, the Dominican friar, the dreamer of the ghetto, assumes an importance in a study of the "friar in fiction" which otherwise it would not possess.

UNITY IN ART

UNITY IN ART

MAN is essentially constructive, instrumentally analytic. The difference between the constructive and the analytic is the difference between regarding a thing from the totality-aspect, the constituent elements of the thing existing only as parts, and receiving meaning only through the whole; and the way of regarding a thing as a group of elements, the total existing to be analysed, the element only being real.

These opposing points of view are the opposing attitudes of the artist and the scientist. By Artist, meaning the poet and novelist, as well as the painter and sculptor, since all of these contribute to the receptive and appreciative personality, all deal with phenomena in a creative way, aiming to give totality-impressions.

The work of the artist is twofold. It is æsthetic, it is also ethical. His æsthetic aim is to set the thing or event before the beholder in such a way that the effect which is produced upon himself shall be passed over to the observer. It is, briefly, to convey the total unitary impression, fraught with his own personality, and make it significant for the observer. The same is true of the ethical activity; its aim is so to present the thing or event, that it shall be effective in directing or transforming the activity of the subject to whom it is addressed.

Not *truth* but *power* is at the heart of the artist's effort. Truth must be there, but it is the truth of impression, not truth of description. The office of the artist is to make an ideal order of existences or values, in the service of which he dissolves the continuity of actual experience, and selects from its elements those which are parts of the ideal order and which will be factors in the production of his desired impression. To this end he employs—Perspective and Unity. By Perspective, meaning the emphasis of the significant and suppression of insignificant elements.

What is intended by Unity is more difficult of definition, both because the thing itself is so elemental and spiritual and because of the confusion so often made between the "unity" and "the unities" of a composition.

"The master of those who know" was not too great a name for the putative author of the doctrine of "the unities." Though in truth Aristotle was chiefly concerned with that internal unity which he claims for Tragedy in common with every other work of art.[1] Whereof this unity consists, and wherein it differs from "the unities," may be more clearly understood by a brief consideration of what has been termed the "English pseudo-classic period of poetry."

The pseudo-classic period of English poetry has been called the age of the supremacy of Alexander Pope, but it began before Pope was born. Dryden, for ex-

[1] Arist. *On Poetry*, VIII., 4.

ample, in the prologue of his tragi-comedy, *Secret Love,* professed allegiance to those ancient law-givers of the poetic art, Aristotle, Horace, Quintilian, Longinus and their modern Gallic interpreter, Boileau, when he claims for his work the merit of having been composed according to the exactest rules, with strict regard for "the unities."

Pope, in the *Essay on Criticism* (1711), makes a like profession of reverence for the ancient masters, though when he names Boileau, he, inconsistently, reproaches French writers for their servility in submitting to Boileau's authority, while at the same time he calls his own countrymen uncivilised because they will not wear the yoke; on the other hand, those English poets who accept the Greco-Roman-Gallic precepts, are "restoring wit's fundamental law." Pope's *Essay on Criticism* did not confirm the vogue of pseudo-classicism in England and give it a reign of nearly a hundred years. It was the example he set of rendering in scintillating verse the very thought of his own age—the thought that is, and the mind of England, as revealed to him in political cabals, literary cliques, frivolous society, and the varied circle of pseudo-philosophers. For him, the poet's mission is to trick out nature in finery and to polish into brilliants the commonplaces of universal morality, the current religion and the received philosophy of life:

> True wit is nature to advantage dressed;
> What oft was thought but ne'er so well expressed.

Admirable, no doubt, Pope is, for he has made poetical the most humdrum sentiments, the most commonplace passions, but they are poor souls and poor wits whom he can content; for it is a low ideal which this poet proposes to himself. Plato classes such artists in speech with pastry cooks. Pope's brilliant antithetic couplets made less artificial poetry seem dull, and the elder poets of nature were for a hundred years neglected and the poetic contemplation of nature repressed; not extinguished, however, either in poet or people, as was proved in 1730 by the success of Thomson's *Seasons,* with its manly sentiment and its native vigour.

Pope himself, in the *Essay on Criticism,* much as he prizes the Aristotelian laws of poetic composition, recognises the supremacy of nature over all magisterial precepts. Nature is, he writes:

At once the source, and end, and test of art;

and of this aphorism he had unexpected proof. Gay's *Shepherd's Week* was written at the instance of Pope to throw ridicule on the *Pastorals* of Ambrose Philips, by introducing scenes from actual pastoral and peasant life in England. Though ludicrous, the scenes were felt to be true to nature and life, and were received with great favour. If ludicrous effect is wanted, we need not seek beyond Pope's own *Pastorals,* where on the banks of "fair Thames" Sicilian muses sing and the swains and shepherd-lasses wear the homely English names, Strephon and Daphnis! This is *reductio ad absurdum* of classicism.

But why should an English poet be required to poetise by Grecian or by Gallic rule? "There is such a thing as reason without syllogisms," pleaded George Farquhar; "knowledge without Aristotle, and there are languages besides Greek and Latin. . . . To different towns there are different ways. . . . We (English) have the most unreasonable medley of humours of any nation on earth. . . . We shall find a Wildair in one corner and a Morose in another; hence the rules of English comedy do not lie in the compass of Aristotle or his followers, but in the pit, boxes and galleries." And herein lay the fundamental difference between French and English literary art. Boileau and his successors in France, until the most recent times, addressed a court circle, an academic clique, or at most a single capital. All literary judgment, all literary taste, emanated from Paris.

The English poet and dramatist addressed the whole people. As long as the taste for poetry in England was determined by the polite circle which admired Pope's exquisitely turned verses and his sparkling epigrammatic style, the native muse unadorned passed for a rustic wench, and unsophisticated nature seemed mere barbarism. In Pope's time Shakspeare was as distasteful to his countrymen as to the French, for whom, as represented by Voltaire, "Shakspeare was a buffoon." And it is an interesting coincidence that Pope's *Rape of the Lock,* his masterpiece, is for the

French critic and historian of English literature, Hippolyte Taine, a piece of "harsh, scornful, indelicate buffoonery."

In the pseudo-classic age, poetry was indeed an art —it was artificial, and for it Nature was an artificial thing. Her face was rouged to make her presentable in polite society; in its presence Nature, naked, was ashamed, so their poets showed them "Nature to advantage dressed." Its conception of Nature and of Man was not drawn from nature or from man, but from literary tradition. The *Gradus ad Parnassum,* and the store of poetic phrases and figures, were no small part of the poet's inspiration. As Coleridge happily characterises some of the most ambitious efforts of Pope, "the thoughts are prose thoughts translated into the language of poetry."

The poet of the pseudo-classic period describe nature with great richness of imagery, but their imagery comes not from nature, being simply a compound of hearsays derived from the poets of classic times. Wordsworth says of Pope's version of the celebrated moonlight scene in the *Iliad,* that "a blind man, in the habit of attending accurately to descriptions casually dropped from the lips of those around him, might easily depict those appearances with more truth." For Wordsworth, it is matter of wonder how an enthusiastic admirer of Pope's *Iliad,* reciting those verses under the cope of a moonlit sky, could fail to notice their absurdity.

The universe which these poets-by-rule evolved was

doubtless very well ordered.   In it "the unities" were sacredly observed; but it was petty compared with Shakespeare's universe, which was God's.   No one is especially anxious about the preservation of "the unities" in God's universe, and, like it, Shakespeare's appears a mighty maze, but is not without a plan.

Truly, for the poet, there is a sublime unity in nature; and his profound sense of this unity and of his own kinship with nature, gives him a passionate sympathy with the whole creation.   He is conscious of a presence in nature that "disturbs him with the joy of elevated thoughts"—

> A motion and a spirit, that impels
> All thinking things, all objects of all thought,
> And rolls through all things.

The poet's vision is, therefore, a feeling, a sympathy, as well as an intuition; the heart has part in it equally with the mind, and his work speaks both to the mind and the heart of those whom he addresses.   It gains admission to mind and heart primarily through sense-impression of a pleasurable kind.   The poet, painter, sculptor, or musician, in order that he may produce such impressions, must himself be in the highest degree sensitive; his mind "a mansion for all lovely forms"; his memory "a dwelling-place for all sweet sounds and harmonies."   Without such native sensibility, he may, indeed, by a *tour de force,* produce a work of art in music, though he be congenitally deaf; but after all, it will be artifice, not art.   It is because all art has its spring in fine sensibility that the artist is held to be by nature an epicurean, a virtuoso of pleasurable ideas and sentiments. Certainly he needs must be a man exquisitely alive to all the joys of sense, whether tranquil or intoxicating. Such must be the sensibility of the artist or poet that, as Sully-Prudhomme finely says, "certain colors, certain lines, certain sounds shall affect him like caresses or like wounds." The poet must, with Wordsworth, have felt the "aching joys" and the "dizzy raptures" of the contemplation of nature.

The reason why sensory experiences thus impress themselves upon the mind of the poet is, that for him they are vocal and emblematic. He does not delight in these excitations of sensibility merely for their own sake; on the contrary, like a true epicurean, he enjoys them only so far as they respond to his inmost emotional and mental states. The flaming of the sunset, foretelling the approach of night, speaks to him of heroic struggles ending in disappointment; the swiftness of the mountain torrent gives him a sense of exaltation; a leaden sky depresses his spirit; that is, the outer world of time and space speaks to him in symbols expressive of man's invisible world, which outreaches space and time; while he contemplates nature, he hears ofttimes

The still, sad music of humanity.

In thus interpreting as symbols the phenomena of nature, the poetic and artistic temperament simply in-

tensifies into a passion a gift which is universal; for
even in the lowest grade, men are sufficiently endowed
with the poetic faculty to discern in physical things
intimations of things spiritual, and analogies with
things and states of the soul of man. Everybody is
poet enough to call a mood "gloomy," or "cold," or
"bleak," or "sunny"; an outburst of anger "fiery."
Were it not for this gift, speech would be impossible; it
would be more difficult to carry on the simplest conversation without metaphor or metonymy than to discourse in words all one-syllabled; we cannot express
modes or states of the soul otherwise than in terms of
sense-impression.

"You have a heart of stone," cries yokel Hans; "and
you a pumpkin for a head," responds his milkmaid
inamorata. In divining the analogy of sensory experiences and affections of the soul, these rustic swains
do for the nonce exercise, the poetic faculty.

> Sunset and evening star,
>   And one clear call for me;
> And may there be no moaning of the bar
>   When I put out to sea,

sings a dying seer; but we need no study to see that
the "sunset" is no literal sunset, nor the "evening
star" a real star, nor the "call" a vocal call, nor the
"sea" a sea; these are all sense-impressions elaborated
in the poet's mind into symbols of things entirely
spiritual.

This faculty, we have said, is possessed by all, but

it is possessed in a high degree only by the artist. To Wordsworth, in the time of his hale, manly vigour, nature was "all-in-all"; the sounding cataract haunted him "like a passion"; the imposing spectacle of creation was to him

> An appetite; a feeling and a love
> That had no need of a remoter charm
> By thought supplied.

But as physical strength declined, he notes in himself an exaltation, a purification of sensibility, and he often is conscious of a Presence that pervades all things. He is still a lover of nature for herself, but he is more, perceiving in

> All the mighty world
> Of eye and ear, *both what they half create*
> *And what perceive.*

Only the poet can interpret the spiritual meanings of the universe of things; he alone has the second-sight. But one need not be a poet to see and feel how true the interpretation is; let it be presented in the poet's verse, and the most prosaic mind will recognise its truth.

To illustrate: Suppose a bark is leaving port on a long voyage. Spectators ashore observe the preparations for departure; the last farewells, the spreading of the sails, the vanishing from view; and each spectator is thinking of the fortunes of that ship, her crew, and her cargo. One, a man of the common mould, a shopkeeper, will carry with him from the scene a few impressions of sight and hearing, and will perhaps think of the dangers the ship will encounter in turning Cape Horn. If asked to relate the incidents of the departure, he will not be able to state a single one proper to that vessel's leaving port, to distinguish it from any one of a thousand like occurrences.

Another spectator is interested in the science of political economy and commercial exchanges; he will have much the same sensible impressions recorded in his memory; but he will probably have made some conjecture as to the ship's tonnage, value of the cargo, risks, profits, and the like. Another is a literary realist, and he will have noted accurately every movement of the vessel and the crew, every sight and sound, and when all is over, will be able to describe the scene vividly and with a particularity sufficient to individualise it among a thousand scenes of the same kind.

A poet, too, is there, and sees and hears just what those others hear and see; but his contemplation goes out beyond the bounds of that harbour and that hour. He sees the bark favoured by summer breezes as she sets out on her voyage; but he sees also the same bark coming back to port after many months.

> How like the younker or a prodigal
> The scarfed bark puts from her native bay,
> Hugg'd and embraced by the strumpet wind.
>
> How like a prodigal doth she return
> With over-weather'd ribs and ragged sails,
> Lean, rent and beggar'd by the strumpet wind.

That is poetry, absolute poetry; yet the most stupid
of mortals will feel its force and its truth, and will
even be sensible of its beauty; it is the very voice of
nature speaking through the poet to the soul and
heart of every man, however low his mental or moral
grade.

In the poet's soul is mirrored all humanity, all nature.
The poet is not a seer for himself; his delight in ap-
prehending the spiritual significations of his sense-
impressions may seem to merit for him the epithets
egoist and epicure; yet if we stop there we attain only
one of those partial truths which are ever deadly false-
hoods. For the poet is more than receptive, and he is
more than a discerner and interpreter of the spiritual
meanings of sensible things; he is also altruistic and
creative; he "half creates and half perceives." The
artist—poet, musician, painter, or sculptor—elaborat-
ing by processes revealed to him alone, the material of
his art, awakens in us feelings akin to his own, when
in "serene and blessed mood" he "sees into the life of
things." He is the interpreter of nature for his less
gifted fellow, whose ear catches not the low, sad
music, and for whom the pageant of nature is "as a
landscape to a blind man's eye."

The poet sees the light that never was on sea or
land, and "in his light we shall see light." The poet
thrills us with a multitude of intimations of spiritual
truths, for his whole soul is concentrated in his work
and labours to have complete expression as far as the
materials under his hand may allow. He educes from

the infinitude of his sensory experiences all whatsoever accords with the tone of some life-truth which he
longs to make known, and this tone, by the aid of his
art medium, he produces in us. If he is a musician,
his artistic creed will be that of Pythagoras as rendered
by Dryden.

> From harmony, from heavenly harmony
> This universal frame began:

he will piously believe the Grecian myth, truer than
any history, how

> Amphion taught contending kings
> From various discords to create
> The music of a well-tuned state.

The sculptor or the painter will combine visual perceptions, such as lines and colours, as subtly as the
musician combines audible vibrations. The art medium of the poet will be words. If he is a master of
the significant, he will reincarnate what he compre-
hends of life and convey his thought to others. To
do this, he is necessarily compelled to create a language
essentially his own; the sap of the word participates in
the vitality of his thought. For there is in language
both personality, fate and inspiration; and words inspire thought as well as express thought.

Thus each artist, giving form in the material proper
to his art, to his individual sense-impressions, according to their expressional value, fulfils the first requirement of all art—that it shall move the spiritual
sensibility by means of pleasurable excitations. Thus,

too, he enables us to enter indirectly into the soul of his work, which he alone can know directly.

Since each of the innumerable sensory concepts given to us by any work of art, for example, the Niobids of the sculptor Scopas, has its separate signification and value; and since each separate signification is spiritual, the expression of the work as a whole must also be spiritual. But the expression of the whole is by no means merely the sum of the significations of the several parts or members of the group, which would be a psychological absurdity. For though the several figures in the group and their several parts, as the feet, arms, breasts, head, of Niobe and her children, be supposed to possess artistic perfection each in itself, yet no association of the various inner or spiritual effects produced by them will enable us to grasp the master idea of the artist—the unity of the group. Unity—not "the unities"—is, as we have said, the soul and life of any work of art; and only the consummate artist can infuse this soul into his work.

Irrespective of the spiritual expression of a work of art, no mere assemblage of its constituent parts will account for our unitary mental conception of it. A work of art must, over and above perfection in its detail, possess unity in expression; *it must say one thing,* and every stroke of chisel, or pencil, or pen, must be subdued to that one purpose. Should the artist fail in realising in his work this unity of idea, then, however great its value may be as proof of skill in detail work, as a whole it is voiceless and expressionless; it says nothing.

But, as will often happen, the artist's conception of the unity of his composition—historic scene, landscape or the like—may be faultless and expressed in his work with perfect fidelity, and yet it will be unperceived to the chance comer, and may require some attentive study to come at it. Works of art are not intended to please or instruct chance comers; truth is often found at the bottom of a well. Works of art are themselves the fruit of deep study and meditation, and they require study and meditation to understand and appreciate them. Meanwhile, they will even by their details give a sensible delight, and by degrees will reveal the harmony of their design.

Standing before the Niobe, if to the mild æsthetic satisfaction we feel at sight of the rippling flow of her drapery, we try to add our sentiment of pity upon seeing her beautiful arm relaxed in pain, and the sympathy stirred by the mother's anguish of her face, we shall never come at the soul and life of the piece; or rather, we shall come at it only in spite of ourselves. For back of our feelings of satisfaction, pity and sympathy, is a larger moral and æsthetic consciousness, which divines the intent of the artist and recognises the unity of the work; its several members are seen to be unified by vital co-operation organically, not by addition of one to another.

From the view-point of the pseudo-classic school, that grand tragi-comedy, Shakespeare's King Henry

IV., appears but a jostling crowd of irrelated characters, of multifarious and incongruous incidents. The plot is incoherent, and the play baffles every search for unity. So well known a French critic as Paul Dupont, steeped in the Grecian and Gallic tradition, complains that there is little action and less interest in this play, that the various circumstances have no relation among themselves, that no person predominates over the others, and that it is "the anarchy of the scene."

Yet to one who reads aright, the character of the King gives obvious unity to the play. Everywhere we feel the dominance of the royal mind, the royal will. His form is ever looming on the horizon. His spirit permeates the tragic and the comic scenes alike. There is, too, a certain unity in the pervading sentiment of life-weariness, which, like the burden of the preacher,

> Vanity of vanities, all is vanity,

is exemplified in the last words of the dying Percy, that

> Thought's the slave of life, and life's time's fool.

It is echoed by Prince Harry, even by jesting Falstaff, and particularly in the closing speeches of the King. There is, too, a deeper unity, a purpose, which gives a psychological oneness more profound and more true than all the unities of the schools. That purpose is to reveal the growth of a spirit, to exhibit the development of a character.

"In the Shakespearian drama," to quote Coleridge, "there is a vitality which grows and evolves itself from within—a keynote which guides and controls the harmonies throughout"—and in this play that "keynote" is the character of Prince Hal. In the opening scene we find him compared, to his disparagement, with young Hotspur. His own father piteously sorrowing

> In envy that my lord Northumberland
> Should be the father of so blest a son:
>
> .   .   .   .
>
> Whilst I, by looking on the praise of him
> See riot and dishonour stain the brow
> Of my young Harry.

Though the king forces "young Harry" from his thoughts and talks of "young Percy's pride," yet the real action of the drama has commenced, and every incident and every personage assumes a proper and necessary place in that harmony of which the keynote is the character of the young prince, and the *motif* is his moral and spiritual regeneration. Even Falstaff, "the unimitated, the unimitable Falstaff," was a creation necessary to the transformation of the madcap Prince of Wales into the kingly hero of Agincourt. Mark the wisdom which assigns to Falstaff the speaking of those words—

> Presume not that I am the thing I was;
> For heaven doth know, so shall the world perceive
> That I have turn'd away from my former self.
> So will I those that kept me company;

Hotspur, too, contributes to the growth in grace of this aforetime roysterer of the Boar's Head, this "mad wag" of Gadshill, who, chivalrous, frees the Douglas ransomless, and to the Percy lying dead, bids—

> Fare thee well, great heart.

"Let the end try the man," says Shakspeare. And when in the last act of the last scene, the new young king says,

> Presume not that I am the thing I was;
> For heaven doth know, so shall the world perceive
> That I have turn'd away from my former self.
> So will I those that kept me company;

we realise that the dramatic action is complete, that the highest unity has been observed.   Henry of Monmouth having learned the great lessons of humanity amidst men with whom his follies made him equal,

> Consideration like an angel came
> And whipp'd th' offending Adam out of him.

Power is at the root of all poetic worth; the words and images of the poet are but symbols used to produce an ideal effect.   He aims to convey human emotion. He is under obligation to no given unity, but uses the material in service of an ideal unity.   Likewise the novelist aims to present an ideal life in such a way that it shall affect his reader as would a real personality. His aim is to reconstruct life and make it significant. He fails whenever description becomes unduly prominent, or when he substitutes psychological analysis of his *dramatis personæ* for the interpretation of life as its significance is revealed to his own soul. He succeeds just so far as he is able to dissolve the continuity of actual experience, and to bring together those elements which, though in fact widely separated one from another, do truly possess spiritual unity.

The true synthetic or unifying element in a work of art is always primarily emotion,—the heart, not the mind. The rational faculty discriminates, arranges, co-ordinates. Its special power lies in analysis; it can only lay parts together, conformably to a plan; as when the anatomist, rearranging the members of the dead body, gives a suggestion of life. But there is suggestion of life, only because the idea of life is invincibly associated in our minds with the human form. Scientific analysis is alien to the artistic temperament; the artist's faculty is intuition, not induction. The difference between the reconstructed cadaver and the living, breathing man, is the difference between a composition by rule-of-art and an imaginative creation.

It is the aim of intelligence to produce results like itself. The soul of the artist animates his masterpiece. To give a dramatic presentation of a situation he must participate in it; he must for the nonce be the character to which he would give life. In that consummate portrait of a hypocrite churchman, *Bishop Blougram's Apology,* every trait is drawn in the clear light of poetic contemplation. Rarely has such a character-study been made; and in making it Browning for the nonce is himself transformed into the very essence of hypocrisy. The poem is a libel, indeed; it is sent to the wrong address; nevertheless it is a work of genius; this hypocrite is no lay figure, no man of straw, but an incarnate spirit, living, breathing, moving.

To the spectator possessed of æsthetic sensibility the portrait of Mona Lisa appears animated by a soul, the very spirit of Leonardo finds expression in those speaking lineaments. The soul of the artist has become one with the soul of his subject; and the spectator feels that he is in the presence of a living spiritual force.

This synthetic element, this element of unity in a work of art we may attempt to define as consisting in the rejection of elements, the data of which do not form part of the ideal order, and the introduction of elements from other data which do form such part. But it is more than that; it is, indeed, something so inward and essential that like all elemental things it is, except in the most vague and negative terms, indefinable. But it is discoverable in any sculpture, picture, poem or person that you really love; and it is the individuality of that work of art or that person—in either case a human individuality, a human personality. It is, in Hazlitt's words, "that fine particle which expands, rarefies, refines, raises our whole being; without which man's life is poor as a beast's"; it is the human soul, the spiritual essence of man. Of this "fine particle" no critic can tell you anything, except that, like Hazlitt himself, or like Lamb, Hunt, Arnold,

he does so indirectly, "in a figure"; when, in words
which are themselves thoroughly imaginative, he
catches the spirit of the thing criticised, as one by
sympathetic imitation catches the inmost self of another. But this unifying "spirit" eludes the analysis
and research of the physicist, the metaphysician, the
psychologist. Being strictly individual, it is not
subject-matter of any science; for science studies
species, not individuals. To know what it is, is to
divine it through sympathy; but only the artist can
express it. A true work of art reveals the artist's soul,
speaking out from passion felt, not feigned; and from
intuition, not hearsay; it is a revelation of the artist's
ideal world and of his own soul.

Mind is the atmosphere of the individual soul; it is
the fire of which thought is the flame; its psychological
significance in art is—personality. "In the depths of
human minds all literatures lie dormant." By presenting life as it is revealed to his own soul, thought
as it is born in his own intellect, the artist will touch a
responsive chord in some other soul, express what
some other intellect has dimly perceived, and awaken
in men's minds feelings that were ready to blossom.

In the art of literature, dominion over the significant can only result from personality, since personality
is the individual conception of the significant, and
power over minds and men is a genius for its grasping
and communicating. The sons of dexterity, and the
imitators, may give us facile prose and flowing verse,
perfection of a thousand details; but failure in this

personal sense for the significant means failure to convey power. In this alone will be found true unity. This alone is impressive and important; convincing, world-changing. Manliness, robustness, effectiveness, the expression of the highest spiritual meaning in so far as it is revealed to the writer, that is personality; life-communicating, life-enhancing. Only through this unifying quality of personality, the power of truth as reflected from an individual soul, can come the realisation of the vision of a glorious, but possible, humanity in literature.

**SINCERITY
IN ART**

SINCERITY IN ART

INASMUCH as sincerity is commonly apprehended as the opposite of feigning, it seems like a contradiction to speak of sincerity in relation to a work of art; art being essentially imitation, or feigning, as Plato defined it, and after him, Aristotle.

The Othello, pacing the stage, his heart gnawed by the venom-pangs of jealousy as he lends ear to Iago's villain slander, is not the Moor, but Edwin Booth, Henry Irving, or some other actor whom we have admired in other characters; yet are we affected by the feigned distress. As we follow the events of his tragic history, we are even moved to tears for the sorrows of the Moor, and express our admiration by applauding the actor who feigns these passions.

Why do we applaud the actor? Because he is a sincere artist. "Ah, but it has been a feigning all the time!" Truly so, but the feigning is in accordance with the artist's nature and aptitudes, with his capacity for feeling and for expression; therefore he is, as an artist, sincere. Were that same artists to assume the part of Rip Van Winkle, probably we should long for our Joseph Jefferson. The actor is permitted to assume the garb, the looks, the manner, the passion and personality of a stage character, but it is not permitted him to be false either to his own self or to his hearers, by counterfeiting any character or personality, that is foreign to his own proper temperament or his own histrionic powers.

All this is palpably true of the art of theatrical representation; it is not less true of all the Arts. A few examples will show that sincerity is a prime essential in works of sculpture and painting.

Consider the Artemis of the Naples museum. Is this figure genuinely archaic, sculptured when Grecian or Italo-Grecian art was still in its infancy? Or must it be referred to a later period and regarded as a studied counterpart of obsolete antique forms—a Brumagem archaic goddess?

With its soulless placidity of countenance, with the stiff regularity of the minute pleats of the robe, which even the hasty stride of the figure cannot disarrange, the Artemis might well pass as a genuine specimen of archaic art.

But if our attention rests on that step which we have purposely described as hasty, and if we note the graceful gesture of the arms, so fittingly accompanying the movement of the whole body, we are forced to refer the statue to a more recent period. Genuine archaic statues are wholly actionless; instance the celebrated funeral stela in the Athens museum. It bears a bas-relief figure of an armed man, known as *Marathonomachos,* fighter at Marathon. Here the sculptor, though he makes the legs divaricate a little, to show that the warrior was marching, nevertheless fails utterly to suggest the idea of motion, that being beyond the capacity of archaic Grecian sculpture.

How and wherefore it came to pass that artists, probably Greek artists, were led to fashion such statues as the Artemis, is a question easily answered when we consider that in Italy, in the last period of the Roman Commonwealth, there were whole populations that held fast to the ancient order and clung to primitive beliefs. These scrupled to pay adoration, or to offer prayer or sacrifice to the graceful statues of gods introduced from conquered Corinth and Athens. The beauty of those figures scandalised the *naif* religious sentiment of these conservatives; they demanded figures of gods such as their forefathers had worshipped. The sculptor, in compliance with the taste of his patron, was then obliged to resort to the trick which many a Florentine workman practises nowadays when he fashions chests and cabinets in thirteenth century styles. But even as the modern woodcarver never can attain the quaint elegance of the earlier artists, so those ancient Italo-Grecian sculptors could not entirely forego their acquired proficiency, nor so completely unlearn, for the nonce, the canons of art as ascertained in their own day, as to render the true spirit of archaism. They produced only pieces of seeming-ancient workmanship, which artistically were not sincere.

Passing from Roman and Grecian art, to the art of the beginning of the nineteenth century, we may instance the works of Antonio Canova. Canova lived in the palmy days of restored classicism. This revival was due to the French Revolution, when France tried to persuade herself that her Commonwealth was a counterpart of the republics of Rome and Athens, and that Bonaparte was Cæsar or Alexander come again. In those days ladies affected Grecian costumes and coiffures; pottery aped the forms of ancient pateræ and amphoræ; articles of house furniture were assimilated to ancient classic forms, and the psuedo-antique dominated public and private life.

Living in a society eager to persuade itself that Grecian and pagan ideals were again to reign, Canova adopted the fashion, and modelled Grecian or pagan deities. Consider his "Venus Rising From the Bath" in the Galleria Pitti at Florence; and, to appreciate correctly its artistic value, it is necessary to remember how the Grecians were wont to represent their Aphrodite.

In the age of Phidias, Aphrodite was indeed the goddess both of love and of beauty; such she appears in the Venus of Milo, a stately figure, divinely fair. To Phidian grandeur succeeded Praxitelean loveliness, which in his disciples and imitators soon degenerated into excessive softness and mannerism. This we see in the Apolline of the Uffizi. We find in the Galleria degli Uffizi a good imitation of Praxiteles, the Venus of Medici. In this statue Venus has lost much of her primitive stateliness; she has become more human; she is still

> hominum divomque voluptas
> Alma Venus;
>
> Joy of men and gods, benignant Venus.—*Lucretius.*

but she is no more empress of earth, and sea, and sky,

> terrum naturam sola gubernans,
> Thou alone all nature rulest.   —*ib.*

imparting fruitfulness to all the denizens of air, sea
and land.   She is now simply the goddess of love,
of human love, gentle and bewitching, but still a
divine being.   Considered from this point of view,
the Medicean Venus is sincere.

To the mind of Canova, living in the Napoleonic
era, how could Venus appear as a goddess?   The
pagan spirit pervading every branch of art and learning with which the sculptor was in contact, might
somewhat weaken, but could not entirely eclipse
modern feeling.   Under these circumstances the prac-
tice of art meant perpetual effort, and not even Canova's skill could conceal the evidences of painful endeavour to seem to be what he was not.   With all his
genius, Canova has utterly failed to give us a Venus;
instead, he gives us a very charming lady of early
nineteenth century, a *dame d'honneur* of Josephine or
Marie Louise, wearing the Grecian headdress which
fashion had made obligatory; but not a Grecian goddess.   The Venus of Canova is, therefore, not a sincere
work of art.

It is due to Canova to concede that the fault was

not, properly speaking, his, but that of the world in which he lived. We have a splendid proof of his genuine artistic genius in the mausoleum of Pope Clement XIII., in the Vatican basilica. Clement (Rezzonico), an old man, is kneeling on a cushion and in prayer. Though he is draped in the pontifical mantle, it is not as Pope that he prays, nor yet is he praying for the whole world; with palms joined, he prays as a man earnestly and devoutly for himself. The conception is grand and in harmony with the idea of a sepulchre—that bourne where all human distinctions of rank and power are forever annulled. Canova might have searched never so diligently among Grecian or Roman models, he could not have found anything like this modern and Christian inspiration; it sprang spontaneously from his own soul, and the work is a beautiful and sincere masterpiece.

Another example is found in the works of Pietro Vannucci, better known as Pietro Perugino. In Umbria, during the fifteenth century, we find, beginning with that painter of Fabriano, so well named Gentile, a flourishing school, an uninterrupted sequence of artists individually little known to fame, but gentle all, and inspired with a religious mysticism. The mood may be traced to the influence of the aspects of nature round about, the quiet grandeur of the surrounding hills and shady valleys; or it may have been fostered by reminiscences of St. Francis of Assisi's preaching, which, in the saint's own epoch, called into being a great school of mystical lyrics. Whatever may have been the cause, it is certain that a spirit of mysticism, if not very deep, at least very genuine, inspired the Umbrian school of the second half of the century in which Pietro Perugino began to paint.

Was Perugino's nature really inclined toward mysticism? It would be worth while to study the man in his personal appearance, "in those features which bear witness to the heart"; and this is easily done in that portrait of him by himself, now in the Sala del Cambio in Perugia. In that rounded, commonplace visage is no suggestion of ideality. In those firm-set lips and those frowning brows, deeply furrowed by anxious worldly thoughts, we read the character of a miser.

Vasari thus delineates the character of the man: "The terror of poverty being always present to his mind, he would for the love of gain do many things which he would never have done were he not so poor. . . . In his hankering after money, he cared neither for cold, nor hunger, nor hard work, nor weariness, if only he might hope to live some day in affluence and well-earned repose."

A covetous man he certainly was; and Vasari tells even worse things about this artist. But we cannot believe Perugino to have been the atheist Vasari would make him appear; yet we may safely conclude that his religious professions were not sincere.

Let us turn to his works, and study the panel representing the Madonna and Saints, found in the

Tribuna degli Uffizi, at Florence. Sitting in front of a double-vaulted portico, an architectural background often employed by Perugino, the Madonna holds the Bambino in her lap. On the curved pedestal we read:

Petrus Perusinus pinxit an. MCCCCLXXXXIII.

The Madonna is as graceful and pretty a woman as Perugino was able to put on canvas; but she is one of those creatures whom nature has gifted with fair, sweet features, rather than with deep and genuine ideality. In a word, a woman such as Leonardo da Vinci, painter of the feeling and the mind, the deepest thinker among all the Italian artists, would never have given to the world as the Madonna.

Perugino has idealised his Madonna by giving her finely-arched brows, languorous eyes half veiled by drooping lids, a straight nose, wreathed mouth, delicate, beautiful face. Expression, there is none, or only an expression of sweet vacuity, betokening sluggish intellect and absence of will. No interior struggle will ever spoil the composure of those suave faultless contours. The Mother holds her Babe with artless grace, but seems not to care much for Him or for St. Sebastian, who, by a hardy anachronism, is pictured standing, pierced with arrows, at her right hand. She would feel pity for him if she were the true Madonna; but, there's the rub. She is not the Madonna, but only a contadina model earning her wages; and when she sits there composedly, with somebody's baby in her lap, she performs her whole duty, and

nothing more is required or expected of her. We find
no fault with the Bambino; he is a nice chubby-faced
child.

On the left is St. John the Baptist, wearing a mantle
over his tunic of goat skin; a fair youth, slender and
well-shaped, as Perugino's young men usually are.
Another bold anachronism, for if the Bambino is
a yearling babe, John must be precisely eighteen
months old. The face of John expresses placid composure, verging on stupidity, but the features are decidedly good. While the gaze of the Bambino is fixed
upon him, what is the Forerunner doing? There
is neither spiritual expression in his face nor spiritual
significance in his gesture.

There is in this youth nothing of the Precursor;
he might stand for an errand boy returning from the
market. Instead of a group possessing a deeply mystic
signification, we have here simply a collection of good-
looking, but vulgar people.

St. Sabastian, with two arrows sticking in his
body, cannot, even in this august presence, be unmind-
ful of his pains, so the artist cleverly combines in the
action of this figure the expression of physical suffering and all-subduing faith. The upturned and fore-
shortened head of Sebastian, considered apart and for
itself, might be pronounced a masterpiece, were it not
that in it we recognise one of Perugino's hackneyed
and stale fetches, not always employed to express St.
Sebastian's martyr-pains.

Perugino's compositions beguile us into an admiration which they do not merit. In each the figures are well painted, and considered individually, are admirable, though somewhat trite from repetition; moreover, the grouping is always graceful. Still this is not high art; it is clever workmanship, artisanship, but it is of the same grade as the mechanic handicrafts; the painter's studio is only a factory for production of religious paintings. So much for Perugino's mystical spirit.

Yet was he a true artist; not because he was a skilled draughtsman and master of all the resources of the palette, but because he had a fine sense of the beautiful, and wonderful skill in grouping his figures; and because all these, his skills, were ministered to by a knowledge of technique that has seldom been surpassed, if ever. But Perugino is more, even than all this would of itself imply. At his best, he is a great painter. Consider the Deposizione in the Galleria Pitti, Florence.

In the centre is the body of Jesus, resting on a stone, and sustained on the left hand by Joseph of Arimathea, who, kneeling on one knee, faces the beholder; near Joseph is St. John and a woman with joined palms raised. On the right, Nicodemus holds the edge of the shroud. Behind the Christ are three figures kneeling; the Virgin in the middle of this group supports one of her Son's arms, while Magdalene, at her side, upholds the head, and the third woman prays. Another woman, standing behind the Madonna and earnestly gazing on the body of the

Saviour, stretches forth her arms, with extended palms, in an attitude full of pity. In the background on the right are three men, one of whom holds on his palm and is showing to the others the nails that have pierced the members of the Crucified.

So much for general description of the painting; let us now proceed to its æsthetical analysis. We admire this composition because it represents a scene full of life and reality.

The minds, if not the gaze, of all the persons in the picture converge on the Saviour. The Madonna, John and the women are looking at him. Joseph and the men forming the group on the right are thinking of him. Thus, and only thus, can the composition of a picture be made synthetical, since it is not enough for two persons to be photographed close to each other or even arm in arm; if both are merely looking at the photographer, they will never form a scene nor even a group. The material bond is of small importance when we fail to realise the corresponding expression, the ideal connection, which in this picture is so evident. The better to appreciate this masterpiece, observe how diversely, but always how sincerely, the feeling of pity is expressed by the several figures. Passionate in the Madonna; sorrowful, yet tinged with feminine gentleness in the Magdalene; blended with manly firmness in Joseph; subdued in Nicodemus, who is busied with cares for the entombment; anxious in John and the woman close to him; mixed with painful wonder in the woman standing behind the Madonna; and piously submissive in the woman kneeling with hands folded.

Turning now to the group of three men on the right, we see one of them pointing out to the others two of the nails he holds on his palm. One of the listeners raises his clinched hands close to his face with a gesture of mingled pity and grief; while the other man looks on with sorrowful astonishment. A brief explanation will show the importance of this group.

One of the first requisites for a work of painting or sculpture is definiteness and clearness of meaning; we cannot admire when the composition is unintelligible to us. This clearness is easier to obtain in literary works, because the spoken or written word traverses a series of moments resulting in one event; while the Fine Arts give us only one of those moments.

Masaccio, Fra Filippo Lippi, Benozzo, Gozzili, and other clever artists of the fifteenth century, resorted to a childishly, simple device to make clear the meaning of their compositions; in the same picture they give two or three successive phases of one act. In the *Tributo della Moneta,* a fresco painted by Masaccio in the Church del Carmine, in Florence, we see in the centre the Apostles surrounding the Saviour, who, being asked by the Centurion to pay the tribute money, sends Peter "to cast an hook and take up the fish that first cometh up," for in the fish's mouth the money would be found. The Apostles are filled with wonder and amazement. On the left hand is shown Peter at the seashore, stooping over the fish and taking the coin out of its mouth; on the right is Peter paying the money to the Centurion.

This device may admit of excuse in the case of Masaccio (born 1402, died 1428), a clever and promising artist, who had not time in so short a life to give the full measure of his power; but the same leniency is not to be extended to Perugino, who had the advantage of living longer and in a more enlightened epoch. The technique of painting had greatly advanced in the year 1495, when Perugino painted this Deposizione.

In putting this picture on canvas, it was essential that Perugino should select some one principal moment in the tragedy. This central group does not, in fact, fix that supreme moment on canvas and upon the attention of the beholder. If, however, the painter, without violating the harmony and integrity of his concept, can introduce into the same something which will suggest some prior or succeeding moment in the same drama, thus synthesising the whole event, he has added to the value of his telling of the story.

Perugino has attempted to attain this in the episode of the man pointing to the nails. It has been objected that "it was an indecency to gloat over those Crucifixion nails at such a time, and it is an anachronism to have men of the year A.D. 33, treasuring as sacred relics those spikes. That sort of thing did not come in till long centuries after." Answer may be made that such a treasuring of the nails as relics would not have been an anachronism in the thought of the age for which Perugino painted. Moreover, there is nothing in the picture to indicate gloating over the nails, nor a thought of treasuring them as relics. Rather does the thought seem to be, "See, here are the cruel spikes with which they pierced the Holy One."

The background of the Deposizione is occupied by a valley in the shadow, gloomy as befitted the sadness of the scene in the first plane, and the fact that it was already eventide when Joseph of Arimathea obtained leave to remove the body of Jesus from the cross. In the distance, the vale expands into a lightsome, sunny landscape. This sunny landscape on the far-off horizon is not necessarily an insincerity or contradiction of the evangelists' account of the Crucifixion. That Perugino intended to indicate that the sun was down, is evident from the shadow of darkness in the valley. But he is mindful that though a Deposizione should represent the body of a man destined for the grave, the painter should at the same time make us see in it the germ of the near and supernatural resurrection of a God. This far-distant glory, a "light that never was on land or sea," is not actual. It but symbolizes the blissful aftermath of redemption, resurrection and endless joy succeeding the passion of death.

In this picture everything has its architectonic reason, every incident is charged with purpose, and the artist who could conceive and realise such an ideal must have been truly great; nothing equal to this ever again came from the hand of Perugino.

Consider further, the "Portrait of a Lady," painted by Andrea del Sarto, in the Uffizi gallery at Florence. What could be more genial? What splendid blacks, and whites, and grays in his "Dispute About the Trinity," in the Pitti gallery. But go to the Church of the Annunziata, and, in the frescoes of the Story of St. Benizzi and the Adoration of the Magi, observe the draperies on the figures. Then go to the Chiostro dello Scalzo and observe how, in the scene of "Zacharias in the Temple," the bystanders dare not move for fear of disturbing their robes. Then, too, what a sad spectacle is his "Assumption." Instead of raising the soul of the beholder toward heaven, as does Titian's "Assumption," Andrea only speaks of tailor's stuffs. By sacrificing significance to pose and tissues, he has become insincere.

Many painters in the sixteenth and seventeenth centuries tried their skill in the treatment of the Last Supper. Several examples of different schools and different epochs may be selected to exemplify what is meant by Sincerity in Art.

In the little refectory of the Convento di San Marco is still to be seen a fresco by Ghirlandaio, representing the Last Supper or Cenacolo. A skilled draughtsman and a clever painter was Ghirlandaio, and he well knew how to group his figures and compose a picture; but his prosaic temperament and his joyous humor scarcely qualified him for a flight of fantasy or for profound meditation. There was in him but little of the poet.

On getting his order for a Cenacolo, the honest Florentine set at work with all the placid industry which characterised him. The Apostles he shows, sitting at three sides of a table, are good folk, every one; even Judas, who is distinguished from the rest only by absence of the nimbus round his head, and by the place which he occupies all alone on the fourth side of the table, opposite to John, who reclines his head on the Lord's shoulder. Ghirlandaio, in the simplicity of his *naïve* realism, has scattered over the table some ripe cherries, and represents a group of honest men partaking of a frugal meal; but he has not painted the Last Supper. Though he is said to have been a very truthful man, and though he never tries to cheat us into believing him anything but what he really is, we are constrained to say that though he has good colour, good portraits, the obvious everywhere, nevertheless as an artist he is not sincere, not faithful, that is, in the treatment of his subject, for he never suggests the significant.

Even more deficient was the painter—probably of Perugino's school—who has left us the Cenacolo in the ancient Monastery of Foligno in Florence. Here Judas is better rendered, because with some betokening of his depraved nature; but the figures of the other Apostles are worse than in Ghirlandaio's picture. Only one of them, sitting beside the Lord and grasping a knife, has something like a flash of pride or wrath in his eye; two others, on John's left, are meant to scowl at Judas, but they are not so incensed as to forget to eat their dinner; another is pouring out wine; while still others are chatting quietly about their private concerns; finally, one who is doing nothing, seems to be waiting patiently for permission to rise from the board.

This Cenacolo is generally admired, and considered superior to Ghirlandaio's. All the figures in it are distinguished by that beauty of feature and form which passed from Perugino to Raphael. To this last master this fresco has sometimes been attributed, erroneously, though nowadays no one believes Sanzio to have painted this graceful but meaningless and insincere Cenacolo.

Turn now to the ample canvas which Paolo Veronese finished, in 1572, and now found in the Academia Belle Arti in Venice. How could this gifted artist, this boisterous reveller, this lover of pomp and magnificence, this painter who succeeded by his magic in dazzling the observer so utterly that all his blunders in drawing and all his anachronisms fail to offend— how could he understand the Lord's Last Supper?

For him the Cenacolo is a sumptuous banquet in a noble palace, under three gorgeously ornamented arches, across which we enjoy the view of a splendid city with pompous monuments. Jesus is a young and fashionable Venetian nobleman; the Apostles are gaudy patricians; and as if this were not enough,

Veronese has filled his picture with a number of people coming and going, ascending and descending the grand flight of stairs—soldiers, a Moor, several turbaned Turks, a cup-bearer in gay livery, a buffoon in motley attire, a dwarf standing in front of a little girl; lastly, a cat and two dogs crouching under the table. Altogether, this is decidedly beautiful to look at; the painting ranks high among the masterpieces of the Veronese, and may in a certain sense be considered sincere, the painter having honestly rendered what he really felt. The question still remains, whether he really felt this subject as it ought to have been felt. And the answer clearly is, No; and hence the decision must be against the artistic sincerity of the painting.

If we turn from the sumptuous Venetian banquet back to humbler scenes and more pious artists, the difference will be startling.

In all that is spiritual, truth comes from God, or from those spirits who have been the friends of God. Of such was that simple-minded, god-fearing Dominican friar Giovanni da Fiesole, who adorned the walls of his convent of St. Mark, in Florence, with many a devout painting, one of them a Cenacolo.

No banquet is this, but a simple repast in a room of bare walls with a rude table, round which some of the Apostles reverently stand, while others, with even greater reverence, kneel and receive from the Lord's hand the blessed bread, and hearken to the sacramental words. "Take, eat. This is my body." The pious Dominican, adhering strictly to the text of St.

Luke, gives to the scene all its mystic significance; it is the institution of the Eucharist. The art-technique is plainly inferior to that in Veronese's picture, painted some 130 years later; moreover, the Cenacolo is not considered to be one of Fra Angelico's best works; but it glows with such certainty of purpose, such sacramental earnestness, that we must proclaim it superior to its more brilliant rival in sincere religious feeling and perfect fitness of inspiration and rendering.

Gifted with higher genius and larger imagination, Leonardo da Vinci, that prince of Italian painters, undertook, toward the year 1497, to adorn with a painting of the Last Supper the refectory of the convent of Santa Maria delle Grazia. Neither as an everyday meal of quiet, good people, nor as the mystic institution of the Eucharist, did Leonardo conceive his subject, but as a momentous drama in which deep feeling and fiery passions are stirred in the hearts of all the actors.

Jesus, sorrowing but resigned, foretells the treason that is to be: "Verily say I unto you, one of you which eateth with me shall betray me." His gestures are most apt. The left hand, with fingers expanded, the palm upward, the finger-tips touching the board, the muscles relaxed, states the fact as a thing that is to be received with submission; the right hand, also with fingers expanded, rests with wrist and thumb upon the board, the palm toward the table and hence away from the speaker's face; the other fingers do not touch the board, but are slightly raised; this attitude of the right hand, by its averted palm, expresses the aversion of the Saviour for the treason, but it is an aversion which is mingled with pity for the traitor, else the muscles of that hand would be tense.

The action of the painting shows the instant effect of the Saviour's words. Turning from the Central Figure toward the left—that is, to the right of the Lord—we have first, John, the beloved disciple, quite overcome with painful emotion; all muscles relaxed, his figure drooping, his head falling to the right, as in a half-swoon, his two hands joined resting on the board with fingers interlaced; a picture of utter dejection.

Next to John is the traitor, dwarfish, ill-favoured of visage, with beetling brows, thick black hair. The announcement has given him a shock and caused him to recoil as far as his proximity to his neighbour, Simon Peter, allows. With his right hand he grasps tightly the money-bag; with his left, he touches the folded hands of the beloved disciple. What means that reaching out to John? Has the Iscariot a velleity of repentance? The expression of that hand is no more than a velleity; perhaps the action is simply reflex and unconscious; there is no muscle in it, no will. But the right hand that clutches the purse!

Next after Judas we see Peter. Peter leans over toward the beloved disciple, and in doing so crowds the form of Judas against the table-edge. Peter has a weighty question to ask, and wants it answered *now;*

so he doesn't mind if he is rude to the ill-favoured Iscariot. He brings his strong, resolute visage alongside the ear of the grief-stricken John, and, summoning him to attention by a prod with the forefinger of his left hand, while the right grasps a knife, he asks in a whisper whether any name has been mentioned; the knife is pointed away from any probable object of Peter's suspicions. *Item,* Peter chooses to keep to himself the secret of the knife; 'but do, John, learn the name of the traitor.'

Next to Peter is his brother Andrew; the expression of his visage, the gesture of his uplifted hands with palms averse and fingers outstretched, tell of his horror on hearing of the perfidy. So far, the action of all the figures, except Andrew's and John's, expresses a two-fold emotion or state of mind, but in John and Andrew one emotion only.

Andrew's next neighbour, James the Younger, while his gaze is fixed intently on the Lord, stretches out, behind Andrew, his left arm and rests the hand on the shoulder of Peter; but he is thinking not of Peter, but of what the Lord may say next. That hand on Peter's shoulder simply rests there; it is not calling Peter away from his questioning of John; it does not clutch Peter's sleeve; it does not press on Peter's shoulder. James will have a question to ask of Peter as soon as the whispered conversation with John is over.

Last on that side of the board is Bartholomew, a noble figure of a man; he stands at the table-end, leaning on it with both hands, and listening eagerly to catch any further word the Lord may utter.

Returning now to the centre, the figure next to the Lord is James the Elder. His action and face expression, or rather facial inexpression, betray amazement, not horror, as in Andrew, whose hands uplifted to one level with palms averse, speak of detestation of the villainy. But James the Elder, is simply amazed, dumbfounded; he knows not what to think of it all. The gestures of his two hands are at odds; so are his thoughts. He is not horror-stricken, else the palms of his hands would be turned outward as though to ward off the horror, and the two hands would be held at one level, as aimed at one object of detestation. James presents a fine contrast to Peter.

See the painfully anxious face of Thomas, next neighbour to James the Elder, behind whose back he bends over toward the Lord; his face as pale as a corpse's, his features sharpened by the fear that maybe he, he himself, is the one that will betray his Lord. Do not the hairs of his head stand erect? Poor Thomas's emotion is, doubtless, the most poignant of all; he, perhaps, is predestinated to be the one to commit the sin that shall be forgiven neither in this world nor in the next. Can we misinterpret the significance of those worn features and of that uplifted forefinger; does not the action of this figure ask more eloquently than would words: "Is it I, Lord?"

Philip has risen to his feet, and with hands pressed

to his heart, protests his fidelity to the Master unto
death.

Matthew, standing also, with face and figure turned
toward Simeon, who sits at the table-end, is assuring
Simeon that those very words, "One of you shall betray me," were spoken by the Lord; that there is no
mistake about it. This is finely expressed by the
gesture of Matthew: "Didst thou not hear?"

But Simeon, with both hands held forth, palms upward, arms bent at elbow, maintains that the thing
cannot be so; "It is plainly impossible."

Between these two sits Thaddeus. Thaddeus has
no doubt about the terrible announcement. Simeon
says, "Impossible, you understand." "No mis-
understanding," says Matthew; "the Lord spake these
very words, One of you shall betray me." "Yes, yes,"
chimes in Thaddeus, as he brings down upon the palm
of his left hand the outspread right with thumb directed toward some one sitting at board with them.
"And I know who the traitor is; I'll name no name,
but it is the fellow back there, our bursar."

Great as is the difference between this and Beato
Angelico's masterpiece, yet in sincerity they are equal.
The genial painter, as well as the humble Dominican,
has truthfully painted in strict accordance with his
feeling for the subject. Each has painted the scene
as it appealed to his own nature. Devout and mystical
the one, powerful and passionate the other. Each has
been faithful to his sense for the significant, and being
natural, he has been sincere; each a spirit of flame,

not only illumined but luminous, shines by his own light; each, by being true to himself, has been true to his art.

The conclusion is evident: whoever purposes to ape another artist, and to imitate a Raphael or a Rembrandt, a Velasquez or a Millet, or to pattern after a certain "School" of Art and to be classed as an Impressionist, or as one of the Preraphaelites, or of the Paris, or Munich, or Glasgow schools, will be insincere in his art.   None of the great painters were imitators; or, if sometimes they were, just so far did they fall below their own greatness, their own sincerity.

Beauty is multiform; each artist should select the expression which best befits his temperament and his artistic powers, since that art alone can be sincere which is the reflection of the artist's inmost self, his soul.

The more the artist depends for style upon his own individuality, the more he depends for inspiration upon the genius of his own age; so much the more widely will he differ from those who have only become models, because they excelled in painting the significant in their own environment and as revealed in their own personality.

Those who are born with visions should paint visions, but luminously; those who are born robust should paint robustly, but temperately; "let those who would soar keep their wings, the others their feet;" each mindful that no one can see except by his own lamp; and, though the goal may not always be reached, it may at least always be striven for.

WOMAN IN
THE ITALIAN NOVEL

WOMAN IN THE ITALIAN NOVEL

L ITTLE more than half a century ago, there were many Italian peoples, but there was no Italian Nation. Out of these petty duchies, kingdoms and states, the ideals of unity and liberty have made the constitutional Kingdom of Italy. Essential differences distinguished the Roman from the Lombard, the Venetian from the Sicilian; and these social, lingual, intellectual and temperamental differences were not obliterated by a stroke of the pen, as the petty political divisions were swept away by a decree. Much, indeed, yet remains to be accomplished; but to-day the whole Italian peninsula is inhabited by one Italian Nation.

Doubtless because of these diversities, the words "Italian woman" do not evoke one clearly outlined figure, though they do suggest a vision of indefinite beauty.

If, indeed, even now, there exists a true "Italian Type" of woman, blossoming from an ancient stock, in a nation new-born, its presentation will be a genuine contribution to "feminism" and a valuable study in social evolution. Especially valuable because the phenomena of Italian feminine development and adaptation epitomizes the story of other slower national evolutions and indicates the direction of certain world-wide currents.

Not only are Italian women everywhere aspiring after better education and seeking for larger personal independence, but, as the pursuit of these aims has established a closer affinity between women's organizations, Italian women have discovered many unsuspected resemblances, which, in the aggregate, make up the "Italian Type"—a type whose psychological and social aspects will be best revealed through the Italian novel, if that novel satisfies Taine's luminous definition, *"Le Roman est la confession d'une société";* because this "confession," besides avowedly and purposely presenting facts, describing customs, painting portraits and landscapes, also unmasks the feminine soul. For the most sincere confession will disclose emotions unsuspected even by the penitent. There is eloquence in omission, and reticence may be as instructive as speech.

How true this is of the Italian novelists! How much they write about their countrywomen! But how much there is which they neither say nor comprehend! D'Annunzio's romances are masterpieces of suggestive poetry; Fogazzaro's novels are philosophic studies; hundreds of Italian novels supply valuable information on many subjects; yet how often do these writers imperfectly understand feminine psychology!

And—fact significant—the more these novels are untrue to the soul of the Italian woman, the more often are they characteristic of Italian life. For the Italian

rarely studies, or cares for, the psyche of his women.
Except for gallantry, the sexes keep much apart. Few
men confide in the women they most love and honour;
few consent to accept advice from them, and scarcely
one will willingly grant them authority.

Of that close communion, that perfect confidence,
which should begin with a mother's kiss to her babe
new-born, and continue to son, brother, husband; vivi-
fying and ennobling, comforting and supporting all
along life's rugged path, even attending the old man
to his final rest, there is a singular lack among Italians.
The Catholic Church is partly responsible for this.
Despite the exaltation of the Virgin, woman's inferi-
ority and the debasing nature of her influence are
preached. It is a corollary to the exaltation of celibacy, and to the teaching that sexual love is degrading
and that the flesh wars against the spirit. Immorality is not checked by such teaching, but tenderness is
blunted and respect for woman is lessened. The
struggle for bread has also brought the sexes into conflict. Everywhere, woman now competes with man.
If masculine opposition is fierce and pitless, Amazo-
nian invasion is bold and eager. Poverty among the
Italian masses and failure to recognize that the success
of the woman does not necessarily imply the defeat of
the man, have accentuated this antagonism.

The moral avarice of the primitive male savage still
poisons Italian social intercourse. There are still ret-
rograde spirits that feel as a loss to one sex every
advantage obtained by the other. All that the Italian

woman has gained, she has obtained by her own un-
aided efforts. No one has smoothed the rough way
for her; no one has cheered her victories or applauded
her bravery. Patient, long-suffering and unpresum-
ing, she has availed herself of every opportunity, and
made marvellous progress in the development of her·
own personality and as a factor in the social economy.
The Italian novel, being the reflection of Italian society, has participated in this misconception, which is
the capital failing in much otherwise praiseworthy
fiction.

Of twin birth with the national ideal of a free and
united Italy, the Italian romance echoed the first heart-
beat of classic patriotism. It sang the passionate
aspirations of those romantic heroes, and played an important part in the general revolt against foreign oppression. This first and heroic period of novel-writing
produced several historic romances, and one of them
was a masterpiece; but in all their pages there is not
one great feminine character. Foscolo's Teresa is
but the mirror of passionate Jacopo Ortis, and Manzoni's religious scruples, compelling him to omit from
his novel all love-passages, have resulted in shadowy
profiles instead of achieved types of womanhood.
Manzoni's imitators have crowded their books with
unreal heroines of foreign pattern, in no wise resembling the typical Italian woman who was then awakening from centennial apathy and earnestly desirous of
sharing in the common danger and common responsibility.

Not until the end of this patriotic and sentimental
period,—in 1859, when Ippolito Nievo produced his
Memoirs of an Octogenarian,—do we have lifelike
feminine portrayal in an Italian novel. Pisana, the
best of these characters, is the typical romantic heroine. With characteristic passionate impulse, reckness-
ness and generosity, she lacks moral principle, is an
unbridled coquette and sentimentalist. Her every act
and word is consistent with her surroundings; yet she
lives, her heart-throbs are real and she possesses a distinct individuality. Like all vital creatures, she suggests a whole series of complementary ideas, which
arouse the reader's criticism and perplex his judgment.
When her generosity becomes folly, when her passion passes into immorality, when she lies and plots,
when she demeans herself to an inexcusable sacrifice,
there is no recognized standard of propriety by which
such a nature can be measured. Pisana is a law
unto herself, as must be every imperial personality.

Underlying all the romantic atmosphere,—so characteristic of the literary moment,—there is a deeply
observed evolution of one woman's soul. The startling
events of the story are logical, if considered as mile-
stones in Pisana's development. Even her adventures
and intrigues are the blind strivings of a soul urged
onward by the thirst for self-sacrifice, and an unsati-
ated craving for love, for love which finally becomes
redemption. So true is this character of Pisana, that
the modern reader, trained in psychological analysis,
better appreciates it than did Nievo's contemporaries.

Half a century of enlightened criticism has sifted the priceless ore from its encumbering romantic rubbish.

Only fifteen years separate Nievo's picture from the first efforts of the Italian realist school. Yet that short interval marks an important change in Italian life and thought. To a period of enthusiasm and heroism succeeded the despondency that so often follows the realization of a dream. The cold light of sordid achievement dimmed the lustre of bright expectation. Poverty, and the limitations of liberty, disillusioned even the most fervent fusionist about the perfections of United Italy. In this dark hour, literary realism, with its pitiless thirst for facts, its pessimistic interpretation of truth, its dogmatism about the scientific redress of wrongs, was accepted by the Italian artist as a necessary reaction from romanticism, and appeared to the Italian novelist an adequate formula for fiction.

This dogma of pure realism was opposed to the serene and poetic traditions of Italian literature. Yet, for a time, realism was rampant; and even when in part displaced by the torrent of new ideas, broad traces of its passage remained in the Italian novel. The clamorous success of Zola's *études de moeurs* (studies of social conditions) was mistaken for Italian preference; but these purposely gross and deliberately vulgar descriptions were so contrary to innate national tendencies as to produce in Italy only a temporary obsession.

Giovanni Verga was the first author of stories and

novels of genuine Italian realism. Wisely he chose
his subjects from the simple Sicilian life. Discarding
facile dialect, he speaks in fragmentary sentences pregnant with the rude passion and confused ideas of the
common people. Unembarrassed by self-conscious-
ness, unrestrained by reticence, the unfeigned feelings
and uncurbed passions of these simple people are revealed in all their impulsive sincerity within a rude
environment of mediæval customs. From this gallery
of pastoral figures emerges a type of womanhood
which is delineated with truth, vigour and originality.
This is the passive, Eastern, almost Biblical, woman.
As in an Egyptian or Byzantine picture, there is the
unconscious hieratic pose; her movements are slow
and dignified; she is not obedient,—since obedience im-
plies the surrender of conscious will,—but she is
utterly submissive. Curbed by fatalism and timidity,
she questions neither the moral law which enslaves her
nor the right and power of man, her master. Her
religion is superstition, her chastity instinctive. Yet
there is in her,—as there is in every Arcadian creature,—a harmony with her environment. She is a
part of her moral world; her beauty blends with the
lines and colours of surrounding sea and sky.

A sunburnt pallid face is illumined by great dark
eyes that gleam under a glossy mass of sombre hair;
a body that ill usage and toil have strained, reveals,
under its rags, the slender elegance of a Tanagra;
the slowness of her gesture attains to stateliness in the
simple rites of her faith; the mellow accents of her

deep-toned voice mingle in concord with the song of the waves on the pebbly shore. Nor is her spirit less attuned to her moral world. There is no vulgarity in her ignorance. She meekly bends to the fatal necessity of her master's will; and when, in blind impulse, she commits some unpremeditated crime of jealousy or lack of self-control, like any other dumb, hard-used creature, she acts instinctively.

Diodata, the farm girl in *Mastro Don Gesualdo* represents this type. To her master, Don Gesualdo, she has granted all that was hers to give, her virginal innocence, her patient toil, her unrequited devotion that shines out of her eyes, doglike in their dumb entreaty, imploring his caress. Yet, when told that he is to marry a noble-born Signora, she makes no protest, scarce dares show her grief, and crouches at his feet, gulping down her heavy tears. With the same unquestioning submission, she had accepted the master's will when that will was to possess her. She now accepts from his hand a complacent lout, who will take her to wife and with her embrace the master's children and pocket the master's money. Fate preordained this arrangement, and in Diodata's soul there is no protest. But when sickness and age have reduced the wretched millionaire to that awful solitude of the unloved and the unlovable, then Diodata returns, bringing Don Gesualdo the balsam of disinterested affection and genuine pity.

In Grazia Deledda's Sardinian sketches, the feminine characters, though delineated in accordance with

Verga's æsthetic principle, are remarkable for originality, sincerity and direct observation.

Centuries of patriarchal life in a land of barren fallows and extensive forests, of traditional superstition and relentless struggle, have powerfully moulded the Sardinian woman. She reverences the head of the family, yet maintains her self-respect; her large share in field labour and cattle tending, the importance which inherited Oriental jealousy gives to her possession, the deadly feuds that any misbehaviour on her part is sure to kindle, endow her with a dignity in singular contrast with her lack of education. Zia Grazia, the stern widow of a brigand, who sits by her fireless hearth and mourns the departed hero and laments the coward spirit of her pious son; Oli, the degraded mother who commits suicide, to save her son from shame and to escape his reproaches, are truly feminine characters and entirely Sardinian.

Federigo de Roberto has in his novels so enlarged the formula of the realists as to present not merely one entire family, or even one entire section of society. In his novel, *The Viceroys,* he includes the whole social world of his native Sicily. This ample reconstruction contains a notable gallery of masculine portraits, but the feminine characters are shadowy representations. In another novel, *Illusions,* where De Roberto presumes to give the complete history of a woman, he only records a series of her love-affairs, from the precocious mishap of her unguarded childhood to the sad fate of the white-haired woman who always pursued an *ignis fatuus* of illusions, and has fallen into moral marsh and mire.

Individualism, that predominant characteristic of the Italian mind, soon invaded the realistic school. Its writers adhered to the fundamental dogma of objective investigation and truthful rendering, but they followed personal preferences and aptitudes. Matilde Serao's emotional temperament sometimes leads her into sentimental wanderings, but she has never swerved from her fundamental conception of the psychology of her sex: love is for Serao the sole master-passion, the only fount of joy or sorrow.

Carmela Minimo, the ballet girl, is a very beggar for love. Her plainness has saved her from temptation, but she has been infected by contact with the wicked world around her; and, when love does come, it is in the poisoned atmosphere of a Neapolitan theatre. The fashionable and adored Terzi ridicules her proverbial chastity. So the infatuated girl takes a lover. This shop clerk, who treats her to cheap suppers and bad wines in tawdry restaurants, who shocks her religious sentiments, and wounds her feelings, dismisses her rudely when he realizes that she is no credit to his snobbery. Carmela, thinking to come nearer to Terzi's ideal, accepts a second lover.

But suddenly the scene changes: the doll becomes a woman! Terzi is dead! He has preferred suicide to facing the consequence of folly and extravagance. In a cheap lodging-house he lies alone. Carmela finds him; she claims the privilege of watching by that

corpse and of weeping for that dead man who now is
hers. By the ruin of her life, by the loss of her hopes
of heaven, she has purchased the right of kissing those
cold lips, that in life gave her only a mocking smile and
a ribald joke. Yet, such is the divine folly of love, she
does not regret the exchange.

The overmastering passion, so enslaving the will
that the entire life drifts like a rudderless boat to
final wreck, is the characteristic trait of Matilde
Serao's women. In *Sister Joan of the Cross,* the object of that passion is changed, but the incapacity for
resisting it remains. By Government decree the little
wizened nun is thrust from her monastery out into the
world. Her soul is obsessed by passion for conventual walls, for the black veil, for the enforced silence,
for all those practices that have lent dignity to her
life. Blinded by her infatuation, she slips down, ever
down, into more miserable situations, serenely content
to accept every humiliation if only she can have a black
gown and shawl of monastic fashion, and save her religious name from contamination. How pathetic the
last scene of all! She sits at a table which charity
has spread for the poorest mendicants, and she par-
takes humbly of these alms; but, when a grand lady
patroness asks for her name, she gives her religious
surname with the pride of a duchess handing her
emblazoned visiting-card.

In the novels of another woman writer,—Neera,—
are to be found more complex types. Teresa is surrounded by that besotted selfishness which crushes the

weak, and burdens with misery the uncomplain-
ing. Even before her tenth year she is the family
drudge, the maid of all work, the sickly mother's nurse.
She rears a brood of younger brothers and sisters,
and patiently endures her father's complaints. That
her marriage portion may be saved for her brother,
her parents refuse consent to her marriage. Teresa's
nature is embittered in resisting the desires of her own
heart and the pleadings of her *fiancé*. She becomes a
fretful spinster, and the man whom she might have
inspired to a useful life, discouraged and unrestrained,
slips into snares and pitfalls.

Lydia, another of Neera's heroines, is petted and
flattered by a brilliant social circle, is led into extravagance, tempted to coquetry, and initiated into the corruptions of the Neapolitan aristocracy, but never
helped toward a more noble life. At first she scorns
the banality of marriage, and when disillusion,
wounded vanity and overwrought nerves finally bring
her to the verge of a darker precipice, she finds refuge
in suicide.

Thus even noble-minded Neera arrives at the
same conclusion as passionate Serao—that, since
woman is only meant to inspire and feel love, it is
useless to study any other phase of her psyche and
superfluous to claim for her any other right than the
free satisfaction of her sensualism.

It was inevitable that the profounder truths resulting from psychological investigation should succeed
the superficialities of realism. The lens and lancet

system was not discarded, but its method was extended to the more complex problems of the human soul. Writers strove to rise above the rude description of obvious phenomena to a consideration of motives; winged imagination and poetical reconstruction added their charm, where heretofore there had only been objective analysis and dogmatic assertion.

To these new elements of the novel Fogazzaro has added his genial philosophy. He is a trained thinker, who, when impelled by his religious convictions to a larger interpretation of life, demands a scientific assurance to confirm his faith. He belongs, with Blaise Pascal, to that *élite* of storm-tossed souls who are perpetually tortured by their craving for certainty and by their thirst for absolute faith in a revealed religion. In his desire to reconcile the Darwinian and Spencerian theories with the Catholic creed, he devised a pretty formula when he defined the evolution of man and the survival of the fittest as the *"modus operandi* of Divinity"; yet no formula can quiet the soul drawn to an ideal, and shackled to reality by scientific training.

This dualism, which informs all Fogazzaro's writings, and peculiarly his novels, is also the key-note of his interpretation of feminine characters. The double current of ideas, ever at war within him, yet ever blending in artistic creations, makes him scrupulously respectful of truth in the rendering of objective elements, and poetically imaginative in their interpretation. This excellent method gives to his delineation of women greater power and completeness, because he perceives that there are other emotions and other desires in a woman's heart than her longing for masculine admiration and love.

Having adopted this view-point, Fogazzaro has not disdained to trace portraits of women who, though they have outlived the age of sexual emotion, are not less interesting subjects of study. Thus, the characteristic traits of Marchesa Scremin, one of the secondary characters in *Piccolo Mondo Moderno,* is pictured in a few vivid sentences which tell of maternal grief borne with Christian fortitude, and silently.

Dowager Maironi, in *Piccolo Mondo Antico,* is a complete and unforgettable character. She symbolizes a fast-vanishing society, yet is she a living and throbbing personality. Her avarice and superstition, her obduracy, her stately manners, and the peculiar authority which she exerts over her entourage, give to her plump colourless face originality and power.

But there are other pictures, full-length portraits, which better illustrate Fogazzaro's feminine ideal,— Elena di San Giuliano, for instance, in *Daniele Cortis.* Nothing can be more realistic than the preliminary analysis of this character. All the biological antecedents of her race, all the conditions and influences of her surroundings, are strongly, crudely presented. Her fatal abasement is a logical sequence. Her own mother's depravity, her slight education and neglected upbringing, culminating in marriage with an irreclaimable wretch; the levity of all her companions, save

courageous though bigoted Uncle Lao, and their tacit
approval of the fault which she has not committed, but
which they imagine inevitable; even the outrage of her
vile husband's jealousy; everything urges her into
sin. Yet she renounces the love that would mean an
honoured and easy life and joy unspeakable; with
breaking heart she condemns her beloved Daniele to
misery, and follows her husband into shameful exile.

Fogazzaro leaves this final step unexplained. Having sounded the abyss of scientific analysis and measured its limitations, for the ultimate result he pro-
vides only a metaphysical solution. At the time he
wrote *Daniele Cortis* his own religious development
would not have suggested a miraculous intervention of
Divine Providence to account for this sudden resolu-
tion of a woman without religious instincts. Yet, Fogazzaro is a Latin, living in a country where neither
public sentiment nor private feelings as to the obli-
gations of the marriage state would suffice to deter a
woman of Elena's rank and education from following
the impulses of her heart. In place of the restraining
influence of public opinion in regard to the sanctity
of marriage, or craven fear of breaking the Decalogue,
he suggests that in every human soul there is an un-
erring guide to right action, a power strong enough to
uplift the world.

Fogazzaro's selection of a feminine character to
exemplify this moral struggle was a promising earnest,
which has been realized in the character of Luisa
Maironi, in the novel *Piccolo Mondo Antico,* one of

the most noble types of womanhood in Italian fiction.
In order to elucidate the one decisive crisis in her life,
with careful analysis Luisa is studied under every aspect of her development. Altruism, the key-note of her
character, informs her every act and thought. Tender
solicitude for her sickly mother, grateful appreciation
of her uncle's protection, encouragement of her husband's plans, unwearied care for her child, everywhere and always she scatters the sun-bright light of
her affection in active charity, kind words and un-
failing good-humour. Her ideal is of justice, courage,
endurance and human love. Her affection for Franco
is strong and passionate, but it has none of that moral
cowardice which bids the intellect and conscience surrender their right of control. The opposition between
her ideas and those of her husband is always conscious; and when the struggle comes, when she has to
choose between Franco's Christian submission to
wrong and her own notion of right, she accepts the
fatal estrangement rather than purchase her happiness
by a renouncement of her ideal.

In the second part of the novel, Fogazzaro strained
the evolution of his character so as to serve his purpose: his moral thesis required that Luisa be "converted," and that Franco's piety triumph. Accordingly, he presents grief, the maddening grief of a
mother who, gazing on her only child's dead body,
feels that she is in part responsible for this loss. Luisa's rebellious spirit at first is crushed, and then come
conscientious misgivings; whilst Franco's pious soul

finds consolation in thoughts of eternal happiness for his dead child, and something of joy in the feeling that his little one has been removed from the temptations of this wicked world. Luisa, in her despair, turns to the delusions of spiritism, but through her love for Franco she finally accepts his theory of Christian resignation and is comforted by the same Faith.

In his last novel, *Il Santo,* Fogazzaro adopted the sterner and more Catholic standpoint, and his Jeanne de Salle appears like an embodiment of Evil, tempting the "Saint" to the sin of love; but, when he wrote *Piccolo Mondo Antico,* he had not yet decided for this interpretation of the great problem. His less prejudiced mind, in its eagerness for the complete truth, could still discern some of the complex changes of the human heart; he could see that, after the softening influence of grief, a woman's craving for pure tenderness and comfort must revive with tenfold power; he could also interpret in its double current of sensations and feelings the conjugal love and the blind maternal instinct that were stirring in Luisa's heart and nerves, after a long period of depression; and above these elements of love, he knew that an infinite desire of making this bond everlasting, beyond the limits of time and space, must lead to a belief in the life after death and the promise of the joys of heaven.

Luisa is not persuaded by argument, nor is she enslaved by an impetus of passion, but she is influenced by a blending of many diverse sentiments. Under the stress of threatening danger, the forebodings of an uncertain future and the necessity of immediate parting, her affection for her husband revives, and in the perfect communion of the two hearts all doubts are dispelled. The importance of the religious sentiment in the relations between man and woman, so conspicuous in many English and American novels, was almost a novelty in Italy, but Fogazzaro pursues it in his subsequent novels.

Elena di San Giuliano, Luisa Maironi and Jeanne de Salle are three important creations in Italian romance. They are impersonations of human tendencies, instinctive desire and every other natural craving which stands in opposition to the pietism and mystic religious exaltation of the three men whom they love, Daniele Cortis, Franco and Piero Maironi.

Despite certain juvenile experiments and the profession of realism contained in the introduction to *Giovanni Episcopo,* few modern novel writers have borrowed less from direct observation than has D'Annunzio, yet in his novels are to be found some of the most characteristic representations of Italian women. This apparent contradiction may be explained by the fact that, although D'Annunzio lacks the aptitude for patient observation, he is richly dowered with the poet's gift of assimilation, with the artistic sense that instinctively grasps the elements of beauty and synthesises them in an æsthetic composition. His right to the epithet of *"immaginifero"* (producer of images) is enforced by the finish of his feminine figures, while his shallow psychology is evinced in his attempted analysis of their feelings.

There is no humanity, no life, in these characters; the clumsiness of their reconstruction dulls the sense of disgust which some of their acts inspire. Thus, Giuliana Hermil, not merely consenting to the death of her new-born babe, but praying for success for the murderous enterprise; thus, Ippolita, in *The Triumph of Death,* always obeying her lowest instincts. *The Virgins of the Hills,* because they never assume to be anything but allegorical symbols, exemplify the author's power for thus creating figures of unparalleled beauty devoid of any psychic life, merely swayed in their actions, or moulded in their appearance, by the reflections emanating from the mind of their lover; ever flitting and changing according to his flitting and changeful moods. Indeed, this essential trait is common to many of D'Annunzio's characters of women. They are phantoms created by the imagination of one man, embodiments of his desire, realizations of his æsthetic dream.

Piacere, one of D'Annunzio's earliest works, wherein he has lavishly scattered the gifts of his poetic inspiration and the dross of his artistic sensualism, contains three very original feminine figures. Around this Child of Volupty these three shadows arise, projected by the fire of his perverted imagination. Maria Fleres, the empress of his higher thoughts, the artist who stirs within him an almost chaste admiration, is the reflected image of all that is still unsullied in his soul. Elena Muti, the queen of volupty, perverted in her refinement, mixing with her utmost depravity a worship for art, is the incarnation of his less avowable feelings. Francesca d'Ateleta is the dimly shadowed profile of his blurred reminiscences of social bonds, family ties and intellectual friendship.

These three personages move clumsily around the man they love, their feelings remain unexplained, their motives confused, and little sympathy is felt for their fate; yet every reader feels that they are stamped with a genuinely Italian physiognomy.

Maria Fleres, of stately beauty, wears her modern gown like the drapery of an antique statue. Her interpretation of music, both passionate and imaginative; her love, both chaste in its spirit and sensual in the deed; her religious scruples and her humbleness before her lover all fix her Italian figure and her Italian mind.

Elena Muti has inherited from the Borgias that perverted sensualism, that intellectual depravity, which blends the most refined æsthetics with the most cruel desires.

Francesca d'Ateleta, too, is eminently an Italian character, an impersonation of that subtle charm, that *gentilezza* which distinguishes the Italian *dama* from every other gentlewoman. She has little of the Frenchwoman's *esprit* and none of the Englishwoman's hauteur. Her attitude and her intonations are less studied, her manners more stately, her smile warmer, her glance more direct; she ignores shyness and scorns etiquette, but has an instinctive abhorrence for vulgarity. It has taken centuries of Petrarchism and Arcadia, of courtly life and seclusion from vulgar contact, of communion with masterpieces of art, to produce this type of *Signora,* and that peculiar character of *gentilezza,* which may be termed a politeness that is sincere, an art that has become nature. It is an untranslatable word, because it answers to a conception of social intercourse without exact equivalent in other countries.

But another woman in D'Annunzio's novels claims, with better right, to synthesise the Italian woman, because, beside all these characters of external beauty, she also possesses—that which the others lacked—a living and throbbing soul, and because this soul is Italian. Foscarina, of *Il Fuoco,* the grand tragedienne, is, like all those things of beauty which have been much incensed and much admired, peculiarly attractive in the hour of her decline. It is as if the beauty of the poetry she has interpreted, the flame of the amours she has inspired, the perfume of the incense she has received, still clung to her, adding to her power of seduction. She shares with the golden sunset on the *laguna,* with the autumnal glory of fiery leafage, and the crumbling magnificence of her Venice, the evanescent charm of that which is doomed to disappear. This charm, made of exquisite sensations and spiritualized impressions, has been rendered by D'Annunzio with his usual power of expression, and also with a sincerity that is novel.

Foscarina is not merely beautiful; she does not

merely appeal to the senses of her lover. She stirs within him deeper feelings, and in her turn she is actuated by higher motives. The dazzling picture of beauty, the delightful symphony of harmonious language, is not the final aim of the book, but only the background to a story of passion, of love and sacrifice. Foscarina, for love, will renounce her lover, and part from him almost without hope of future meeting. And this devotion, this tragic crisis, shows how essentially Italian she is: Italian in the stately pose which no emotions can ruffle, Italian in her unconscious preoccupation with beauty, Italian in her forgetfulness of reality, in the triumph of love over the long-enslaved flesh.

After the barren attempts of realism and the clumsy studies of pure psychology, this poetical reconstruction of the feminine type indicates a new manner of interpretation. Neither cold observation nor scientific analysis has produced any satisfactory literary representation of the Italian Woman. Has not the time come for trying a new method? The preliminary studies have indicated some of the elements of reality. It now remains for some comprehending spirit to seize them and idealize them in a poetic reconstruction. If this shall happen, it will have been once more the poet's glory to show the way and indicate the method. Others will follow, and, considering the activity of Italian novelists since the great war, will perchance promptly achieve that only picture which is yet wanting in the gallery of Italian fiction: the true portrait of the Italian Woman.

THE HEARING OF
MUSIC AS A
SENSUOUS AND A
SPIRITUAL PLEASURE

THE HEARING OF MUSIC AS A SENSUOUS AND A SPIRITUAL PLEASURE

A DEEP-TONED BELL has for years pealed daily and hourly from a stone steeple; in a garrison near a suspension bridge military bands have for years sounded their blatant martial music. One day it is found that strands of the steel cable which sustains the bridge are broken, that the steeple is in danger of disintegration. And science, when asked the cause, points to the military band and to the bell.

I may not understand how sound can accomplish the destruction of a bridge that bears without hurt the measured tramp of a marching regiment, or how the same cause can threaten wreck to a steeple which might withstand a cannon-shot. Sounds, however long continued, have not that effect upon me. I find pleasure in the lively band music, and in the deep tone of the bell. What is sound that it should have those differing results?

Steel rope and steeple have heard no sound. If they could speak they would ask me what I mean by "hear" and "sound." They might perhaps tell me how this succession of more or less energetic vibrations—this motion repeated day after day, effects their gradual disintegration, but of sound they could give no idea, for them it is naught; these vibrations are nothing but physical tremors, in the absence of an organ of hearing and a brain.

The same succession of vibrations, the same motion, which reaches the iron rope, reaches me also; and I, having what the rope has not, an organ of hearing and a brain, am conscious of sound. But how? Let us begin our inquiry by considering the phenomenon of sound in detail.

The phenomenon of sound, considered objectively, is perceived to be a simple physical phenomenon of motion, a regular and more or less rapid succession of undulations or waves. The vibrations of the body in which the sound has its origin are borne, through the medium of the air, to my external ear, thence to the middle ear or tympanum, and thence to the internal ear or labyrinth, in which is the terminal of the auditory nerve, which extends to the brain. The statement is simple; but as the sound-waves make their journey, the phenomenon is transformed; it is no more a purely physical phenomenon, it has become physiological, though it still remains a phenomenon of motion. The vibrations are now conveyed through the highly specialised nervous cellular tissue. Still, they are only motion, and it is as waves, that is, as motion, that they, by means of the auditory nerve, reach the particular organ of the brain with which that nerve communicates. There a further change occurs. In my brain the phenomenon is again transformed. It was physiological; it becomes psychological, and I hear.

In hearing I perceive sound, not motion. Yet I may perceive both if I choose; I may touch a violin-string and feel the tingling, quivering sensation of its vibrations, at the same time that my ear transmits a perception of the sound of that string. But would the vibrations of that string mean sound to the sensoria of all animated creatures? Science seems to tell us that certain insects have no perception of sound except as a sequence of shakes. And there are grounds for believing that some animals perceive as sound, vibrations which are either too rapid or too slow to be perceived as such by man: just as the ultra-violet and ultra-red rays of the solar spectrum are not seen by the human eye, though they are clearly evidenced by actinography. Vibrations slower than forty per second, and more rapid than thirty-eight thousand per second are heard with difficulty by man, and do not convey a true tone-sensation. Man's perception of such slow vibrations is perception of motion rather than of sound. But do all vibrations, do all aerial waves produce sound? That is one of the unsolved problems of science.

What effects this mysterious transformation? The spiritist tells me that it is effected in the passage of the phenomenon from the brain to the spirit; the positivist explains that it is merely a function of the brain. Let us leave them to their conjectures and pass on to our argument.

The aerial waves, transformed, have reached my brain. I hear, and with the hearing comes a further sensation—a sensation, perhaps, of pleasure.

The sensation of pleasure which any given cause arouses in me may be one or the other of two things, a sensuous pleasure or a spiritual pleasure. The sensuous pleasure depends immediately upon the cause which has produced it, which has been apprehended by the inner self and received as an agreeable or a disagreeable feeling. If the sensations are those of taste, smell or touch, no scientific distinction can be made between the agreeable and the disagreeable. What is good to me may be distasteful to my neighbour. No *gourmet* can by scientific rule prove to me the goodness of a taste I dislike. I abhor the scent of magnolia, yet many people think it agreeable. One acquaintance is disagreeably affected by the touch of very smooth surfaces, another by the touch of rough ones. Who is right? None can decide. We are wrapped in a subjectivism from which no science can free us. For each individual those sensations are good which are in harmony with the feeling produced by the activity of his whole organism; and in judging the sensuous pleasures of taste, smell and touch we can perhaps find no better rule than this—"Good is not what is good, but what is pleasing."

May we apply this rule to the pleasures connected with the two remaining senses, sight and hearing? Leaving the former out of consideration, and coming directly to our subject, the sense of hearing; the answer to the question will depend on our ability to make a scientific distinction between sensations of hearing; to establish a criterion by which to determine what sounds should give pleasure and what should not. Consider the most elementary principles of musical sound, and see whether science points out to us one sound rather than another as of a nature to cause pleasure.

Physical science fixes with exactness every musical tone by determining experimentally the number of vibrations of which it is the result. Thus every tone is, in a sense, a number. On considering those numbers with relation to each other it is perceived that certain of them stand to the others in an arithmetical ratio more or less near, that is, are more or less nearly related, while certain of them are totally unrelated. The notes, therefore, represented by those numbers— the notes produced by vibrations of the rapidity fixed by those numbers—ought to be related more or less nearly, or totally unrelated, according as the numbers are related or unrelated. And a combination of tones most nearly related ought to give most pleasure.

The related tones are by this process found to be, generally speaking, the octave, third and fifth, together with the note taken as a basis for calculation. A combination of these notes ought therefore to afford pleasure to the ear; and the sensations of a hearer should range from the maximum of pleasure produced by the full chord—the maximum of consonance, the combination of tones most closely related—to the disagreeable sensation produced by a dissonance, a combination of unrelated tones.

We thus find some reason for liking certain com-

228 The Friar in Fiction and Other Essays

binations and for disliking others; and this reason holds equally, whether the hearer's sensations are or are not what this rule indicates they should be. For instance, one may determine experimentally certain related notes which, sounded together, should cause him pleasure; but his actual sensation may be utterly at variance with what he perceives he ought to feel. He should like a combination of related tones, he should dislike those unrelated; but a pure harmony may be to him nothing but noise, and he may be equally unaffected by a discord.

Again, the pleasure of a hearer varies with the quality of the tone; and tone-quality depends upon the addition of harmonics,—related notes which are called into being by the sounding of the fundamental note, and which blend with it. To the number and relative strength of these harmonics tone-quality is due, and we should expect to find most pleasure in hearing that tone richest in harmonics, that tone evoking the greatest number of related tones. But while such would be the sensation of a hearer, he may be in fact indifferent to a tone which this rule shows to be beautiful, and may receive a sensation of pleasure on hearing a vulgar, strident, blatant or throaty tone from instrument or voice.

When we pass from the single note or chord to notes sounded consecutively, a further condition confronts us. Notes may be sounded one after the other irregularly, at haphazard, or there may be a mathematical symmetry by which each has its value of duration with relation to every other that precedes, accompanies, or follows it. They may thus be grouped into bars or parts of bars, into phrases, or successions of bars, into movements or portions of movements, successions of phrases, and so on. And a symmetrical grouping ought to give more pleasure to the hearer than any mere chance arrangement. Yet he may be unresponsive to symmetry and unable even to keep time to a march played by a brass band.

We know that no intellectual process can give this idea of pitch, this discrimination of tone-qualities, or this sense of rhythm. Yet these faculties—certainly the first and last—are essential to every listener who would perceive the beauty of what he hears. The sensation of sound is not to be ruled by subjectivism like that of smell. It is only when affected by sensations produced in us through the medium of hearing or of sight that we use the term *beauty*. We cannot call beautiful those things which seem beautiful to us, unless they obey a rule outside of us. Our perception of beauty is controlled not merely by subjective appreciation, differing from individual to individual, but by fixed and objective law.

"I never could understand," said Richard Cobden to D'Azeglio, during a concert given in Florence in honour of the great economist,—"I never could understand what sort of pleasure people find in all this noisy thumping and grating." And clearly it was impossible for him to understand. Like many other

clever men he associated no psychical activity with the
simple sensation of hearing.

We find accordingly that a perception of pitch—
relative pitch, that is, or the ability to determine
whether notes are played or sung in tune,—and a
sense of rhythm, or time, are and must be the inheritance of every one who would listen to music and
judge its beauty. Here we are lifted above mere sensation, since these things cannot be apprehended by
sensation alone, but must be perceived by one of those
elements of thought which Emanuel Kant calls *pure*.
As these faculties, if possessed, have been, in substance, always possessed, as no element of experience
is mingled with our original possession of them, and as
when originally entirely lacking they cannot be acquired, they may be considered to be what Kant de-
nominated pure intuitions.

We are now on the borders of the realm of music.
We will only glance within.

When a musical composition is heard as a composition,—as something more than a combination or
succession of notes produced in rhythm,—there are
blended with the primitive sensation, and with the
intuitive element, both of which we have considered,
countless new psychical elements, differing from individual to individual. The higher the percipient element of æsthetical enjoyment in the hearer,—that is,
the greater the activity of his thought,—the greater
this resultant pleasure; but it is always an æsthetical
pleasure, never entirely sensuous, if he possesses the

essential intuitive qualities. Does your neighbour tap
his foot in a futile effort at time when the band plays
"Yankee Doodle," and does he slumber through a symphony? Then perhaps he prefers corned beef and
cabbage on a deal table to a dinner with Lucullus.

Yet we are still only part way on our road to complete spiritual enjoyment of music. Our primitive
sensation, acted upon and transformed, first by our
intuitive faculties, and still further by our psychical
elements, has resulted in perceptions.. The perceptions, thus aroused, are, by the mental activity, transformed and remodelled into concepts, and these concepts may in a thousand ways be united or opposed by
the endless working of the power of ratiocination.

And herein lies the point. The hearer will not find
spiritual beauty in music unless he himself possesses
those intuitive qualities and those psychical elements
which enable him to perceive it, and unless he rises
above the merely sensuous impression. And he will
not find it except as he finds the expression of a concept; as such alone can beauty spiritual exist.

Fine arts can claim that name only as they give
expression to a concept. Not every art is equally
apt to express a definite idea, as painting, sculpture
and poetry can. It is not given to all of them to express all sorts of ideas.

Architecture is more vague in meaning than poetry;
but are we to say that it has no meaning, that its
beauty cannot be expressed in concept? Consider for
instance the gorgeous church of the Annunziata in

Florence. For all its gorgeousness it lacks that concept of a temple which the Cathedral of Santa Maria del Fiore, notwithstanding its bareness, embodies.

Is not the meaning of music more definite than that of architecture? And must not music disclose its spiritual beauty by the expression of concept?

In the mind of the creator of the music the concept arises, and through the expression which he gives it, through the performance it receives and through the mind of the hearer, it is imparted exactly or approximately,—the cause and the effect of the noblest psychical activities of composer, performer and listener. When the concept is thus expressed and thus perceived, the hearing of music is something more than a sensation; it is truly and really an æsthetical, a spiritual, pleasure.

NICCOLA PISANO, THE FATHER OF MODERN ITALIAN SCULPTURE

NICCOLA PISANO, THE FATHER OF MODERN ITALIAN SCULPTURE

A S EARLY as the reign of Constantine, Roman sculpture was in hopeless decadence; in the sixth century it gave some faint signs of lingering vitality in the bas-reliefs of certain Christian sarcophagi; it then became involved in the "universal and unillumined night," and so remained for six centuries. In that period all artistic expertness was lost; all skill in hewing and carving marble was forgotten.

In the Duomo of Pisa is seen, affixed to a wall, a bas-relief representing the "Descent from the Cross", it is the work of Benedetto Antelani and was executed between the years 1178 and 1198; it is the earliest evidence we possess of the reawakening of this long-dormant art. Its most striking feature is the ugliness of its figures, which suggest the rude wooden *dramatis personæ* of a puppet show rather than the venerated forms of the saintly men and women, the angels and the Saviour, which constitute the group. Nevertheless, we view with more tolerance this crude composition when we reflect that the figures in Antelani's "Descent from the Cross" do not by any means bear the palm of ugliness among the productions of Italian sculpture in his time.

And indeed Antelani's bas-relief, though crude in

235

conception and rough in execution, is a distinct advance beyond all similar works of earlier dates; for in those earlier works the figures are not only false in delineation—in fact, more like monsters than normal human creatures—but also they are invariably carved in rows, all in one attitude, as though cast in one mould; there is no individuality, no character, no action, no movement, any more than in a row of hairdresser's blocks. Therefore, in spite of all his shortcomings, it is greatly to Antelani's credit that at least he could so far disregard conventions as to attempt the representation of a dramatic scene.

But though in Antelani's work indications of progress are not wanting, it is all too evident that he art of carving marble with a chisel was still in a very primitive state. On the other hand, in striking contrast with sculpture in marble, the art of moulding and casting in bronze, in which the later Byzantines attained a high degree of perfection, was, under the tuition of Byzantine masters, making rapid progress at this time in Italy.[1] But through the Byzantines could teach the

[1] Of this noble workmanship there remain three celebrated examples. 1. The bronze door of San Zeno in Verona, the most ancient portion of which dates back to the eleventh century. 2. The rear door of the Duomo of Piza, called Porta di San Raniere, which is ascribed to Bonanno; its probable date, 1180. There is good reason to believe this Bonanno to be the same architect who, assisted by Guglielmo d' Innspruck, had already begun the erection of the celebrated Campanile. When three tiers of columns had been erected, the building, because of the uneven settling of the foundations, was seen to lean to one side; and this inclination the architects who undertook the completion of the tower deemed it advisable to continue for the upper five tiers. 3. The bronze gates of the Duomo of Troja, wrought by Oderisino of Benevento. In beauty of design and excellence of workmanship, this door excels that of Pisa as Pisa's door surpasses that of Verona. The superior skill

Italians to cast bronze and to carve ivory, they could not instruct them in the art of carving marble with hammer and chisel, for that was an art unknown in Constantinople.

Hence, the early Italian sculptors, those worthy of the name, had no aid either from teachers or from tradition, in the art of representing the human form in marble; they had to work out their own ideals, to discover the principles of art expression for themselves, and to formulate its percepts. At first they chose to hide their deficiencies by attempting only what was easy, as the carving of roses and foliage on the cornices of framework with which they surrounded their crude essays in bas-relief; occasionally they blended decoration in mosaic with this carved ornamentation.

Such was the condition of sculpture in Italy at the advent of Niccola Pisano and the renaissance of the art which was, rather more than two hundred years later, to recall the glories of the ancient Grecian schools.

Of the life and studies of Pisano there is no authentic record; his birth is referred to the year 1206, and he died in 1278; his birthplace is in doubt, the quasi-surname, adopted by himself, Pisanus (of Pisa) indicating the scene of his artistic labours rather than his native place. It is doubtful if he had any master; but

shown by Oderisino is a proof of the powerful influence exerted in Southern Italy by the Constantinopolitan Greeks, an influence which was not only far stronger there than in Northern Italy, but also lasted a century longer.

the influence of the remains of ancient Roman sculpture is evident in all his works, even the earliest.

It would be foreign to our subject to dwell at length upon the work of Niccola as an architect, that is worthy of a separate study. The Castel Capuano and the Castel dell' Uovo at Naples; the Basilica of St. Anthony at Padua; the Church of the Santa Trinita at Florence, and the Church of San Domenico at Arezzo have been attributed to him. The *alto-rilievo* of the "Deposition from the Cross," still to be seen in the lunette of one of the side doors of the Duomo of San Martino at Lucca, and the statuettes on the outside of the Misericordia Vecchia at Florence, are also reputed to be his work; but it is not certain that he executed them, nor is their precise date known.

It is in the Battisterio of Pisa, a beautiful Romanic temple, that we find the first intimations of Pisano's genius as a sculptor. The Battisterio was commenced in 1152 by the architect Diotisalvi. On entering this exquisitely beautiful building, the object which first commands attention is the gorgeous baptismal font in the middle; but another work of art, and one far more worthy of study, though too often it is left unnoticed, because of the imposing grandeur of the font, is the pulpit erected by Niccola Pisano.

Throughout Italy, and especially in Tuscany, are seen many carved pulpits of marble of date anterior to Pisano's pulpit at Pisa; but these are all built after one conventional model without a touch of original genius; they are invariably rectangular in form, at the back built into the wall of the church, and in front supported by brackets or by columns.

Nicola showed the originality and the boldness of his genius as an architect, for here was a problem for the architect rather than for the sculptor, by erecting an hexagonal pulpit, entirely isolated, and supported wholly by nine columns, six at the angles, two at the back, supporting the stairs, and one in the middle. Of the columns, two rest upon the backs of lions and one on the back of a lioness, giving suck to her cubs. At the feet of the lions crouch smaller animals, seeking protection. To develop the symbolism of these figures and groupings would involve a closer and larger study of this work of Pisano's than can be given to it in the present essay.[1]

The central column is set upon a group of men and animals. The six incorrect Corinthian capitals, which crown the columns of the six angles, support rounded arches, each of which is divided, after the ogival style, into three smaller, rounded arches. From the corner capitals, between the arches, rise pillars faced with caryatid-like statues, which serve as supports to the cornice. The triangular spaces between these caryatid pillars and the arches are adorned with bas-reliefs of the evangelists and of doctors of the church. Above the cornice rises the parapet of the pulpit, at each angle

[1] The lion is the accepted symbol of sacerdotal wisdom and watchfulness; he always in traditional story accompanies the wise Solomon. Christ, of whom the Jewish King was a type or figure, is represented as attended by twelve lions—the twelve apostles. In the Apocalypse of St. John the Divine, Christ is called the Lion of the tribe of Judah.—Kreuser, Vol. I., p. 189.

of which are three columns. At one of the six spaces between these triple columns is the stair; the faces or compartments of the parapet in the other five spaces are beautifully carved in bas-relief. In the angle called *cornu evangelii,* or the gospel corner, the columns are cut somewhat shorter than in the other angles of the parapet, and support an eagle which holds in its talons a rabbit, and on its outspread wings sustains a reading-desk or lectern.

Not all of the architectural ideas realised by Pisano in this work are original with him; he may not have borrowed them from the remains of Greco-Roman art existing in his country; and we have no reason to suppose that he had any knowledge of ancient art derived from literature; but in the beautiful bronze door of the Duomo of Modena (about 1120), in the church door of San Zeno in Verona (about 1140), and again in the door of the Duomo of Ferrara, of the same date, he might have seen columns resting on the backs of lions. So, too, the pulpit of a church at Barga (1200), and that of San Bartolomeo in Pistoia (about 1250), presented the figure of an eagle, and had at the angles pillars faced with statues.

But herein is no disparagement of his originality. An artist does not create the elements of which his art consists. His genius is shown in his mastery of those elements, in the skill with which he manipulates and orders them, in his power to pronounce the creative *fiat* which makes them things of life.

Pisano showed his independence of convention and

demonstrated his architectural genius by raising his pulpit above the floor of the Battisterio with no other support but its own columns; and by adapting from the ogival style the division of the one rounded arch into three smaller ones; thus is given to this work a peculiar and original character which distinguishes it sharply from all works of French and German architecture.

We will now give some account of the bas-reliefs which decorate the five panels of the parapet; and first of the "Nativity." The most notable figure in this group is that of the Madonna, who is semirecumbent on a couch. Near her, swaddled and in a cradle, is the Bambino, sleeping, while beyond is the Angelic Host, a shepherd and his dog. Plainly the sculptor does not yet recognise the limitations of his art, and attempts in one composition to represent two distinct moments of the story of the Virgin and her Son. Thus, while to the left of the Madonna we see the Babe sleeping and cradled, on her right is the same Babe attended by two women, one of whom holds him upright in a basin and washes him, while the other pours in water from a pitcher; the figure of the Babe is the most exquisite piece of modelling in the whole composition; unfortunately the head of this figure, as well as the arm of the woman holding him, is lost. To the right of this woman sits St. Joseph, an ill-modelled, stiff, uncouth figure, with a disproportionately large visage. On the left of the woman pouring water is seen a part of the shepherd's flock—sheep and goats, coming to the front from under the bed of the Virgin. The three sheep strike the modern critic as tediously identical; the three goats are effectually individualised in action and attitude. Taking this bas-relief as a whole, it must be said that in diversity of form, feature and attitude, it far surpasses all previous works of mediæval sculpture. Pisano had, at least in part, shaken himself free from the tradition of the schools; for in the bas-reliefs of previous Italian artists the composition was simply a procession of figures, men and women, with as little difference of features, action or expression as in Egyptian sculpture. In Pisano's "Nativity" there is a wonderful advance upon this poverty of invention, though the force and originality of the artist's ideas are limited by lack of technical skill and power of expression; he still needs also, as we have seen, a clear perception of the true province of his art and its limitations.

A serious fault of this work, in the estimation of us moderns, with our studious regard for "the truth of history" and "local colour," is that the figures are never Jewish, but always distinctly and typically Roman, ever grand and dignified. Pisano's pulpit at Siena, which we shall examine later, has the same defect, though in a less degree.

Take for instance, in the work before us, the figure of the Madonna; it renders the familiar conception of the Roman empress or the Roman matron. The female figure behind the Madonna, and pointing her out to the angel, is just as thoroughly Roman; as is also the angel himself. In the adjacent compartment, containing the bas-relief of the "Crucifixion," the Christ has the thews of a Hercules; and again the two women who support the swooning Virgin are truly Roman in feature and in massiveness. The same Romanesque stateliness is seen in the bas-relief representing the "Adorazione dei Magi"; indeed the Madonna in this compartment is neither more nor less than a copy of a Phaedra carved on one of the ancient sarcophagi in the Campo Santo of Pisa.

It is evident, therefore, that from whomsoever Niccola learned the rudiments of his art, and the use of hammer and chisel, his real masters were the specimens of decadent Roman sculpture existent in Pisa in his time, and which are now preserved in the beautiful Campo Santo, the most interesting museum of ancient art in the world, and of modern art also, as far as sculpture is concerned. It was from the ancient Roman school that Pisano derived that stateliness and forcefulness which, when thoroughly attempered, constituted one of the chief excellences of his style. In the bas-relief of the pulpit in Pisa, we recognise the work of a genius; but his art is still in its infancy, and its technique is still to be developed.

In this, one of his earliest essays, Niccola made a great advance beyond his predecessors; but an examination of the pulpit in Siena, executed by him some six or eight years afterward (1268), shows a remarkable development alike in technical skill and in artistic sensibility. This pulpit was built and ornamented by

Pisano in collaboration with his son Giovanni, then eighteen years of age, and with Arnolfo di Cambio.

Being octagonal in form, this Siena pulpit differs in architectural character from the one in Pisa. An experienced eye at once perceives that the stairway is of later date than the rest of the structure. It was built in 1500 by the *maestero Riccio,* and is thus three centuries later than the pulpit proper; the bas-reliefs of this addition, the pure Corinthian capitals and the columns of the balustrade are painfully at discord with the main work.

But it is with Niccola's pulpit that we have to deal. Among its bas-reliefs we will study first the "Nativity." In the handling of this subject there is but little difference between the pulpit at Pisa and that at Siena, but the changes are happy. In the place of the woman pointing out the Madonna to the angel, we have here a more homely and idyllic motive—an aged woman welcoming another elderly woman, whose hand she presses fondly between her own; possibly the prophetess, Anna and Elizabeth, mother of John the Baptist. The Madonna, who again, as before, occupies the central place, reclining on a couch, is no longer the stately Juno-like Roman matron; here she is seen in the langour and feebleness of her young motherhood; her eyes are closed, she is unconscious of the scene around her; she is absorbed in contemplation of the new era which opens with the birth of her Babe; but she is still *Ancilli Domini,* the handmaid of the Lord. St. Joseph occupies the same position as in the corresponding bas-relief of the pulpit at Pisa; here the visage of St. Joseph is in better proportion, but the expression of the face is simply fatuous. The figures of the two women washing the Babe are commonplace, but even so they are an improvement on those of their predecessors in the corresponding bas-relief at Pisa.

Instead of the shepherd and dog as in the Pisa "Nativity," we have here two shepherds in an attitude of wonder and admiration, gazing upward toward the angelic host, seen above a bank of clouds in the background. Three oxen, from their stalls behind the Virgin's couch, project their heads into the sacred scene.

The years that have intervened between the pulpit at Pisa and that at Siena have produced a great change, and that a change for the better. In the former work Pisano was like an apprentice, in much following reverently the teachings of the masters of Roman art in its decadence; too respectful of traditional authority to give free reign to his own originality, and, moreover, sorely hampered by his not having thoroughly mastered the technique of his art. But in his later work he soars on the wings of genius, and, disdaining imitation, turns for inspiration to the fountain-head—to Nature—which he now feels competent to interpret.

In the pulpit at Siena there is but little imitation of decadent Roman art, and the result is that, taking the same subject as before, Pisano produces, instead of a bastard classic scene, a domestic picture which, in detail at least, is true to nature and to life, though not conformed to the canons of art in the *ensemble*.

In the "Adorazione dei Magi" of the pulpit at Siena, the visage of the Madonna is indeed coarse and vulgar, but her figure and attitude are graceful; and the modelling of the Bambino is very good, except the head and face (which are not infantile) and the abnormally large ear. Of the kings and their ministers and attendants, it is to be said that they are dignified figures of men, but that they ride ridiculously small horses and ill-shapen camels. The horses have the merit of being at least symmetrical, and are carved with a just apprehension of their natural form; but not so the camels. Niccola had probably never seen a camel, and so evolved that animal out of his imagination.

Of the statues standing at the right and left of this compartment, the Madonna with the Bambino in her arms is admirable, her long, flowing robe being rendered with fine effect. The figure of Moses bearing the tables of the law, which bounds this compartment on the left, is far less successful; the expression of the great lawgiver's countenance lacks force and dignity.

The "Giudizio Finale" is worthy of admiration. The Blessed and the Damned are shown separated by the sentence of Christ the Judge, the blessed on his right, the damned on his left hand. Christ's tribunal, with figures—eagle, ox, lion, and man—at its four corners, is erected near the middle of the background, and Christ the Judge separates the good from the wicked, the good being arrayed in orderly lines before him and to his right, the wicked on his left, without order and convulsed with terror and despair. The ratio of the good and the wicked in this bas-relief is not without significance; the saved are to the lost in the proportion of three to two. This subject, as well as the "Adorazione di Magi," is also treated in the pulpit at Pisa.

While engaged on the Siena pulpit, Pisano undertook, at the request of the people of Bologna, to carve for them a shrine to hold the relics of San Domenico. What part he had in the execution of this work cannot be definitely ascertained; he may have simply sketched the dominant *motif,* and left the development of it and the execution of the design to one of his pupils, the Dominican friar Guglielmo; certain it is that Fra Guglielmo had some share in the work; but it is highly probable that the more important parts were carved by Pisano and the rest by his pupil.

The larger sides of this rectangular shrine are decorated with two bas-reliefs each, the shorter with one only. In the left-hand compartment of the front or façade, a miracle is represented—San Domenico recalling to life a youth that was killed by a fall from his horse. In the right-hand compartment the scene is the trial by fire of Manichean and orthodox books; the fire is consuming the books of the heretics, while those offered by San Domenico for the ordeal remain unscathed by the flames. The first of these bas-reliefs is the more beautiful because of the spirited rendering of the sympathetic emotions of the people who crowd around the fallen youth. This note of tenderness has given cause for doubt as to whether the work is really Pisano's, his chief charactertistic being, as we have

seen, severe, stately grandeur. But it must be remembered that this stateliness belongs most markedly
to the master's early manner, and that by the time of
the carving of the shrine he had to a great extent
emancipated himself from the dominion of decadent
Roman classicism.

The beauty of the composition is in itself a strong
argument in favour of Pisano as its author, and the
note of tenderness which pervades the work may well
be taken as an index of the artist's evolution.

The Fountain of Perugia, a masterpiece of architecture as well as of sculpture, was executed by Pisano,
then nearly seventy years of age, with the assistance of
his son Giovanni and the same Arnolfo di Cambio,[1]
who had been his collaborator at Siena. It is most
probable that the plan of the fountain was drawn by
the aged artist, who had already at Pisa and Siena
given such splendid proofs of his genius and practical
skill in architecture, especially for small monuments intended to be adorned with sculpture.

Four steps lead up to a great polygonal crater or
basin; at the angles are groups of spiral columns.
Each side is divided by a small pillar in the middle into
two compartments. Within this basin is a series of
columns rising from its bottom; these sustain another
basin, also polygonal, but of smaller dimensions. The
angles of this basin are adorned with statuettes. From
the bottom of this second basin rises a column support-

[1] It is to the glory of Arnolfo that he was the architect who traced
the first plan and directed the construction of the beautiful church of
Santa Maria dei Fiori in Florence.

ing a bronze basin, in the middle of which are three nymphs standing shoulder to shoulder and partly back to back, and supporting three griffins; the griffins uphold a tube from which issues a jet of water. All the bronze work of this monument was cast in 1277 by the *maestro* Rosso, a brassfounder of Perugia.

The panels or compartments of the two greater basins are adorned with bas-reliefs, and most of the scenes represented are secular. Only the statuettes at the angles of the second great basin are reputed to be the work of Niccola. These figures, praiseworthy though they are, are plainly too short and too stout, and show an incorrectness of proportion much more marked than do the other figures. This incorrectness of proportion is doubtless due to the fact that Niccola, notwithstanding his technical skill, was still in ignorance of many useful expedients that were not unknown to more ancient artists, and which by the moderns are rightly considered indispensable. One of these is that of modelling the figure in clay, then having it cast in plaster, and from the cast copying the figure in marble. By employing this method and bearing in mind the proportions prescribed by the block of marble and the place which the statue is to occupy, the artist has every opportunity to reduce or to enlarge his model before commencing on the marble.

Niccola and his contemporaries laboured at a great disadvantage in having to begin work directly on the block of stone or marble that came to their hand. With hammer and chisel the head was first roughly shaped;

if its vertical dimension was too great, the sculptor had perforce to shorten some other part of the figure; hence oftentimes incorrect proportion.

But if under Niccola Pisano the art of sculpture did not reach its apogee, some important steps were made in the right direction. Stiff stateliness yielded little by little to the gracefulness of human faces and figures copied from life. The progress made by Pisano through study of living models may be traced in the statuettes which adorn the fountain of Perugia; more marked still does it appear when we compare the figures of the fountain with those of the Pisan pulpit.

The fountain of Perugia was certainly Pisano's last work; there is even doubt whether it was yet finished in 1278 when he died.

Pisano's name has an eminent place in the history of art. He it was who opened men's eyes to the degeneracy of Byzantine art, and that directed them to the true school, the antique, and to the only fount of inspiration, Nature. As Cimabue and his pupil Giotto were the heralds of the renaissance in painting, so was Niccola Pisano the father of modern Italian sculpture.

**EDMONDO
DE AMICIS**

EDMONDO DE AMICIS

WHEN a man has written books, which, of all books written in his own language, are the most widely read; when he sees them translated into other languages and praised all over the world; when the profits earned by this work of his pen far transcend the most sanguine hopes of any other writer in his country; when critics have been hymning dulcet strains of mild praise, and readers of all classes, gentle and simple, old and young alike, have been faithfully buying the whole long series of his volumes as they issued from the presses; does he not seem justly entitled to rank as a great master of his profession and a genuine artist? Yet we doubt if Edmondo de Amicis is a great master in literature or even a genuine literary artist.

His power of arresting the attention and arousing the interest of the reader is conceded. His quickness of perception and his exquisite moral sensibility, responsive to all noble emotions is admitted. He can picture a landscape better than any other living prose writer of Italy; as a stylist he is inferior only to a few of his Italian contemporaries; and he has the knack of making something out of nothing—of winding off page after page of pleasant reading upon the most trifling matters. Turning his pages, one easily grows into a liking for the author; pleased with his buoyant hopefulness, convinced of his genuine sincerity; yet all the time conscious that something is wanting to our perfect satisfaction, something which none but the really great writer can impart. Wherein lies the fault?

A careful examination of the work of De Armicis will reveal why, liking it so well, nevertheless it does not satisfy.

The year of revolutions, 1848, was critical for Italy; her divided populations aspired to freedom and national unity; it was a time when high hopes were entertained of a complete Italian renaissance—political, religious, social, moral, intellectual. Milan threw off the yoke of the Hapsburgs; Carlo Alberto cast the weight of his sword into the balance in favour of the popular aspirations; a Pope stood forth as sign and proof of the Church's sympathy with the national sentiment; young Italy dreamt dreams and entertained confident hopes that were not to be realised, but while the generous illusion lasted, the skies seemed to promise an eternal Springtide, a new birth and a rejuvenescence of the race which once had been the world's master. Into this moral atmosphere was De Amicis born; and the warmth and enthusiasm of that day-spring of liberty in Italy wrapped his infant soul and stamped it with the character of perennial youthfulness and antique Roman simplicity.

His birthplace, Oneglia, has little fame in history. It was founded early in the tenth century and till the

end of the thirteenth belonged to the bishopric of
Albenga; then for near three hundred years it was a
dependency of the Duchy of Genoa, and then the
Dorias sold it to Emanuel Philibert, Duke of Savoy,
in 1576; in the fortunes of war thereafter it changed
masters repeatedly, as Savoyard or Spanish or Genoese or French arms or craft prevailed. It is a snug
little town of 7000 or 8000 inhabitants, cosily en-
sconced amid the hills bordering its bay in the Ligurian
sea. Its chief architectural monument is a noble
church edifice, San Giovanni Battista, designed by
Gaetano Amoretti. The olive plantations of Oneglia
and the adjoining town and district of Porto Maurizio
yield the finest oil exported from Italy. It is a picturesque region, bright with a variegated wealth of
flowers, but with a soil that yields scant returns to
the labour of the husbandman. Such is Oneglia, famous of old as the birthplace of the great Genoese ad-
miral Andrea Doria and in our time of the genial,
kindly novelist Edmondo de Amicis.

Edmondo was intended by his parents for a soldier,
and his education was completed at the military school
of Modena. Such a special training means, the world
over, short measure of classical or literary study, and
his scholarly attainments at graduation were neither
more nor less than those of the average military cadet.

As an officer in the army he first saw active service
in the battle of Custozza, and with the national army
tasted the bitterness of defeat on that disastrous day
when no degree of personal courage could compensate

for inefficient leadership. The campaign which followed opened with the most brilliant prospects, but a series of reverses ensued, which gave weight to the dark insinuations whispered against the leaders in this ill-managed war. De Amicis had shared in the high hopes entertained of the spirit and efficiency of the army and he shared also in its reverses; but no shame of unmerited defeat, through the incompetency or the treachery of the commanders, could shake his confidence in the soundness of the national cause or abate his loyalty to his king; indeed his attachment to the military profession grew with the disgraces which had befallen the army.

From 1867 to 1870 he was in the garrison at Florence, and employed his leisure hours in writing short stories for the periodical *Italia Militaire,* of which later he became editor. His *Novelle* and his *Bozzetti Militari* appeared first in that journal and were instantly received with public favour. They were then published in volumes; and as the editions were speedily exhausted, he recognized in that fact a sort of call to a literary career, and soon he resigned his commission.

He has told us, in his *naïve,* artless manner, of his hesitation before taking this step. He had scruples of hault courage, thinking that "none but masterminds have the right to renounce the active life, and to presume that, by giving forth their thoughts in writing, they may pay the debt every man owes to society." He modestly considered, however, that even

very humble and simple souls have wants and aspirations which none but a congenial spirit can understand;
and he believed that he might give utterance to their
unspoken sentiments, and direct upon their grievances
the current of human sympathy. From that moment
the history of his books is the history of his life. He
goes abroad and gives us the journal of his travels
in the volumes *Spain, Morocco, The Netherlands,
London,* and *Paris.* At every return home he finds
his fame and popularity ever greater; so he feels encouraged to attempt new work, as in *Cuore, Alle
Porte d'Italia,* and *Gli Amici.* His *Sul Oceano,* a
lively record of a voyage to America, reveals the
author's sympathy for socialistic doctrines. In this
voyage De Amicis had an opportunity to observe the
condition of emigrants, and his interest in their fortunes is awakened. At home, he studies the life-
problems of schoolmasters and schoolmistresses, and
the results of his observation are found in the works
Fra Scuola e Casa and in *Il Romanzo d' un Maestro.*

Since he first entered on the literary career his social
and political views have undergone a change, which
has been differently judged by the supporters of opposing schools of political doctrine; but no one has ever
challenged his absolute sincerity. His Italianist patriotism and his more or less cosmopolite socialism
are but two aspects of his generous, hopeful nature;
he has no rancour for the class which he regards as
the oppressors of the mass of the population; but he

believes that their rule is coming to an end, and that a new era of peace and justice is coming.

He labours for redress of wrongs, without invoking vengeance upon the doers of wrong. He has thus been consistent with himself throughout, whether he glorifies militarism or lauds the blessings of peace, whether he exalts the royal throne or pleads the cause of the lowly millions; he never veers with the wind of opportunism, but is always responsive to the cry of the distressed.

In a parliamentary crisis he was induced to stand for election to the Chamber of Deputies as a representative for Turin; but on being elected he was unwilling to bear the responsibility and resigned the deputyship. Indeed, in disposition and temperament he is ill-fitted to be a wrestler in the parliamentary arena.

It is a fast popular belief among the Italians that some persons are born lucky, others unlucky. It were doubtless nearer the truth to say that in the struggle for life a man is generally victor or vanquished according to the measure of his pluck, perseverance and good sense. If success is a matter of good luck, then De Amicis is to be reckoned a lucky man. But the secret of his constant good fortune lies, possibly, in the fact that he has never aimed too high, never undertaken to do that which he was not fitted by nature to do; good luck is sometimes only another name for good sense.

From the outset of his literary career he has been

conscious of his power and of his limitations. At first he wisely confined himself to the only subject with which he was conversant—military life. Meanwhile he did his utmost to compensate for his initial deficiency, his want of a solid classical education, so necessary to a man who would write pure and elegant Italian. To an extended course of miscellaneous reading he added a careful study of Fanfani's *Vocabolario,* and bent all his efforts to the acquisition of a refined literary style.

His long residence in Florence was of decisive moment in fitting him for eminent rank in Italian letters. Like his greater countryman, Manzoni, he was aware that a Lombard "must needs wash his garments in Arno's wave." The rude dialects spoken in the north of Italy, or worse, the idiom of barracks and camps, receive scant toleration in Italian literature; and De Amicis was practically under the necessity of learning literary Italian, a new language. A comparison of his earliest with his latest writings will show how much he had to learn and to unlearn.

Yet, despite their provincial dialecticism, his first writings, the *Novelle* and the *Bozzetti Militari* were hailed with delight all over the land. The chord of patriotism was still vibrant in every Italian heart, and with it De Amicis' strain was fully accordant. Diplomacy did more than arms to bring about the happy consummation—Italian independence. But the end having been secured somehow, anyhow, and the people being now liberated from foreign bondage and united under a popular monarch, the army, which had, though indisciplined and ill-led, striven valorously to achieve independence, was, for the many, an object of patriotic pride; and the praises lavished on the soldiers who had laid down their lives in their country's cause, were grateful to their companions in arms and their countrymen, and were not too scrupulously weighed.

In truth, the heroes of those battles as portrayed by De Amicis were mostly of a kind which does not stand criticism unscathed. His soft-hearted officers and thick-brained devoted soldiers are not real flesh and bones, to be turned round and viewed from every side and studied like living, throbbing humanity; they are of such unsubstantial stuff as dreams are made of, images reflected by a mirror, rather than men.

Our author's writings at this period present a fairly accurate portraiture of the outside, but of the soul, spirit, character within, not a glimpse. The fault was hardly detected by his countrymen, because the same slurring of psychological analysis is usual in modern Italian literature. Liveliness of conception and keenness of appreciation of the beautiful in nature we find in these Southern artists; but that very gift disqualifies them for minute observation of the hidden springs of action. Psychological analysis has seldom proved attractive to these life-enjoying, pleasure-seeking Italians. In examining the more recent productions of Italian painters and sculptors, we are struck by the absence of any suggestive or deeplying intention. They are clever artists, artisans.

They understand both the harmony of colours and the purity of lines. Their benches and chisels are in their hands pliant tools to produce the effects conceived in the artists' minds. Their works please the eye and the fancy; they excite admiration; but they do not make us think. The beautiful masterpiece has not been meditated deeply enough, and hence does not tempt us to search into its innermost meaning, and to trace its genesis back to the primal idea in the artist's mind. And this is true of Italian artistic expression, alike in painting and sculpture, music and literature.

In the works of De Amicis we find this want of spiritual or psychological depth, yet rare skill of artisanship withal. As critics have pointed out, his effeminate officers are always ready, on the slightest provocation, to shed a tear or utter sentimental bathos; but at the same time we are required to believe that in the stress of battle they are veritable lion-hearts.

Unacquainted though we are with the intimate life of young officers, we will grant that De Amicis relates correctly the doings and sayings of his young officer heroes; we only ask that he shall help us to recognise their doings and sayings; we wish to have the impression removed from our mind that these figures of young officers are only puppets. When Kipling's Mulvaney and his comrades sit around a fire, discussing their own and their officers' affairs, we get such intimate acquaintance with those rude, honest, prejudiced hearts that we easily read their motives and interpret their actions; but when De Amicis, in the *Figlio del Reggimento*, shows us a group of lusty young officers fondling and petting a little street urchin, stroking his unkempt locks and gushing over him with long speeches of motherly tenderness, our feeling is rather one of disgust than of sympathy; one cannot regard such a scene as true to nature and fact.

"Carmela," the prettiest of these short tales of the *Vita Militare,* is the melancholy story of a peasant girl, heartbroken and demented in consequence of an unhappy love affair with an officer. She lives in a dreary islet inhabited only by some scores of convicts and a small military guard. This rustic Ophelia's chief delusion consists in mistaking for her false lover every officer who succeeds him. How a youthful lieutenant is moved to pity for the unhappy girl; how pity changes to love; and how he contrives to cure her of her insanity by re-enacting, in every particular, the scene of her first lover's departure. All this is told with ingenuity. As we read, we grow curious to learn how this novel experiment will result; but all the time we are conscious that these far-fetched emotions, these extravagant moral feelings, this unreal world of sentimentality, has no point of contact with our own moral world; and that the actors are shadowy creations of the author's mind, not human creatures.

Their sorrows or their joys are not our sorrows or our joys. The scenery, the landscape, the figures, we clearly distinguish; but the souls animating these puppets are for us enigmatical. Even if the story be founded on fact, it is presented in such guise that to us it appears as a creation of fancy.

If we use the word Poet in its primary significance of creator, De Amicis will have no claim to that title; but if by Poet we mean one highly gifted with imagination and fancy, De Amicis has about the same right to the appellation as, say, Coppée or Felicia Hemans.

While he possesses in liberal measure the imagination and the fancy of the poet, Nature has denied him the *primum mobile* of all poetic genius,—restless, passionate desire of realising an ideal. De Amicis is blessed with a healthy, joyous, one is tempted to say, a bovine contentment. He lacks the stimulus of a passionate desire for higher and highest things; it never occurs to him that he must "look before and after and pine for what is not." To his eyes come no visions of a supernal, an ideal world. Poets have been great only when they have agonised; painters and sculptors have created immortal masterpieces, when, comparing their dream of the Beautiful with their surroundings, they have blended harmoniously the outer and the inner vision. This power of conceiving an ideal, actuated by an impulse to express it in words, lines, colours or musical sounds, will make a great writer out of a ploughman, will frame the divinest of musicians out of a deaf man, and will fashion a world-famous preacher out of an uncouth fanatic. Dante is the greatest of Italian poets, because none agonised as he did to give expression to ideas from the supernal world of the spirit.

Now, De Amicis has never been tempted to meddle with spiritual problems; the heights and the depths of poetic and philosophic contemplation are ignored by him; he is concerned only with the interests of the passing day, and he amuses the passing generation; his works are for present consumption; none of them is "a possession for ever."

For him, religious belief, as is often the case with his countrymen, is a matter of no importance. He does not care to make profession of atheism; he just pays a pretty compliment or two to Providence in his earliest writings, and there an end.

Had De Amicis been born a few years earlier, he might, fired with patriotic enthusiasm, have sung with Berchet, if not with higher-soaring Niccolini, the golden vision of Italian liberty. That dream is now realised, and, like many other realised dreams, has lost much of its dreamland brilliance. Italy has been freed from the Austrian yoke and from the oppression of native tyrants, and no longer requires the services of her sons on the field of battle; the task set to the present generation is to educate this newly united people and to contrive means of making the nation better morally, socially and economically. De Amicis has given his best endeavours toward forwarding these ends; the dominant note of all his writings is that sentiment of Italian nationality which, as the result of the Great War and the incorporating into the

Kingdom of "Unredeemed Italy" has at last been satisfied, and of which Mussolini and his government, triumphing over all the forces of disintegration, is the symbol.

The other affections predominating in his soul are an exquisite, almost feminine, tenderness for his mother, and an accurate perception and appreciation of the many shades of friendship. These, he has, in his several works, rendered with appropriate delicacy and clearness; these feelings are not dramatic; they grow to full blossom and fade away without ever provoking passionate struggle. We may be interested in the description of such sentiments, but we are neither stirred in our own souls nor brought into communion with the soul of the writer.

Even socialism becomes with him a bland aspiration for the amelioration of society, unmixed with any idea of warring against unfavourable environment. De Amicis is peculiarly lucky,—or wise,—in this: he knows his power and his weakness. He never tests the strength of his wing by attempting a soaring flight, but is satisfied with warbling his dainty sonnets and clearly modulated epistles of simple sweetness.

Among the poetical works of De Amicis, the best of his sonnets are those inspired by the ardent patriotism of his early years, *Come vorrei morire* . . . (how I wish to die) being the most popular. The idea is indeed trite, but it is expressed with grace and in a manly spirit. In the two sonnets entitled *La Grandináta* (the hailstorm), the poet with a few simple but effective touches realises for the memory and imagination of any one who has lived in Northern Italy the phenomena of one of those brief, angry and ruinous storms not infrequent in that region.

De Amicis' filial tenderness is delicately expressed in a sonnet beginning with praise of his mother's beauty and ending with the wish that he might, by himself growing old in an instant, see his mother young once more, at the price of his self-sacrifice.

If delicacy of feeling and exquisite poetic form were all that we require in a poet, then De Amicis must be accounted a genuine poet; but the poet's bays are not so easily won. He possesses neither that knowledge of the heart of humanity which was the heritage of Shakespeare, nor does he perceive the soul of nature as does Wordsworth; neither has his spirit travailed with personal sorrow as did that of Leopardi when he wrote *Le Remembranze,* nor has he been maddened by the black vision of some national wrong as was Niccolini when he summed up the misery of Italy in his *Arnaldo da Brecia.*

To return to the prose works of De Amicis, and in particular to his stories of military life, we readily see why these fail to awaken our interest; we do not take his military characters *au serieux.* We cannot bring ourselves to believe that those officers and troopers of a generation ago were, every man and boy of them, in all circumstances absolute stoics, counterparts of Socrates at Delium. Did De Amicis never hear of officers committing suicide rather than

obey commands they knew to be cruel and dishonour-
able? But our author's military characters know
nothing of the conflict between conscience and necessity, between duty and possibility; these impossible
automatons, having received the word of command,
always on the instant proceed to execute it, as blindly
obedient as the subject of a mesmerizer.

In *"Camilla"*—one of his *Novelle*—he shows us a
young conscript who resorts to mutilation to escape
from duty in the army. This poor wretch is painted
in the darkest colours; the author takes such pains to
bring public odium upon this worst kind of malingerers
that he effectually quells any feeling of compassion one
might have for the unhappy wretch. No extenuating
circumstance is allowed to have any weight in excusa-
tion, no mercy is shown for the culprit. Dostoiesky
can have sympathy with the vulgar murderer; but
De Amicis would deny all the offices of humanity to
the offender against the military laws.

The records of travel—*Morocco, Spain, Holland,* and *Souvenirs of Paris and London*—are the
most valuable of the works of De Amicis. In these
his talents find free scope, and his limitations and his
temperamental defects are less obvious. He looks
around him with the keen glance and quick perception
of all Italian artists, and describes his impressions in a
charming, lively style. He is a delightful *raconteur,*
himself deeply interested in all the strange and novel
experiences of travel in foreign lands, and awakening
an interest no less lively in his readers. As we turn

these entertaining pages over one is continually reminded of *raconteurs* of like gifts, encountered in many an out-of-the-way corner of Italy; genial natures, who will talk for the sake of talking, will laugh at their own jokes, smile at their own conceits, and altogether amuse themselves so heartily that they seldom fail to amuse their hearers.

De Amicis never takes a short cut through any subject or narrative; he never hurries along the main road, but follows every promising by-path, lingering wherever the vista invites, describing minutely not only the things he sees, but the dreams they recall and the wishes he has cherished. Before entering a town he usually describes it as it is painted in his fancy; then he will give us first impressions, and lastly a minute account of everything. As a fair specimen of this manner, let us open the volume *Holland* and read his description of Broek. Ever since his arrival in Holland he had been, in fancy, planning and building this curious village. He had been inquiring everywhere about it, noting not only the answers he got, but also the looks, smiles or shrugs that accompanied them; and when at last he is come to the much-talked-of locality he peers through the screen of forest with eager, playful impatience, and this is what he sees:

"After half an hour's walk, although no sign of Broek appeared beyond the top of a tall steeple, I began to see here and there signs which announced the neighbourhood of a village. As I went on I saw rustic houses with their windows ornamented with net curtains and ribbons, with little movable mirrors, and toys hung up; their doors and window-frames painted in bright colours, and finally, strangest of all, trees with their trunks coloured bright blue from the root to the first branches.

"Laughing to myself at this last oddity, I looked about and discovered a boy lying on the grass. 'Broek?' inquired I. 'Broek,' he responded, laughing.

"Imagine a city made for the show-window of a Nuremburg toy-shop, a village constructed by a ballet-master after the drawing on a Chinese fan, a group of houses made for the scenes of a puppet-theatre, the fancy of an Oriental drunk with opium, something which makes you think of Japan, India, Tartary, and Switzerland all at once, with a touch of Pompadour rococo, and something of the constructions in sugar that one sees in a confectioner's window; a mixture of the barbaric, the pretty, the presumptuous, the ingenious, and the silly, which, while it offends good taste, provokes at the same time a good-natured laugh; imagine, in short, the most childish extravagance to which the name of village can be given, and you will have a faint idea of Broek.

"All the houses are surrounded by small gardens, separated from the streets by sky-blue paling, each in the form of a balustrade, with wooden apples and oranges on the top of the pales. The houses, for most part built of wood, and all of one story only, and very small, are rose-coloured, black, gray, purple, blue and

grass-green; every door painted and gilded, and sur-
mounted with all sorts of bas-reliefs representing
flowers and figures, in the midst of which can be read
the name and profession of the proprietor.

"The gardens are not less odd than the houses.
They seem made for dwarfs. The paths are scarcely
wide enough for the feet, the arbours can contain two
very small persons standing close together, the box-
wood borders would not reach the knee of a child of
four years. Around houses and gardens stand trees
cut in shape of fans, plumes, discs, etc., with their
trunks painted white and blue, and here and there appears a little wooden house for a domestic animal,
painted, gilded, and carved like a house in a puppet-
show.

"One expects every moment to see the doors fly open
and a population of automatons come forth with
cymbals and tambourines in their hands, like the
figures on hand-organs. Fifty paces carry you around
a house, over a bridge, through a garden, and back
to your starting point.

"After having walked about for a while without
meeting anyone, I began to wish for a view of the
inside of one of these houses. Whilst I looked about
in search of some hospitable soul, I heard some one
call 'Monsieur! Would you wish to see a private
house?' She was a poor widow, she told me, and
had only one room; but what a room! The floor was
covered with clean matting; the furniture shone like
ebony, all the little points of metal here and there

looked like silver. The fire-place was a real temple, lined with coloured tiles, and as clean and polished as if it had never seen a fire. She showed me the utensils for cleaning the room—enough to set up a shop; brooms, brushes, cloths, scrapers, dust-pans, pokers, shovels, feather brushes, aquafortis, Spanish white for window-panes, Venetian red for the knives, coal-dust for the copper vessels, emery for polishing the iron things, brick for rubbing the pavements, and sticks for poking out microscopic straws that get in the cracks of the floors.

" 'In former times,' she said, 'the mania for cleanliness arrived at such a pass that the women of Broek neglected their religious duties for it. The pastor of the village, after having tried all means of persuasion to end the scandal, took another way. He preached a sermon in which he said that every woman who faithfully fulfilled her duties toward God in this earthly life, would find in the other world a house full of furniture, utensils, and trifles various and precious, in which, undisturbed by other occupation, she could sweep, wash, and polish for all eternity, without ever coming to an end. The image of this sublime recompense, the thought of this immense felicity, infused such ardour and piety into the women of Broek, that from that moment they were assiduous at religious exercises, and never had need of further admonition.' "

De Amicis tells us that further along in this village is preserved a miniature representative of one of the houses and gardens as they appeared in ancient Broek, "preserved by the proprietor as an historical monument of past folly. Here are bridges a palm long, grottos and cascades of miniature proportions, small rustic chapels, Greek temples, Chinese kiosks, Indian pagodas, painted statues; tiny figures with gilded feet and hands, which bounce out of flower-baskets; automata of life size that smoke and spin; doors which open with a spring and display a company of puppets seated at a table; little basins with swans and geese in zinc; paths paved with a mosaic of shells, and with a fine porcelain vase in the middle; trees cut into a representation of the human figure; bushes of box carved into the shapes of bell towers, chapels, ships, chimeras; peacocks with spread tails, and children with arms stretched out; paths, arbours, hedges, flowers, plants, all contorted, tormented, twisted, and bastardised. And such in former times were all the houses and gardens of Broek."

Thus does De Amicis in his travels muse, talking to himself, laughing aloud, very much like an overgrown schoolboy, which, after all, he is; and somehow this familiar prattle is right welcome; we take a strong liking to this ingenuous traveller and we willingly follow whither he leads.

As we wander with him in Spain, assisting at a bull-fight, *correada de toros;* seeing through his eyes we miss no episode of the gala spectacle. When we follow him to Morocco, so life-like is his picture of the brilliant and gorgeous fantasies of the Moorish capital that one is inclined to regard De Amicis as at his best when painting gay pageants and festivals; but when we turn to the homely, sober descriptions of neat, toy-like Dutch houses, and the impressive picture of a dark gray sky lowering on the dull, sombre waves of a bleak northern coast, we pause and ask which we like best, and are ready to acknowledge that no other books of travel afford so much delight as these.

The reader of the volume *Constantinople* will not easily forget the clever little sketch of those dogs that "will hardly stir even if they see a four-in-hand coming down upon them at full speed," and which will make a move only at the very last moment, when the horses' hoofs are ready to come down upon their heads; even then only dragging their laziness a few inches farther, just the necessary distance to get out of danger.

"They will crouch in the middle of a street, in a circle or in a row of six, ten, or twenty of them, so doubled up that they look much more like a heap of filth than living animals; and there they will sleep the whole day, amidst people going to and fro in a deafening turmoil. . . . Neither rain nor snow nor scorching sun nor chilling cold can move them. When snow falls, it falls on them; when it rains, they lie there sunk in mud up to their muzzles; and when at last they rise, they look like dogs moulded in clay, but with eyes, ears and faces hardly distinguishable."

That is a picture from the life, and a like accuracy of description is seen in all of our author's books of travel. Notable, too, is his avoidance of monotony in his descriptions of many similar landscapes or scenes;

whether he describes winter scenery, or Dutch cottages, or rows of ships at anchor in Flemish harbours, there is never repetition.

It would be ungracious to remark upon what De Amicis might have told us, but has not told; how he has overlooked weightier matters in thus giving attention to homely things, or to what is simply picturesque or curious.

De Amicis, as appears from his books, is just the sort of man one would like to have for a fellow voyager. He has that fund of good humour and that faculty of being happy and at home everywhere, without which travelling, though with portemonnaie packed with bills of exchange, is a dreary experience. His radiant cordiality seems to have on occasion melted the icy barrier of reserve with which the untravelled Englishman fences himself round. While De Amicis was riding on top of an omnibus in London, a young man sitting beside him addressed a remark to him in English, which to our author was an unknown tongue. The story must be given in the author's own words, or rather in an English version of them: "My only reply was a nod and a smile; and thus encouraged he went on. Seeing that he was pleased to find me in agreement with him, I made a show of understanding it all, and treated him to a series of nods, smiles and indifferentiated gestures that might answer to anything. When I grew tired of my part, I thought that, since I had been conversing in an idiom I could not understand, I had some right to address him in a language of which he was ignorant, so I began to talk in Italian.

"It was like groping in the dark, yet he laughed, clapped his hand on my knee, and sat listening as though I were singing an arietta; then he fell to talking English again; and so we went on till the omnibus stopped."

Happy the traveller who meets with such adventures, or rather who can carry himself through such adventures so prettily by sheer force of his good humour.

The most popular of all of De Amicis' writings is *Cuore;* indeed it may be said to be at this moment the most popular prose work in Italy. With a view to excite and stimulate a feeling of comradeship and fellowship among young Italians, it calls into being a whole world of schoolboys, in which the true, natural and moral relation of individual to individual, and of individual to society, are illustrated. This world of boys bears a strong impress of truth and realism in the pages of *Cuore;* we feel as though we were really living with them, joining in their sports, sharing their amusements, striving with them to form ourselves to a manly character. We know them all by name, and, as it were, personally; Garrione, the sturdy protector of the little ones; De Rossi, the boy of gentle birth, whose superior breeding is recognised, not envied by his comrades; the funny Garoffi, a born shopkeeper, keen for profitable trade. We pity the crippled boy, son of a convict. We share their troubles and their simple joys.

Though fiery patriotism may ofttimes be lacking in world-worn men, and the world-wise sceptic may smile at their heroic feats, we are sure that many a gallant hero of eleven has glowed with admiration for the brave little drummer or the daring Lombard boy whose stories are told with a simplicity more impressive than De Amicis' usual florid style.

Yet when we consider how difficult it is for grown people to understand children's minds, and how general the failure to produce in English, books designed to promote the healthy, moral, social and mental development of boys; we naturally hesitate to admit all the claims made on behalf of *Cuore*.

In Italy *Cuore* certainly enjoys unparalleled success, and the book or its 'system' is believed to be a step toward the solution of one of the problems of true education—education for moral and social ends.

A man of De Amicis' magnetism and geniality is sure to have many friends, even chance acquaintances are apt to be demonstrative. Though ephemeral, the attachments are pleasant to remember. When time has snapped the slender tie, there still remains the fragrant perfume of memory, mellowed by easy oblivion of any former bitterness. In swarms these phantoms of old friendships haunt the mind of De Amicis; day by day as they pass he fixes the pleasant vision and notes down his emotions until he has accumulated material for those two bulky volumes *Gli Amici*.

Naturally we do not find that analysis of friendship which Montaigne has given us in a few pregnant sentences. The faculty of exploring the human soul is denied to De Amicis; whenever he has undertaken to write a pathetic tale it has been a failure. Heroes like Albert and heroines like Camilla—in the volume *Novelle* are second-rate mouthpieces of persecuted innocence and bombastic sentimentality.

Under the influence of Zola he has in *Un Dramma Nella Scuola* tried his hand at a realistic rendering of passionate grief in a girlish heart. Anyone must remember the masterful pages in which Zola shows how a sensitive and refined little girl breaks her heart and dies of grief for her mother's fault. The same subject tempted De Amicis, and he tells us how a schoolgirl is tortured by her mother's shameful life and how after having been rudely told how matters stand she becomes ill and dies. Whilst Zola in a few masterful strokes sheds such vivid light on little Pauline's feelings that we learn to understand her slightest word, nay, her every look—as when she recoils under the doctor's physical examination; we utterly fail to penetrate into the heart of De Amicis' heroine. The whole management of the plot is clumsy; a crowd of useless characters encumber the scene, adding nothing to the realisation of the psychic moment, diverting our attention from the principal figure which grows hazy and loses all individuality.

The ideas crossing that dying girl's mind are enumerated at length by the author, and we are not called to behold the soul-struggle which alone must be interesting in its cruel effects. We read a tale, we neither see nor feel a human heart.

The success of his *Travels* indicated to De Amicis wherein lies his power, and he wisely abandoned the field of sentimental fiction and confined himself to that branch of literary art in which he is unrivaled— description of social types and exposition of actual social conditions.

Sull' Oceano is the best example of this talent. Confident in his own original power as observer and artist, and encouraged by the unvarying success of all his books of travel, he boldly dispenses with the historical allusions and the lumber of geographical description, with which those earlier writings were filled, and in this volume is simply a painter of every changing scene. The book is not unlike an album of photographs of classes and groups of passengers—tourists, merchants, emigrants—taken on shipboard in a voyage to America. The first-class passengers are described with fine satirical humour; the miserable emigrants with sympathy deepening into compassion, and at times rising into indignation over the miseries which compel them to quit their native land, and to seek new homes over sea. Passages of broad humour are happily intermingled with deeply affecting scenes; and such is the author's lightness of touch and his exquisite sensibility that we are never shocked by any jarring note.

On this voyage his eyes were opened to new problems of society. Henceforth these problems are chiefly to engage his attention, and he will devote all his energies to social reform, and will labour to bring about the social revolution.

The two volumes which succeeded *Sull' Occano,* viz.: *Fra Scuola e Casa* and *Il Romanzo d' un Maestro,* are a study of the social and economic conditions of schoolmasters and schoolmistresses in Italy.

In these works De Amicis does not presume to investigate the historic causes of the present conditions; he simply shows what they are, without offering any project of redress, enough for him that he paints the situation faithfully, so as to call public attention to evils that cry out loudly for a remedy.

The plot of the *Il Romanzo d' un Maestro* is loosely developed; it is little more than a slender thread connecting together a number of scenes in school life. The perusal of this book has a saddening effect; even the buoyant spirits of De Amicis sink as he contemplates the hard and cheerless lot of Italian teachers. A man rising from such a study must become a pessimist and abandon hope and effort, or he must become an earnest advocate of reform.

And it is in Socialism that De Amicis puts his trust for the cure of this and all other ills of society. He has accepted the doctrine of the socialists, it is true; but he is of too mild and gentle a nature to harbour feelings of rancour against the oppressor while he broods over the wrongs of the oppressed. In his youth he was the enthusiast of patriotism; afterward an ardent socialist; whether as patriot or as socialist, he acted from passionate feeling, sympathy, rather than from calm reason. He was a socialist for the same reason that he was a nationalist; because at that time socialism was in the moral atmosphere about him, as patriotism was then; and in the political life of Italy no party interests, save those of socialism, could have strong attraction for a man of the moral constitution of De Amicis.

In his latter days his voice was often raised and his pen was ever busy in appeals to the working classes to unite against what he terms "the common enemy" —Capitalism; but De Amicis was not, indeed could not be a leader; like Doctor Faustus, he had seen the good and the evil of the world of man and of the spiritual world; like Faust, he dreamed a beauteous dream of peace and righteousness.

SOME EARLY
PRINTERS AND
THEIR COLOPHONS

SOME EARLY PRINTERS AND THEIR COLOPHONS

I

SO long as literature shall exist, so long as books shall be printed and read, so long, doubtless, will the origin of "The Art Preservative of Arts," the methods of the production and distribution of the earlier printed books, and how the intellectual life of the world was sustained and nourished before their appearing, be subjects of perennial interest. Only one corner of this large subject can be touched upon in this book. An out-of-the-way corner, it is true, yet full of information, at first hand, as to the beginnings of great things. Full too of quaintness, of humour, of pathos, these autobiographical side-lights of those early printer-publishers, whose foibles and vanity, keen appreciation of the dignity and importance of their work in selecting and rendering available for mankind the literature of the world, and no less keen perception of the failures and impudent pretensions of their fellow-craftsmen and would-be rivals; and sometimes, too, most touching instances of their own humility; all these appear in turn in the colophons which they affixed to their books.

These colophons are revelations of character; they

are full of *humanity*. They are no less valuable for their information as to the introduction of the art of printing.

Of course, there were books before the days of the early printers, and it would be interesting to consider the history of their production, preservation and distribution from the earliest Egyptian dynasties down to and through the period of intellectual activity in Greece and afterward at Rome; to speak of Alexandria as a centre of book production and distribution and to continue the sequence down to the days of Guttenberg.

But though in the Alexandria of the Ptolemaic kings and during the Augustan age in Rome there was effective book-publishing and book-selling; yet, in attempting to trace the continuous stream between these early sources and the first printer-publishers, we should be led far afield from the specific subject of this essay.

Even in limiting ourselves to the early monkish scribes we might justly include the literary work done in those early monasteries of Africa and Asia Minor, to which we owe the preservation of so many Greek classics and the writings of the early fathers.

Yet the thread between the literary work of those early scribes in African and Asian monasteries is too slender and our knowledge of their methods too slight to warrant considering them in connection with the early printers.

Not so the *scriptorium* of Viviers, under the direction of Cassiodorus, and the establishment of the monastery of Monte Cassino, near Naples, in 529. From these *scriptori* to the workshop of Guttenberg the line is direct, the nine hundred intervening years being represented by the period of the monasteries of Western Europe, the period of the older universities and the period when the manuscript trade of Venice and Florence became important and the fairs of Frankfurt and Nuremberg distributed their books, not only among *clerics* and *magisters,* but among those larger circles of the community who required books written in the language of the people.

Reference will be made in the text to this close connection between the monkish-scribe and his immediate successor, the first printer. To appreciate these colophons that connection must be kept in mind. The text-type was a copy of the scribe's handwriting, the size of page, width of margin, style of illumination, manner of decoration—all was done with the thought of producing a printed imitation of the original manuscript.

Of course, in time came a less slavish following of the written page; there were obvious improvements. From Italy came the three most valuable text letters: the *Roman,* first founded by Sweinheym in 1465, and perfected by Jenson in 1471, then the *Italic* and *small capitals,* introduced by Aldus Manutius, at Venice, in 1501, and modelled on the handwriting of Petrarch. To these early forms modern taste is returning.

Delightful it would be, too, to trace the history of those early printer-publishers—the Estiennes, of

France; Aldus Manutius, of Venice; Plantin, of Antwerp; Froben, of Basel; the Elzevirs, of Leyden and Amsterdam, and the Kobergers, of Nuremberg. Interesting, too, the consideration of the influence of Luther and Erasmus on early printing and the importance of the "divine art" in the propagation of their doctrines and the spreading of the Reformation. With the requirement came the men and also the invention.

Interesting, too, would be a more exhaustive study of the colophons affixed to manuscripts by those poor monkish scribes and their influence on the colophons of the first printers; and how their reverence for the printery was a direct inheritance from those devout scribes who regarded their *scriptori* as holy places and at their consecration used to pray:

Benedicere digeneris, Domine, hoc scriptorium famulorum tuorum, ut quidquid scriptum fuerit, sensu capiant, opere perficiant.

We recall, too, that zealous scribe in the monastery of Wedinghausen, in Westphalia, to whom it came upon a day when his weary hand ceased to copy, his eyes closed in the last sleep and the angels received his spirit. His body was committed to the ground and mouldered into dust. But not altogether, for a score of years after, when the grave was opened, behold, the right hand was found as firm of flesh as the day he relinquished the pen. And, that the infidel may see and believe, are not the hand and the pen preserved unto this day as holy relics and may be seen in the reliquary under the altar of the monastery chapel?

Then, too, there was Dietrich, the first Abbot of St. Evroul, filled with holy zeal for the transcribing of manuscripts and making of books. In order that his monks might work more earnestly he used to tell them this story:

Once upon a time there was a wicked monk. At his death the devil claimed his soul. He thought he had a sure thing. Now, it happened that just before his death the monk had completed the copying of a great folio volume. This book the angels brought to the judgment-seat of God, and for each letter written in the book one sin was forgiven. When the recording angel had added up the two sides of the account, behold, there was one little "i" left over, and the monk's soul was saved.

Here, again, is the colophon, or finis, which a monkish scribe of St. Jacob's Monastery, in Liége, added after finishing his manuscript:

Jacob Rebeccæ dilexit simplicitatem,
Altus mens Jacobi scribendi sedulitatem.
Ille pecus pascens se divitiis cumulavit,
Iste libros scribens meritum sibi multiplicavit.
Ille Rachel typicam præ cunctis duxit amatan,
Hic habeat vitam justis super astra paratam.
[The Hebrew] Jacob loved the simplicity of Rebecca;
The lofty soul of [the monk] Jacob [loved] the work of the
    scribe;
The former accumulated riches in pasturing his flocks;

The latter increased his fame through the writing of books;
The former won his Rachel, loved beyond all others;
May the scribe have the eternal life which is prepared above the
    stars for the just.

These are instances, to be sure, of reverence for the
"holy art" of transcribing manuscripts. But the
printer considered that, though of a higher order, he
was the direct successor of the scribe and deserving

of the same and even greater honour, inasmuch as by
his art the boon of books was brought to a greater
number of people. His printery was a sacred workshop and he himself engaged in holy work, for which
the reasonable reward was, as the scribe of Liége
wrote, "the eternal life which is prepared above the
stars for the just."

We have mentioned the types used by the first printers. It would be interesting to consider their origin and history and how the modern printer, after wandering in the desert for so many years, is awakening to the fact that Aldus and Jenson and Caslon and

To the Reader. Who faulteth not, liveth not; who mendeth faults is commended: The Printer hath faulted a little: it may be the Author oversighted more. Thy paine (Reader) is the leaste; Then erre not thou most by misconstruing or by sharpe censuring; lest thou be more uncharitable than either of them hath been heedlesse: God amend and guide us all. ❧ ❧

the Elzevirs and what are called real Old English types were full of beauty and have not been surpassed or improved upon by modern founders.

A fair copy of the Old Flemish Black letter is the colophon to Caxton's *History of Reynard the Fox,* printed in England in 1481. It is particularly interesting as a specimen of the type first used in printing in England, and was probably imported by Caxton from the City of Bruges. It is quite different from either

290 The Friar in Fiction and Other Essays

modern Flemish or German text-letter and was
anciently known in France as *grosse bâtarde.*

In contrast, and as an example of a modern Black
Letter which shows originality, the "author's apology"
is here offered in a type designed by Mr. Will H.
Bradley, and the words are the words of the colophon of Robartes quarto volume on *Tythes,* printed
in Cambridge in 1613.

Without answering for the shortcomings of the
printer, the author knows well that he has "oversighted" much that he will be glad to mend if further
editions of his work are called for.

II

IN the first age of Typography printers were deeply
impressed with a sense of the importance of their
art, and gave expression to it in terms that often
evoke a smile from the modern reader of their colophons. Printing is "a new manner of writing, and
almost divine;" it is "the master art," an art "holy,"
"divine," without qualification; a "marvellous art."
Yet while thus fully conscious of the sacrosanct character of the Art Preservative of Arts, so engrossed
were they with the work they were doing that, self-
forgetting, they at first neglected the opportunity of
associating their names with the immortal writings of
classic poets, historians, philosophers, and orators
issued from their presses. Many of the earlier printed

books appeared without the printer's name or the time or place of the printing.

This self-effacement gave occasion to the controversy that has now for four hundred years been waged over the question, Who was the inventor and first maker of types of cast-metal, John Guttenberg or Coster, of Haarlem in Holland? For though there are other claimants of the title, Father of the Art of Printing, Coster is the only one who in recent years has seriously disputed the claims of Guttenberg; and even Coster's claims are now generally discredited.

Soon, however, the typographers bethought them of the oversight, and began to couple their names with the works they were sending forth; and that in no demure, self-denying way, but with pretty loud trumpeting of their artistic skill and the correctness and elegance of their work: all this in the *Colophon* or *Finis;* for it is usually there, and not on the first page—which was not yet in all cases a title-page—that the first printers of books made themselves and the city of their domicile known to the reader. Usually the printers hired a poet's pen to celebrate in verse the glories of typography in general and their own artistic eminence in particular.

Alrich Hahn, for example, in the colophon of his edition of Livy's *Histories* (Rome, 1469), orders his office poet to address the Guardian Goose of the Tarpeian Jove and bid her be of good cheer:

"O, Guardian Goose of the Tarpeian Jove! why dost flutter and beat thy wings? The Gaul (Gallus) is fallen: thy venger is here, Ulricus Gallus [*gallus* is Latin for hahn]: he has proved that there is no longer need of thy quills; in a day he prints more than can be penned in a year."

Ulrich's poet was surely a fellow of rare wit; but though by his verses he insures immortality to his employer's name, he fails to tell in what year Hahn printed his edition of Livy, which, by the way, is the *Editio Princeps* of that classic; and because the verses do not give the date of printing, the right to the title of Princeps had to be established by research.

Windelin of Speier practised the art of typography at Venice, in succession to his brother John. Windelin's poet puts in the mouth of the reader of his edition of Q. Curtius Rufus' *History of the Deeds of Alexander the Great* this apostrophe to the honest German typo:

"O, Windelin, this breath shall fail me and return to the airs of heaven and quit my tenantless corpse, ere thine high worth and virtue and thine illustrious fame, my noble friend, shall be by me forgot."

This bard also fails to state the place and date of printing the work; but the place is Venice, and the date almost certainly 1470.

The *History* itself begins abruptly on the first page without title or heading of any kind and without mention of the author's name—a thing usual enough in old MSS. Hence the once customary mode of quoting books, as papal bulls and legal instruments are still quoted, by the first word or two of their text, *e. g.,* the bull in condemnation of Martin Luther, *Exsurge Domine,* and as the Hebrew sacred books are quoted and named by Hebraists and Jews, *e. g., Bereshith Bara,* the book Genesis: the same usage is seen in the names we give to judicial writs, as *Habeas corpus, Fieri facias.*

At Rome, in 1471, was printed an edition of the works of Ovid, by Conrad Schweinheim and Arnold Pannartz. The printers' poet makes a graceful apology for the outlandish surnames:

"Illustrious reader, whoever you be that look into these volumes, if you wish to know the names of the printers, read: you will smile at their harsh sounding Teutonic cognomens. Mayhap their art will make less uncouth these vocables all unknown of the Muses: Masters Conrad Suueynheim and Arnold Pannartz imprinted many such copies as this at once. The brothers Pietro and Francesco Massimo provided offices suitable for the work."

This is the *Editio Princeps* of the complete works of Ovid.

In the same year, 1471, was produced at Bologna an edition of the same Roman poet by

"Baltasar Ozoguido, Citizen of Bologna, born in most honourable station," and what is of more consequence, "the first inventor of the printer's art in his city."

This printer's prose, it is seen, in claiming for Baltasar the honour of inventing the art, makes a more daring flight of fancy, or of some other faculty, than the verse of the poets hired by the German printers of Rome and Venice.

Modestly dignified is the colophon of Jacobus Rubens,

"By nation a Frenchman, who, when the renowned Nicola Marcello was doge of Venice, 1471, imprinted Ovid for the behoof of the living and those to come after them."

His hired poet then takes up the pen and thus addresses the reader:

"O reader, if you desire admission to the Muses' fountains, peruse the divine poems of Ovid. Through Ovid is the surest way to all other poets, for he first broke a path through trackless regions."

Then, after an enumeration of the beauties of the *Metamorphoses, Art of Love,* and the rest, he declares this edition to be a work of

"Marvelous perfection."

This is very tame compared with the verses in which are sung the praises of Augustin Corneri, who, in 1476, printed at Ferrara an edition of the *Metamorphoses:*

"Were Ovid still breathing this air of the upper world, thy fame, Augustin, would never sink into oblivion; for not less would thy art be extolled than Corinna's charms."

Antonio Zarotto published the same work at Milan the next year, 1477, and in the colophon bluntly characterizes himself as a

"Distinguished printer."

But the poet's judgment on his employer's work may be suspected of bias, and still more open to suspicion is the printer's judgment on his own work. Here, for example, is Matteo Capcasa, who, in the colophon of his edition of the Works of Ovid, printed at Venice in 1489, assures us that the printing was done

"With most scrupulous accuracy under happy and favouring auspices."

But when the critics come to pass judgment upon it they find it to be teeming with error of every possible kind—errors and blunders of editor, compositor, proof-reader, pressman, the D——, the binders—in short, of everybody that had a hand in it. A copy of this notable edition of Ovid is in the library of Heidelberg University.

Warned, doubtless, by the unfortunate result of poor Capcasa's effort to produce a correct text of the bard of Love, another printer, Filippo Pincio, to whom we owe an edition printed in Venice in 1491, sought help and guidance from heaven, still keeping his powder dry, however, for though he invoked "the aid of God most high"—at least he tells us that he sought such aid—he did not fail, on his own part, to give the work

"Most scrupulous care and great industry,"

with what effect the historians of printery report not.

The fair presumption is that Pincio's work had some blemishes, for the printer of another Venice edition of Ovid, though doubtless he had Pincio's Ovid before him, seems to doubt the possibility of any considerable degree of critical accuracy:

"If, perchance, any change of letters, or transposition, apposition, omission, or other perversion of the same offend the reader's eye, let him charge that to the account of the difficulty of the proof-reading."

The printer who thus prays for a charitable judgment is Simon Bibilaqua.

The next printer to get out an edition of Ovid makes no address to the reader. He doubtless had his trials and troubles while doing the composition and press-work, for in the colophon, as though with a sigh of relief, he exclaims:

"Praise be to God Almighty; printed at Venice by Bernardino Benali."

He neglects to note the year, but it was 1494.

A singular conjunction of callings and avocations is seen in the colophon of Paulus Suardus' Commentary upon the *Metamorphoses* printed

"At Brescia by the most skilful typographer the priest Baptista Farfeugo, doctor of pontifical law, in the year MID."

Dr. Farfeugo deserves credit for writing the year 1499 so succinctly: his three letters say precisely the same as the long formula of his contemporaries, *e. g.,* MCCCCLXXXXVIIII. Such is the date formula of an edition of the *Tristia,* printed by

"The most diligent and industrious Joannes de Cereto at Venice."

It is almost as long as the year number written out in full in Latin—millesimo quadringentesimo nonagesimo nono. Doubtless our ingenious priest-canonist-printer would have employed the more compendious form, millesimo undequingentesimo, which expresses precisely his MID—one thousand five hundred less one.

The next year, 1500, an Ovid printed at Lyons

"By the labour and skill of the careful printer Jean de Vingle,"

has the date MCCCCC instead of the correct brief form MD. But the vagaries of the old printers in dating style are sufficiently curious to be studied apart, and some specimens will be presented later.

The *Editio Princeps* of Livy was got out at Rome, in 1469, by Ulrich Hahn, and contains the famous apostrophe to the feathered watchman of the Tarpeian Rock. In the next year the *Histories* were printed at Venice by Windelin, of Speier. The text was edited by a poet and scholar, Joannes Andreas, bishop of Aleria, and he gave the typo a grand send-off in two-score and six spirited elegiac verses. Apostrophizing the Roman historian, he tells him that it is honest Windelin that rescues his fame from oblivion.

" '*Magna loquar sed vera tamen*'—big words, but true. If some one, O Livy, were to save the lives of your children, would you not say you owed that man more than you could repay?

Now here is Windelin, who has saved your great works, your progeny, has beautified them and multiplied them: You will surely be grateful to the artist."

Another celebrated printer, Antonio Zarotto, of Milan, is content to have his praises sounded in prose. In the colophon of his Livy we find:

"Printed at Milan by the most consummate artist, Antonio Zarotto, in the reign of the most illustrious dukes Bona and Giovan Galeazzo Maria Sforza 1480."

A printer at Milan, Alessandro Minutiano, who was also a classical scholar, but whose duties at the case left him little time for critical work on his texts, thus brushes away all the pretensions of scholars and editors to scrupulous exactitude, telling them in effect that they were but literary pharisees, puritans, hypocrites, mugwumps:

"He is no imitator of the insolence of those who, that they may appear to be knowing, give out that they correct and amend every text."

On the contrary, passages that appear to him doubtful or obscure he leaves untouched, so that the true and genuine reading may be investigated in the light of ancient copies.

Windelin, of Speier, is in all probability the printer of the *Editio Princeps* of Tacitus. It has no title prefixed, nor does it give either the year or the place of printing. In the colophon is a tetrastich devoted equally to praise of the historian and of the printer.

"Tacitus is the father of history and all posterity will do him honour: the printer is he of Speier, and he is the chiefest glory of his art."

The place of printing is almost certainly Venice, and the year almost beyond a doubt is 1468; there is some uncertainty about the personality of the printer— whether he is Windelin, or Windelin's brother John, of Speier, who died about 1468.

The *Editio Princeps* of Horace appears without any indication of place, or date, or printer's name: it has not even a title or heading, nor are the pages numbered. It would seem to have been printed at Milan, in 1470, by Antonio Zarotto. Some scholar, noting this omission of the printer's name, has added, in the place of the usual colophon, four elegant and spirited verses, in which he prays that

"Whoever gave out the Venusian bard's poems in a copy so correctly printed, might live in the memory of all generations even as the immortal poet himself."

But an ungrateful posterity, looking the gift horse in the mouth, finds it a botchwork, full of all kinds of errors and defects: *e. g.,* the initial letters of the several poems are omitted or not supplied; the long *f* is used as a final letter; letters are often transposed; words are dropped out so as to destroy the metre; and so on. Plainly there was no editor; the ancient MS. was given to the compositor and there was no competent revision. Such is the *Editio Princeps* of Rome's greatest lyric poet!

The next edition of Horace's works was certainly printed by Zarotto, at Milan, in 1474. To this he fearlessly, nay proudly, signs his name. In the colophon we have:

"All the works of Quintus Horatius Flaccus, carefully corrected, and by Antonio Zarotto elegantly and faithfully imprinted, March 16, 1471; Whoever buys this will never be sorry."

In the same year, at Ferrara, Augustino Corneri printed an edition of Horace. In the colophon is an elegant tetrastich, telling that:

"At Ferrara, in the reign of the godlike Ercole, consort of the queenly Lionora, it was imprinted by young Augustino Corneri, son of the honest bookseller, Bernardo."

Between the time of the introduction of typography and the year 1500, the works of Horace seem to have been published far more frequently than those of any other Latin classic except Virgil. An illustrated edition of Horace was got out at Strasburg in 1498— the second instance of the use of woodcuts in a classic author. Terence had been similarly honoured in 1496. Both the annotations and the woodcuts were by "Jakob Locher, poet laureate and professor in the University of Freiburg;" and the pictures are in the title described as very beautiful; but a later age pronounces them to be "crude and often simply ridiculous, like those in Crüninger's Terence."

The colophon of the *Editio Princeps* of Persius consists of one hexameter verse:

"Explicit ignotus per totum Persius orbem,"—here endeth Persius, a poet quite unknown to the world.

The volume is without date, name of printer and locality. Its title of *Princeps* is given to it by inference from the ambiguous word "unknown"—taken to be equivalent to "unpublished" or "unprinted."

But the printer's poet may have writ better than he knew or intended; at all events we are free to give another meaning to the word unintelligible. For however widely the satires of Persius may be diffused, they will be still "unknown," or not understood. If the anecdote told of St. Jerome is not true, it is at least a happy invention. Jerome threw his copy of Persius into the fire, saying:

"The flames will understand him;"

and addressing His Obscurity, he added:

"If you don't want to be understood you ought not to be read."

In this severely just judgment Jerome was at one with Persius' best friend and trustiest counsellor, Cornutus, who, after Persius' death, gave up to the flames a number of the young poet's writings. Unfortunately six of the Satires escaped that most righteous doom, to pester all generations of schoolboys and scholars of a larger growth in the ages that followed.

The *Editio Princeps* of Sallust was printed at Paris by three Germans, Ulrich Gering, Martin Kranz and Michel Freiburger, about the year 1470; but all these particulars are got from inference only, for the work itself gives neither date, printers' names, nor place of printing. But in the colophon, the printers' poet has an octastich, the first couplet of which is believed to refer to the year 1470, when "the world's greatest King" [Louis XI] was "assembling armaments and men and threatening destruction to his ancient foes" [the Burgundians]. The martial spirit of the people of Paris is then lauded, and they are asked "to number among their champions the Germans who printed these histories of Sallust." If this Paris edition is not the *Princeps,* then the primacy belongs to the Venice edition of Windelin of Speier, the date of which is without controversy 1470. Windelin's office poet in a hexastich, after mention of the history and fate of Jugurtha, rather petulantly addresses the reader:

"Windelin has produced 400 copies of Sallust, O reader! and can you think of looking at books written with the pen when the work of the types is so much more elegant?"

Here is the record of a faithful friendship between two German printers settled in Venice. It occurs in the colophon of a Sallust printed in 1474:

"Printed at Venice under the direction and at the cost of John of Cologne and John Mantheim, of Gerretsheim, who live together in true accord."

Two other German printers of Sallust, Petrus Kaiser and Johann Stoll, are memorable for us solely because of their curious business signs, the Green

Bellows in St. James Street, Paris. Their poet contributes a clumsy and ungrammatical octastich lauding both Sallust and the two printers.

Here is a very curious colophonic tetrastich appended to an edition of *Speeches taken from Sallust's Histories:*

"O Christ, true God, for the love of thy holy Mother, guard me in body and soul: from all the wiles of the Fiend shield thou me this night. I am a sinner: that I do confess: do thou have mercy upon me."

The work does not give the name of the printer, nor the date, nor the place of printing.

Though an entry on the title-page of a book has no rightful place among these notes on colophons, one may, in passing, notice the edition of Sallust published at Edinburgh, in 1744, by William Ged, goldsmith. It is

"Printed not in the usual way from movable types, but from cast tablets or plates."

This Sallust is unquestionably the first of the classics to be printed from stereotype plates. By the way, William Ged had the usual fate of inventors: "died of a broken heart."

To the "duumviri of the art of printing in Italy," Conrad Schweinheim and Arnold Pannartz, is due the credit of having been the first to print some of the writings of Cicero. The Orations were printed by them, at Rome, in 1471, and in the same year at Venice by

Christopher Waldarfer. In the colophon, Christopher's laureate has a tesseradecastich in which first he lauds the inventive genius of the Germans.

"Who is there that admires not the acuteness of the German mind? The German does straightway whatsoever he essays to do. See with what marvellous skill Christopher Waldarfer, native of Ratisbon, the great glory of his fatherland, has printed books, how speedily he has reproduced so many monuments of antiquity."

Then the printer's versewright pronounces an encomium on Cicero, and finally apostrophizing the great orator says:

"Whoever studies thee, Tully, will be without more ado, eloquent."

Another German printer, Adam of Ammergau, robs his fellow-countryman of two verses of his tesseradecastich, and solders them on to a couplet which very plainly is shop-made and original with Adam.

"O, thou who readest this bulky volume of causes forensic and discourses addressed to the Senate and to the people."

So much Adam purloins from Christopher surnamed of Waldarf or Waldorf:

"Know that they are printed from metal types by a man of Ammergau: lo, here is Master Adam."

Another instance of this stealing a fellow-typo's thunder, or his wind, is seen in Antonio Zarotto's edition of Justin's *Histories.* Zarotto conveys from the Frenchman Nicolas Jenson (Venice, 1470), the first half of a tetrastich:

"I, Justin, present to you the ancient historians and recount the world's story: read me, I am Trogus in brief;"

and tacks to it a distich in praise of himself. Zarotto's Justin appeared in 1474 at Milan. It was a great scandal that one of the most eminent Italian printers should commit so mean a theft.

Schweinheim and Pannartz produced Cicero's *Letters to Friends,* at Rome, in 1467. This is the first of the ancient classics printed by them at Rome. Previously they had had a printery in the great Benedictine monastery of Subiaco. In 1467 these printers were not yet fully established in the eternal city, and they had to be content with a less flamboyant *envoi* or send-off in the colophon than was given them a little later when they could afford to employ a first-class versifier. In the colophon of the Epistles of Cicero they simply say that

"Conrad Schweinheim and Arnold Pannartz, partners, got out the work with wonderful perfection."

Another edition of the *Letters,* printed by Emiliano of Foligno and Johann Numeister, appears without date or place of printing, but the number of copies struck off is stated in the colophon to have been 200. The art of printing, and all the arts associated with it, have made great progress since that time, but a book of say 500 octavo pages, of which only 200 copies were printed from movable type, would probably cost much more now than then. On the other hand, a copy of a mammoth sheet like one of our daily newspapers would cost in those old times several dollars.

The *Editio Princeps* of Valerius Maximus cannot be traced with certainty to any printer, date or place; it has the title in full on the first page, therein differing from many other books printed in early times; but the initial letter of chapters is nowhere printed, being filled in by hand. The only marks of punctuation are the colon and period. The date is believed to be 1470, and the place of printing Strassburg. The edition of Valerius Maximus, which came out very soon after this, is very distinct, nay emphatic, in setting forth the printer's name, the time and the place. In the colophon we read:

"The present most celebrated work of Valerius Maximus! completed in the noble city of Mainz! in the year 1471 on the 18th before the Kalends of July! by that excellent master of the art of printing Petrus Schoyffer of Gernsheim! happily is consummated!"

This is followed by the arms of Fust and Schoeffer. Windelin of Speier is less boastful in the colophon of his Valerius Maximus than he is wont to be; he has simply

"The end, 1471,"

followed by a distich which tells that

"This work of art, printed with types and shining with splendour, was produced by Windelin."

Posterity endorses Windelin's judgment of his work, it is *"splendida editio,"* a splendid edition.

Schoeffer's colophon of Valerius Maximus, which we have just noted, with its exclamation signs, is imitated by Petrus Kaiser and Johann Stoll in their edition. Their colophon has:

"The present most celebrated work! . . . most noble Paris!" etc.

A more servile imitation is seen in an edition got out by the bachelor of arts, Martin of Würzburg, at Leipzig; he has all the exclamation signs, but he forgets to give the date.

The Frenchman Nicolas Jenson appends to his edition of Suetonius, in 1471, four graceful verses, in which he modestly enough names himself as the printer —but alas! tramples on prosody to fit his name into the first verse:

"Hoc ego Nicoleos Gallus cognomine Jenson."

Then he asks whether any one will dispute the neatness of the artisanship, and thus addresses the reader:

"While you are perusing at ease your Suetonius, I beg, O reader, that you will love the name of printer."

Now that is perfection! Nicolas, a mere artisan, whose education was got doubtless in the printing-office, is a gentleman.

How different the address of Simone Paschale

Giodertino in his Suetonius, printed at Bologna, in
1488:

> "Whoever you are that desire Suetonius of most absolute
> correctness, buy this and go your way assured; for Simone
> Paschale Giodertino—he is the delight of his countrymen—has
> purged it of every error; so that ye shall seek in vain anything
> that makes difficulty for readers: take ye therefore a copy of
> this edition, or cease to look for a faultless copy."

The next year, 1489, a Suetonius published at Venice
seems, in its modest colophon, to rebuke the extravagant pretensions of the man of Bologna:

> "Here you have, good reader, the lives of the Cesars, long
> earnestly desired, at a small price and corrected with the utmost
> care by the most competent scholars, and printed most accu-
> rately by Bernardino of Novaro."

And now comes a printer who, though he will not
have his work praised in verse, takes extraordinary
pains with the style of his prose colophon. He is a
purist, a classical Latinist, at least he will tolerate no
barbarisms. He rejects such neologisms as *impressor*
to express "printer," *prelum* for "press," and so forth.
As for him, he is no "impressor," he is *biblioponus,* a
bookwright in good Greek; he prints not with *typi*
(types) but with *aes signatum* (stamped metal); nor
does he use a *prelum* (press), but *torcular* (having the
same meaning); his very name, whatever it may have
been to his good old Deutsch mother and his school-
fellows, is now, in ancient Latin style, as when Plancus
was consul, Cneius Appius.

He had to leave the name of his city little altered; under his pen it became Erphord, but we know from history that ever since 1505, at least, the name has been Erfurt; he reverts to the ancient Latin manner of the epistolary imperfect tense instead of the present: in short, he achieves this exemplary colophon:

"Τελος. *Cn. Appius Biblioponus Erphord Aere.*
SIGNATO TORCULARIQUE TRANSCRIBEBAT, Meuse Junio M. D. VIII."

This seems to have been Cn. Appius' début—it appears to have been also his finale.

In the same year, 1509, appeared at Paris an edition of Suetonius with a text freed from the "monstral monsters" *(monstris monstralibus)* of corrupt readings, formed in previous editions, and restored to its original purity. Of this edition the great critic Ernesti says—just what might be expected of a rival editor:

"What a succession of editorial *Sisyphi* we have been reviewing."

Now let us see what was the judgment of critics upon the work of Ernesti himself. He puts forth a Suetonius in 1748, at Leipzig, and of this the critics say: "His text is carelessly edited: his annotations are unworthy of his fame as a scholar."

Distasteful indeed it must have been to purge the texts of the ancient classics of the errors of copyists, printers and editors. Even when the story of this herculean labour is told in verse, as it is in an octastich by Christopher Crassus, it excites a feeling of disgust that can hardly find adequate expression in our language without giving offence to the proprieties. This Christopher, in singing the praises of Cuspiniano, "favourite of Apollo and all the Muses," and editor and corrector of the text of Florus, declares that said Cuspiniano (here English is unequal to the occasion)— *ulcera defricuit multo stillantia tabo.*

It is with a grateful sense of relief that we turn away from this vision of a lazar-house to the sunshine and flowers to which we are invited by another printer's poet. In the colophon of a Florus published in the same place, Vienna, and the same year, 1511, as that other:

" 'Studious youth' is invited 'to accept budding and blooming Florus, whom chaste Minerva in chaste wedlock bore.' "

And we can pardon the vehemence of the curse that follows the poet's distich:

"Therefore, whoever thou be that shall call this edition adulterine, be thou accurst"—*sacer esto!*

Apuleius is represented by an extraordinarily large number of copies in MS.: his *Metamorphosis,* or *The Golden Ass,* was among the first books to issue from the printing-press.

And the way in which the authors of Boccaccio, Don Quixote, Gil Blas, and their modern imitators, "borrow" their choice episodes from the Numidian philosopher, even as he "borrowed" from Lucian, though it would make the modern plagiarist-hunter shudder, yet indicates his perennial popularity.

The *Editio Princeps* of the *Metamorphosis* was printed at Rome in 1469 by Schweinheim and Pannartz. In the colophon of an edition published at Vienna in 1497, the printer, who calls himself in Latin Johannes de Hiberna Arce (Winterthur?) tells us that his native place is—

"Not far from Rhine's banks and the city of Mainz, inventress and mother of the art of printing."

Some of the editions of the *Metamorphosis,* whether in the original Latin or in translation, have, either in the colophon or the title-page, extravagant laudations of the work as a book of religious and moral edification; but it would not be safe to expose for sale as a devotional work *The Golden Ass* unexpurgated. In the German translation of 1588, made by

"Johann Sieder, erstwhile secretary of the right reverend prince and lord Lorenz von Biber, bishop of Würzburg, duke of Franconia, etc., and imprinted by Alexander Weissenhorn, at Augsburg,"

we are told that in

"this beautiful fiction men are taught how, with God's help, they may be no longer like the horse and the mule, which have no understanding, but may become well pleasing in the sight of God and rational and upright."

The predecessor of Windelin, John of Speier, his elder brother, printed the *Editio Princeps* of Pliny's

Natural History, at Venice, in 1469. A hexastich in the colophon introduces Pliny, or rather his great *"Historia Naturalis,"* giving praise to the honest printer:

"Me whom the eager reader erewhile could so seldom take in hand, and who, indeed, was hardly intelligible, John of Speier has restored to integrity and has written out with metal types. Let the tired hand and the quill have a rest, for toil gives place to study and genius."

That was in 1469. In 1470 an edition of the writings of St. Augustin, *Civitas Dei,* printed at Venice, has in the colophon a hexastich recounting the principal achievements of John of Speier in printing, his death, and the succession of his brother Windelin:

"John of Speier, who proved to the Venetians that in three months a hundred volumes of Pliny a month and as many big volumes of Cicero could be produced, had made a beginning on the writings of Aurelius Augustinus, when sudden death carried him off. But Windelin, his brother, is here in his stead, in the art not his inferior: He will live in the memory of Venetians."

This vaticination of immortality regards Windelin, not his deceased brother, but both brothers are of the band of the immortals. As for Windelin, he is doubtless the greatest genius that ever lived: He himself has said it.

In the colophon of his edition of Virgil, published in that same year, Windelin's poet thus lauds his employer:

"Windelin of Speier printed these works of Virgil, at Speier; so let others praise the Polycletuses and the Parrhasiuses and such like artists: but whosoever loves the gentle arts of the Muses will extol Windelin with highest praise; and that not so much because that he has produced many volumes as for that his volumes are at once the most correct and the most elegant of all."

And here be it confessed that the good typo did produce editions of exemplary correctness and of undeniable artistic merit.

Windelin's rapturous thurification of himself in the verses just quoted, his pelting himself with bouquets, might justify one in taxing him with a little vainglory. And see the effects of bad example and the contagiousness of our vices. Windelin's too enthusiastic hymn to himself is of the year 1470. The very next year Adam Roth, almost as good and great a man as he, in the colophon of his Virgil (Venice, 1471) sings, or sets his office poet a-singing:

"Whoever desires to read the poems of the bard of Mincio, let him read me."

It is the book that addresses the reader.

"Not Solomon, nor Hiram, nor the Sibyl, nor famed Greece with all her sages, nor Rome mighty in arms and peer of gods, ever could boast that they possessed so grand an art. We are the progeny of that ADAM whose name recalls the first parent of all."

In the same year, but without mention of printer's name, or place of printing, appeared an edition of Virgil's acknowledged works, with some spurious pieces of an obscene character, at that time commonly believed to be Virgilian. In the colophon is a distich:

"You ask why these poems, though obscene, are printed? Excuse them: they were writ by Virgil."

In the character of the typography and in certain peculiarities of the composition, the hand of Adam Roth is discerned: another Fall of Adam,

"whose name recalls the first parent of all."

Christopher Waldarfer, or Waldorfer, was the printer of a volume of Commentaries on Virgil, by Servius Maurus Honoratus, published at Venice, 1471. A decastich in the colophon celebrates the absolute flawlessness of the text, the great learning of the editor and the skill of Christopher:

"If any one desires books that are well printed, books in which from beginning to end there is no blemish, let him examine this: The text was corrected by thine hand, Great Guarino! and the proofs were read by thy son, Baptista. These commentaries never saw the light before. It cost money and labour to get them: hustler Christopher alone could secure them —Christopher, of the Waldarfer line, native of Ratisbon. The Latin tongue approves the inventor's work."—*inventoris opus lingua latina probat*.

There is a book sent forth under the fairest possible auspices! The next year another edition was printed: proof, you will perhaps say, of high public appreciation of the critical, commentatorial and correctorial talents of Great Guarino and Little Guarino? Hardly. The new edition has a different editor, and in it are cor-

rected the errors of the inerrant Guarino. An octastich proclaims the unapproachable excellence of the
new edition, while not a word is said of its faultless
predecessor.

"Many a book, O Christopher, the glory of Ratisbon! hast
thou given to the press for the common good: Now thou givest
furthermore the commentaries of the learned Servius upon Virgil's poems, thus making accessible to all a work that used to
be a rarity. O youths! buy this book, it has been corrected
with the utmost care by Ludovico Carbone, and will be of great
service to you."

O Christopher Sisyphus, beware, beware! They
are fooling thee, those pretended great scholars!

The printer of a Virgil rated very low the talents
and learning of the literary hacks of his day. He signs
himself B. H., but gives no particular of date, of place
of publication; but B. H. is supposed to signify Benedetto Ercole, a printer of Ferrara. He thus addresses
the reader:

"Reader, if you wish to read the works of the greatest of
poets, Virgil, then read them here, for here they are, redolent of
the grandeur of antiquity. Here you have none of the polishing,
furbishing, correcting, emending of Roman and Venetian
editors: away with that laborious scrupling and judging of
critics: away with their pretended corrections: here you have
Virgil's own copies that were treasured in the church of St.
Paul, at Rome: here is the complete, true text: if you would
be convinced, read, Farewell, B. H. A. D. 1472."

An edition of Virgil, printed at Venice, 1472, by
Leonard Achat, has in the colophon:

"I am of the city of Basel. Leonhardt Achat is my name. I printed thy poems, O divine Virgil."

In the same year three partners, Jacopo, Baptista and Alexandro, printed at Fivizzano, in Tuscany, the works of Virgil. They thus commend themselves to the reader in a pretty pentastich:

"With nimble fingers and stout heart the works of Virgil, a poet famed beyond the skies, were imprinted by these three: Jacopo, the eldest; Baptista, a priest, and Alexandro, comrades living in kindly accord at Fivizzano, a town worthy to be named above towns."

Alrich Hahn, he of the Guardian Goose, finds himself, in 1473, associated at Rome with Simone de Luca, and the firm produces an edition of those obscene short poems unjustly fathered on Virgil. The colophon is in prose, but is not less noteworthy for all that. It reads:

"This present impression of the most renowned poet Virgil was made in the kindly city of Rome; not with ink and a quill pen, nor yet with a pen of metal, but by a certain device for imprinting or making letters was the work done unto the praise of God."

A curious fulfilment of the Apostolic counsel, "whatsoever ye do do all to the glory of God."

Nor is Ulrich Hahn the only one of those ancient printers who reproduce obscene poems "unto the glory of God." But no suspicion of impiety attaches to a similar pious phrase in the colophon of an edition of Virgil's complete works printed at Milan.

"Happily imprinted at Milan with God's help and by the industry of Germans at the cost of Master Leonhardt Pachel, of Ingolstadt, and Master Ulrich Schinzenzeller, in the year 1478, in the reign of the most illustrious prince Giovan Galeazzo Maria Sforza, Viscount, and the most unconquered Duchess Bona, his mother. Unto the praise of the Most High, the glory of the whole heavenly court, and the benefit of mankind. Amen."

A Virgil printed at Strassburg, in 1502, is memorable chiefly for having illustrations designed by the celebrated Sebastian Brandt, author of the *Ship of Fools*. In the colophon these woodcuts are described as being "most artistic figures and images." At Strassburg also appeared, in 1515, an edition of the *Aeneid,* printed by Johann Knoblouch, as appears from a tetrastich written by Othmar Nachtgall—appropriate surname for a poet! But Othmar was hardly even a poetaster. He brings the very name, Knoblouch, into his verses—verses by courtesy. They can no more be scanned than the daily stock reports:

"John Knoblouch, excelling in his art, imprinted this book from selected types; also, he freed the Roman Homer from blemishes so that now he appears in irreproachable form. No neater edition exists."

Soon after this, Knoblouch christened himself in Latin, Cnoblochus; which is greatly to his credit.

We have not yet noted any colophon written in English. Here is one, appended to an English Virgil printed by Caxton in 1490:

"The Boke of Eneydos, compyled by Vyrgyle." "Here fyn-yssheth the boke of Eneydos, compyled by Vyrgyle, whiche hath be translated oute of latyne in to frenshe and oute of frenshe reduced in to englysshe by me Wyllm Caxton, the XXII daye of Juyn the yere of our lorde MiiiiLXXXX."

And while we are in the neighborhood we may just glance at another translation of Virgil. It is entitled:

"The XII Buckes of Eneados of the famose poete Virgill."

Translated into Scotch metre by Gavin Douglas, bishop of Durkeld; its date is 1553, printed in London.

In the year 1524 was published at Rome a work entitled *Dissertations upon Ausonius, Ovid and Solinus,* by Mariangelo Accursio. This scholar being accused of plagiarism, makes an impassioned protestation, which, though it lies a little outside of the field which we are exploring, nevertheless shall have a place here as a literary curiosity. The accusation was that this author has "conveyed," as the wise call it, the labors of another scholar, Fabrizio Varani; the defence is made in the form of an oath, a pagan oath, in these terms:

"Let Gods and Men and Right and Truth give ear. Under the religious sanctions of the Oath and of whatever is higher, if higher there be than the Oath, I do affirm, and this I solemnly and sincerely wish to be received as true: That never have I read, nor so much as seen any writing that could give one title of suggestion of help to me in writing those lucubrations. And if I am perjuring me, then let the Supreme Pontiff see to it, and may the lucubrations be, at the Devil *(malus genius diatribis contingat)*; so that if aught in them be good or even tolerable, the same shall be esteemed of by the unschooled vulgar as the worst possible and by the learned as worthless; and if any reputation is left to me, that it shall be wafted by the winds and made nought."

The *Editio Princeps* of Lucretius appears without date, place of printing, numeration of pages or of signatures, without catchwords; but the printer signs his name in the colophon:

"Thoma Ferando."

Now, Ferando practised his art at Brescia, and his Lucretius would seem to have been printed there in 1473.

In the colophon he is not at all boastful of the correctness of his text. After diligent search he was unable to procure more than one copy of "this exceedingly rare work." It was a faulty one, but he made such corrections as he best could and put it in type. He says in the colophon:

"The reader surely will rather possess this copy, faulty though it be, than no copy at all: Should other copies chance to be found he can by comparison with them correct the errors of this."

The sisyphean striving after irreproachable correctness of text goes on forever. Here is Heinrich Quentell, of Cologne, who in the colophon of his Virgil, printed in 1506, says that

"the text has been freed from many slight blemishes"

found in his previous edition: these were due to the

"inadvertence of the compositors;"

but in this revised edition the work of correcting was done by

"a certain scholar who was by much importunity prevailed upon to undertake the task."

Ludwig Hohenwang, native of Elchingen (as he informs us in the colophon of his Virgil, though he does not give its date nor its place of printing), seems to have concluded that in the matter of the true Virgilian text finality had been reached; so he sets about ornamenting his edition with a woodcut portrait of the poet and orders his colophonic versifier to make honourable mention of it, which the man does very neatly in the distich:

"Subduxit morti vivax pictura Maronem,
Et quem Parca tulit reddit imago vivum."

(By lifelike portraiture Virgil is snatched from death and given back to us as he was when rapt by Fate away.)

Neat verses they are indeed; but the colophonist, in his use of *tulit* takes a liberty with Latin that Virgil would hardly approve; also he has a false quantity in *vivum*.

Just as happy is the distich of another printer's poet, appended to an edition of the historian Eutropius:

"Hactenus Eutropii titulum nomenque, sed ipsum
Nunc demun, lector, conspicis Eutropium."

(Hitherto, O reader, you have had Eutropius' name and title, now at last you have Eutropius himself.)

The reader will have noticed here and there in the colophons frequent pious ejaculations and precatory formulas: in fact, for the first fifty or sixty years of the history of printing, such prayers, or perhaps we should rather call them ominations, were the rule rather than exceptional. The printers were the immediate successors of the monkish copyists, and it was customary with those humble transcribers, when their stint of work on a book was finished, to give thanks and praise to God and his saints, and to entreat the prayers and "suffrages"—as the term was in those times understood—of whoever should read the books, on behalf of the souls of the transcribers. The request was made at the end, in the colophon. Naturally the printers, using as "copy" the work of the monks' hands, followed the custom established by the monks; and, like their predecessors, they regarded their labour and their art as something sacred, holy, non-secular, and looked on themselves as a sort of "clergy" as well indeed they might, if they esteemed aright their calling.

Well did the Cardinal de Cusa, a devout, learned and enlightened churchman, and an alumnus of the school of Deventer, call printing a "sacred art:" he was instrumental in procuring for the duumviri of printing in Italy a local habitation at Subiaco. Peter Schoeffer, in the colophon of his edition of the Justinian *Institutes of Law,* in the year 1468, declares that the inventors of printing were given to the world by the divine Head of the Church himself:

"Hos dedit eximios sculpendi in arte magistros."
(He gave those great masters of the art of printing.)

A surviving memorial of this old-time view of the sacredness of the art is seen in the term "chapel," as used by printers, viz.: first, to designate the typographical workshop, the printery; and then the assembly or lodge of the journeymen employed in a printery. Another vestige of monachism is the official designation of the head of such a chapel, viz.: "father;" but perhaps this designation is now obsolete. The "devil" of the printing-office may be a survival of the slang of the mediæval scriptorium, or copying-room in a monastery.

Touching is the simplicity of the honest soul who some time before the era of printed books wrote this at the end of a volume containing Sallust's *Histories,* and Cicero's *Old Age:*

"Quis scripsit hunc librum sua anima in paradiso."
(He that wrote this book, his soul is in paradise.)

His grammar is shockingly bad, but to his sentiment we may say amen.

Did he mean the soul of the pagan author, or the soul of the coypist?

Who is there that will not approve heartily the sentiment of "Leofric, bishop of the church of St. Peter, at Exeter," who "gives for the behoof of his successors" a copy of Sallust, adding this anathema:

"If any one shall take it away hence let him be under a curse."

The good bishop made that entry first in Latin, then in Saxon. In Saxon the curse could not miss being understood; even the Maid of Orleans, though probably she knew not five words of our language, understood enough of it to fashion a name of her own to designate Englishmen—"godams" she called them always, even amid the dread solemnities of her trial and at the *auto de fe*.

And here is the colophon of a book written in English at the time of Chaucer:

"Here endeth the book of Revelations of Juliana, the Norwich anachorete, to whose soul may God be merciful."

Thus in nearly every MS. that came into the hands of the early printers were found such prayers or pious ejaculations; and the printers for a time continued the laudable custom. Here are some of the formulas used by them. This one we have already noticed:

"Imprinted to the praise of the Almighty God and to the glory of the whole court of heaven, and the good of mankind. Amen!"

The piety and the orthodoxy of that ascription of praise are unexceptionable.

But what shall we say to such as these:

"May the Gods bless our labours."
"May the Gods prosper the undertaking."

We shall see other heathenish formulas employed. Very usual is the ejaculation, "Thanks be to God,

Amen;" "To God be praise;" "God Almighty be praised;" "To Christ alone be praise;" "Thanks to the Most High God;" "With God's help happily completed;" "The end, praise be to God." At the end of a copy of Ovid's *Metamorphoses,* with its fables, never very edifying, of gods and goddesses, we find:

> "In honour of God and the glorious Virgin Mary."

If an individual saint of rank in the celestial hierarchy inferior to that of the Virgin is named, it is always, so far as the present research goes, St. Anthony, presumably not the founder of monasticism, but St. Anthony of Padua, the worthy disciple of St. Francis of Assisi, and a popular saint in Italy. He is invoked only by Italian printers. The usual formula is:

> "Guard us, blessed Father Anthony."

There is in the colophon of a Virgil a trace of the worship of the Heavenly Hosts of the Stars:

> "Imprinted under a lucky star."

But the printer compensates his Sabianism with an even superlatively Christian date-formula, viz.:

> "On the eve of Peter and Paul, apostles, in the year 1516, from the most Christian birthday"—*natali christianissimo.*

But then he throws somewhat into the opposite scale by styling Virgil's poems "divine." Verily it is with this printer a case of good God, good Devil. In view of this opposition of incongruous things, one is led to suspect that our mediæval forefathers had no sense of humour.

Typical of their obtusity in that regard is a volume printed in 1503, which contains those bawdy pseudo-Virgilian little poems and one more poem of a like kind. "Bacchus and Venus," along with "Brother Baptista of Mantua's Votive Poem to the Blessed Virgin Mary." Such conjunctions of irreconcilables are so frequent both in these colophons and in the architecture and painting of the Middle Ages as to be almost a "note" of that period.

Wonderful and fearful are the modes of dating employed by these ancient printers, as a few examples will serve to show.

Paul Friedberger, native of Passau, domiciled at Verona, thus succinctly notes the date of publishing an edition of Lucretius:

"The 1486th year from the incarnation of Christ, the 28th day of September, the kalends of October."

An impossible month-date, by the way, for September 28th is not the October kalends, but four days before the kalends, as the Latins used to count, but three as we reckon.

A book in German, printed at Augsburg, in 1482, has the date in this form:

"The year of our Lord CD in the LXXXII year, Wednesday before the conversion of St. Paul."

i. e., June 25th, A. D. 482. A rather early date for a printed book.

Another printer gives this date:

"Year 1584 after Christ's birth, Wednesday after St. Gertrude's day."

It was a roundabout way of writing November 18.

Instead of Anno Domini or A.D. we have such formulas as "year of grace," "year so-and-so of the *Reconciled Nativity*," and other uncouth date styles.

Curious, indeed, is this date in French:

"*L'an de grace M. quatre cents iiii. xx. et iiii*"

literally, year of grace one thousand four hundred fourscore and four.

The French language has no other word for 80 than *quatre-vingt*—four twenties or fourscore.

Here is a day-date showing very accurate knowledge of the dogma of the divine incarnation:

"Day before the annunciation and the Lord's incarnation."

Less precise, theologically, are these:

"Day before the birth of the Lord;"
"Wednesday after the day of Mary, Mother of God, in the year of our Saviour so-and-so;"
"Day next after the day of Vitalis the martyr;"
"Year—after the birth of our dear Lord;"
"Year—from the incarnation of Jesus Christ our Saviour."

But the foregoing instances are examples of shorthand dating, as it were; here are formulas in longhand:

"Year—from the incarnation or nativity (unorthodox theology) 1496;"

"The next day after the epiphany of the Lord, which is the seventh day of the month of January."

In justice to this "datist" it must be said that the "which" of the last clause relates to "next day," and not to "epiphany." The ambiguity does not exist in the Latin.

It would not be easy in our time to find anywhere a person, however familiar with the church calendar, who could offhand tell on what day of what month falls

"Eric's day after St. Egidius' day,"

which is the day-date of a book printed in the year 15 A.D. The year number is important if true; but there is reason to believe that the true date is 1515. With the help of a perpetual calendar one ascertains that

"Monday after St. Valentine, year 1489, after the birth of Christ,"

was February 16, for in that year February 14 was Saturday.

We find such a style as this:

"The 1515th year of the sending of the Divine Word into flesh,"

and we admire the ingenuity of the mind that invented it.

The consummate genius among all devisers of

soundly orthodox and catholic date forms is unquestionably Heinrich Quentell, printer, of Cologne. Here
are two specimens of his finest work:

"Year of the virginal childbearing next before the centenary
jubilee," *i. e.,* 1499.
"Festival of him who forbade marriage to persons vowed to
God, year of the virginal childbearing next preceding the centenary jubilee."

The answer to the puzzle would seem to be "May
25, 1499." This printer died, if we may venture to
imitate his style of dating, "in the year next after the
centenary jubilee of the virginal childbearing," but on
what festival, or eve, or octave of what festival, history has not recorded, though it was fitting that the
day should be the festival held everywhere on April 1.
After his death his printery was known as that of
"H. Quantell of pious memory."

The curiosities of dating are not yet exhausted.
The peculiar Roman division of months by kalends,
nones and ides made a great deal of trouble for the
old-time printers, as we have already seen in the case
of Paul Friedberger, when he made September 28 and
October 1 the same day. Impossible dates are exceedingly frequent. Examples:

"20th, before the ides of June;"

but the highest possible number of any day before the
ides of June is 8th. Similarly we find

"18 ides of July,"

which is equally impossible. More curious and interesting is the mixing of Roman, Grecian and Christian
chronological styles, *e. g.:*

"1472 7th ides December 2d year of the 295th Olympiad from
Christ's birth."

Instances of blunders of notation, like that from
Paul Friedberger, might be cited by the dozen; two
or three will suffice here: "MCCCCV," to express
MXDV, or 1495; "MLXXXXVI" (1096) to express
MXDVI, or 1496. And they sometimes made a similar error when they wrote the number out as ordinals,
e.g.: "Anno millesimo (quingentesimo) undecimo"
(1011), the word in parentheses (500) being omitted;
similar is *"Millesimo decimotertio"* (1013), the word
for 500 being again omitted.

To the year number the name of a pope or of a
secular prince is very often added, as—

"1513 Leo X, supreme pontiff, governing the Christian
Commonwealth;"
"Year of Salvation 1490, Innocent VIII being supreme pon-
tiff, his sixth year."

We have reserved as our last, and to an English
reader the most interesting of all colophons, that to
Caxton's *The Recuyell of the Historyes of Troye,*
which, as we have already stated, was the first book
printed in English. Of this book Caxton was not only
the printer, but translator from the French. He is
not content to end with a long colophon in English

prose and Latin verse, but must divide his longwindedness between it and the prologue. Then, to be sure that he has given the reader the worth of his money and omitted nothing, he prefaces the prologue with an introduction or title-page. Verily this was before the preaching of "the strenuous life" and the doctrine that "time is money."

This introduction (or title-page) and prologue are interesting not only for their subject-matter, but as marking the conception of a title-page and preface.

Of course, in the earliest of printed books there was no title-page, its place being supplied, as we have seen, by the colophon. Later, when the title-page and preface were firmly established, the mission of the colophon ceased, and it passed into desuetude.

Caxton had so much to say in this first printed English book that he required title-page, preface, and colophon to tell his tale.

In the introduction or title-page he says that the book was

"translated and drawen out of Frensshe in to Englisshe by Willyam Caxton, mercer, of the cyte of London, at the comaundement of the ryghte hye, myghtye, & vertuouse pryncesse, hys redoubtyd lady, Margarete, by the grace of God Duchesse of Bourgoyne, of Lotryk, of Braband, etc. Whiche sayd translacion and werke was begonne in Brugis, in the Countee of Flaundres, the fyrst day of Marche, the yere of the Incarnacion of our sayde Lord God a thousand foure honderd sixty & eyghte, and ended and fynysshyd in the holy cyte of Colen the xix day of Septembre, the yere of our sayd Lord God a thousand foure honderd sixty and enleuen."

Passing to the prologue, he says:

"Whan I remembre that euery man is bounden by the comandement & counceyl of the wise man to eschewe slouthe & ydlenes, whyche is moder and nourysshar of vyces, and oughte to put my self vnto vertuous ocupacion & besinesse, than I, hauynge no grete charge of ocupacion, folowynge the sayde counceyll, toke a Frenche booke & redde therin many strange and meruayllous historyes, where in I had grete pleasyr and delyte, as well for the nouelte of the same as for the fayr langage of Frenshe, which was in prose so well & compendiously sette & wreton, whiche me thought I vnderstood the sentence and substance of euery mater."

So he begins the work, and with courage of a doughty knight

"toke penne and ynke and began boldly to renne forth as blynde Bayard in thys presente werke . . ."

Then remembering his

"symplenes and vnperfightnes"

both in French and English, he

"fyll in dispayr of thys werke, and purposid no more to haue contynuyd therein . . ."

and laid aside the work,

"Tyll on a tyme hit fortuned that the ryght hyghe, excellent, and right vertuous prynces, my ryght redoughted lady, my lady Margarete, by the grace of God, suster vnto the kynge of Englond and of France, my souerayn lord, Duchesse of Bourgoine . . ."

At the command of this lady Margaret, whose many titles Caxton recites with the gusto of the modern Englishman, who so dearly loves a lord, he finished the translation, and three years later it was printed in Bruges, in 1474.

In the colophon Caxton says:

"Thus ende I this book, whyche I have translated after myn auctor as nyghe as God hath gyuen me connynge, to whome be gyuen the laude and preysing."

The father of English printing tells us with touching simplicity that, because his pen is worn, and his eyes dimmed with long looking on white paper, and because he had promised to give his friends copies of the book at the earliest possible moment, therefore

"I haue practysed and lerned at my grete charge and dispense to ordeyne this said book in prynte after the maner and forme as ye may here see, & is not wreton with penne and ynke as other bookes ben, to thende that euery man may haue them attones. For all the bookes of this storye named the Recule of the Historyes of Troye, thus enprynted as ye here see, were begonne in oon day, and also fynysshid in oon day."

Then he prays all who read this simple and rude book, including his "redoubted lady," to whom he has offered it, and who has largely rewarded him, that they may not disdain it. This "redoubted lady" was, as we have seen, Princess Margaret of England, the sister of King Edward IV. As the wife of the new Duke of Burgundy, Charles the Bold, she took great interest in her fellow-countryman Caxton, who, as governor of the English *nation,* as they called the English mercantile colony in Bruges, was the leading Englishman in the entire duchy of Burgundy.

But *revenons à nos moutons*—the colophon to the first book printed in English. Caxton continues that, though Dictes and Homerus incline to the side of the Greeks and "Dares wryteth otherwyse," yet all agree as to the destruction of the

"noble cyte of Troy, and the deth of so mony prynces, as kynges, dukes, erles, barons, kynghtes & comyn peple."

These "comyn peple," though counting doubtless ninety-nine per cent. of the combatants and of the slain, one may infer were of secondary importance to Caxton, a thousand of them not being worth one "kynghte."

With all the earnestness of a member of the "Peace Society" he reflects upon the dreadful example and warning of this destructive war, and piously concludes:

"Therefore, thapostle saith All that is wreton is wreton to our doctryne, whyche doctryne for the comyn wele I besech God maye betaken in suche place and tyme as shall be moste nedeful, in encrecyng of peas, loue, and charyte, whyche graunte us he that suffryd for the same to be crycyfied on the rood tree, and say we alle Amen for charyte."

If goodman Master Caxton had been satisfied to end with this preachment, we should have felt that he needed no apology.

But look at this final flourish in fourteen lines of

rhymed doggerel Latin with which he closes the colophon to the first English printed book:

> *Pergama fiere volo, fata Danais data solo*
> *Solo capta dolo, capta redacta solo*
> *Causa mali talis, meretrix fuit exicialis*
> *Femina letalis, femina plena malis*
> *Si fueris lota, si vita sequens bona tota*
> *Si eris ignota, non eris absque nota*
> *Passa prius paridem, peridis modo thesia pridem*
> *Es factura fidem, ne redeas in idem*
> *Rumor de veteri, faciet ventura timeri*
> *Cras poterunt fieri, turpia sicut heri*
> *Scena quid euadis, morti qui cetera tradis*
> *Cur tu non cladis, concia clade cadis*
> *Femina digna mori, reamatur amore priori*
> *Reddita victori, deliciis que thori.*

Now, is not that very bad?—this beggarly play upon the word *solo,* in its three senses—*solo solare,* to solace; *solo,* alone; and *solo,* evil. *Peridis* and *thesia* are not Latin at all. Such trifles of bad grammar as *qui* for *quae,* of *qui* for *que,* and of *ne* for *ni,* pale into insignificance compared with the puerility of the expressions as to Helen, *femina letalis,* "woman full of mischief" who escapes all harm, and *reamatur amore priori,* "loved again with the old love." *Reddita victori, deliciis que thori,* is "given back to the conqueror and the delights of the marriage-bed."

We should like to believe that this rubbish was the product of Master Caxton's office poet; but in default of evidence to the contrary must leave the onus on

Caxton himself, remembering that he was not content simply to print, but that the majority of the works issuing from his press (including the one to which this colophon is added) were his translations, and that in his edition of *The Golden Legend,* in the life of S. Roche, he says:

> "Which lyff is translated oute of latyn into englysshe by me Wyllyam Caxton."

Yet was he a worthy man, and, in spite of his slight Latinity, with him

> "saye we alle Amen for charyte."

And well we may, for he was not given to boasting. In the colophon of *Tully on Old Age* he says:

> "Emprynted by me, *symple person,* William Caxton."

The modesty of this "symple person" is in refreshing contrast with the flowers which most of the German printers present to themselves.

We have seen how the thurification of one printer is the bad example to another; so this publisher's modesty is perhaps the inspirer of John Lydgate, who, in the same year (1481), issues from Caxton's press his *Cura Sapientiae,* or "Court of Sapience," and in his bow to the public says:

> "I am a monk by my profession,
> Of Bury, called John Lydgate by my name,
> And wear a habit of perfection,
> Although my life agree not with the same."

The *Cura Sapientiae* has for us a more serious interest, as the poem was written only about twenty years before the printing of the book, and shows Caxton's willingness to venture on printing literature both contemporaneous and in the vernacular, whereas other early printers, almost without exception, printed in Latin or Greek, their works in general being the early classics, or else theological tomes.

The *Morte d'Arthur* is another book that was fairly contemporary, as Malory states that he finished it in 1470 and Caxton published it in 1485. *A propos* of the subject of the beginnings of rights to literary property, it would be interesting to know whether Malory was alive at the date of publication, and whether Caxton paid him anything for "copyright."

Of the book Caxton has this to say:

"In these playsaunt historyes may be seen noble chyvalrye, curtosye, humanyte, frendlynesse, hardynesse, love, frendship, cowardyse, murdre, hate, vertue and synne. Doo after the good and leve the evyl and it shal brynge you to good fame and renommee."

As good advice to-day as when it was written.

This giving of good advice, this telling the reader why he had printed a book, and the benefit which would accrue to the reader in its perusal, was a weakness of Caxton's. Here, for instance, is the "apologie" with which he prefaces his translation of *Blanchardin and Eglantine*. Its interest lies in that, so far as we know, it is the first printed defence of novel-reading.

"A book joyful to be read by all virtuouse young noble gentlemen and women, as for their pastime. For under correction, in my judgment, histories of noble feats and valiant acts of arms and war, which have been achieved in old time of many noble princes, lords, and knights, are as well for to see and know their valiantness for to stand in the special grace and love of their ladies, and in like wise for gentle young ladies, and demoiselles for to learn to be stedfast and constant in their part to them that they once have promised and agreed to, such as they have put their lives oft in jeopardy for to please them to stand in grace, as it is to occupy the ken and study overmuch in books of contemplation."

Peace to the ashes of the first English printer!—sturdy, always prepared to defend his position, and to give a reason for the faith that was in him. Unlike most of his brethren on the other side of the Channel, he seems to have been a good business man, paying his way as he went, and asking no favour from patron or lord. He died in 1491, working until a few hours of his death on his translation of the *Vitae Patrum.*

For our final colophon we can do no better than give that written by Wynken de Worde, Caxton's assistant and successor:

"Thus endyth the moost vertuous hystorye of the dewoute and right renowned lyves of holy faders lyvynge in deserte, worthy of remembraunce to all wel dysposed persones which hathe be translated oute of Frenche into Englisshe by William Caxton of Westmynstre late ded, and fynysshed at the laste daye of hys lyff."

We are nearing the end of this stroll among the book treasures of the time of Europe's awaking from her millennial sleep. Truth to tell, it has been in a way somewhat like a stroll through an old graveyard: there, on the more pretentious tombs, we read ascriptions of all the virtues, natural and supernatural, to the fathers and mothers, husbands and wives, sisters and brothers, that lie there. The monuments of the old-time printers are the books they produced, and noble monuments they are; but the epigraphy of many of them is Gothic, not to say Gargantuan.

If those early printers had had the sublime confidence in themselves and in the greatness of their works which the great painters and sculptors of antiquity had—and the modern artists, too—and simply subscribed their productions with a "Fust printed this," or "Udalricus Gallus fecit," after the style of "Zeuxis painted," or "Pheidias, sculptor," they would have assured immortality to their names; but then they would not have afforded to irreverent posterity so much amusement by their *naif* vainglory.

We only smile, however; we do not scoff. Those good and faithful artisans, themselves living in intellectual darkness, in poverty, hardship, and all sorts of discouragements, laboured day and night, as never men before, except the very *élite* of men, to spread the light of civilization. Poor fellows! their honest pride in their noble art sticks out in every one of their colophons. Well might they all, as some of them did, regard themselves as "of clergy;" yet one does not anywhere read of the sacred order of Typographi being erected into a Fourth Estate.

But the whirligig of Time brings his revenges: the spiritual posterity of those ancient printers to-day are more powerful than king or church or parliament. It is not so very long since the printery was as dingy and obscure a place as the cobbler's or the tinker's shop, though from it went forth currents of a force that was transforming government, science, creeds, everything human. Without the printing press, Luther would have left no impress on the world's history. Well might those old printers be proud, for they had some dim consciousness of the greatness of their art; they were as proud as Diogenes and as poor as he in worldly goods.

The art having been invented in Germany and its secret guarded for a while, most of the artisans were in the early years of typography Germans. These German printers, wherever they exercise their art, do themselves honour in the honour they never fail to render to their fatherland and to their native cities. Their names are uncouth to the Italians, the French, the Spaniards, but as Schweinheim and Pannartz tell their Italian patrons, their art will conciliate favour even for such outlandish names.

Sometimes they latinize their surnames, *e. g.,* change Lichtenstein into an equivalent Latin form—*Levilapis;* Hahn into *Gallus,* and so on, but usually they preserve in the Latin countries the German form; and not content with that sign of their *Deutschthum,* they in nearly every instance name, and usually with some honourific epithet, their native province or their native town—plainly, they loved the Old Land, and were but sojourners in the land of the stranger. One of them is named Franck, and he invariably qualifies himself as Allemannus, "the German;" another, Sixtus Riesinger, at Naples, is "a Strassburger;" and we have John "of Westphalia," John "of Cologne," John "of Vienna," and so on. If a printer is from Mainz, it is for him "the noble city of Mainz;" and we have "renowned Basel," "holy Cologne," "princely city of Landshut," etc.

A really touching instance of their fond regard for the Old Home is seen in one of the colophons—that of Friedberger "of Passau in Germany." Plainly he knew no Latin, but enough of Italian to know that in that language Deutschland is *Allemannia*. He somehow got the name of his native town latinized fairly enough into *Passavium,* but to latinize Deutschland was beyond his powers and the best he could do or get was Alla Magna—*"Passavium Alac Magnae."* Be that Latin or no, "he got there all the same," and Deutschland is honoured of her son.

Those poor printers! They knew neither Greek nor Latin, but they were the cause of Latin and of learning in others. While they were diffusing intellectual light over all Europe, they were themselves nearly as ignorant of the true meaning and fruit of their labour as the blind horse that turns a mill of the office it is performing. What would have been their sense of personal dignity had they known the intellectual contents of the works they set in type; and with what delight would they have prosecuted their labour if, as they progressed with the copy, the intellectual lights of the ancient sages and poets had irradiated their minds! *Sic vos non vobis.*

These poor printers were doing in truth the work of clergy: but the titular clergy—drones they, or worse— were enjoying the honours and the emoluments provided by the piety of ages and by the toil of the passing generation, for the spiritual and intellectual nurture of Europe.

THE FALLEN GOD

THE FALLEN GOD

PART I

How art thou fallen from Heaven,
O Day-Star [Lucifer], Son of the Morning!

. . . .

Yet thou shalt be brought down to hell,
To the uttermost part of the pit.

THE legend of The Fallen God,—a common character in all recorded myths, is probably based on the phenomenon of the falling meteor. Hephaestos, the elemental fire god of the Greeks, was hurled from heaven by his father, Zeus. A similar story crept into the Christian mythology, and the fathers to account for it, though justified undoubtedly by the Apocalypse of St. John the Divine, twisted a text of the Hebrew prophet to their required meaning. The story does not seem to have taken so strong a hold upon the Latin peoples and upon the blue-eyed children of the northern wilds,—perhaps because the phenomenon upon which it was based was accounted for by the pagan myth that was never thoroughly eradicated from the imagination of the common people. In England, years before the Restoration, there was a mystery played at Chester which enacted the fall of Lucifer. For Piers Plowman he is as real as the lordly bishops whom he typifies. In a deep dale this symbolist saw a dungeon, called the Castle of Care.

Therein woneth a wight, that wrong is i-hote
Fader of falsness, he founded it himselven,
Adam and Eve he egged to do ill
Counseilede Cayne to cullen his brother
Judas he japede, with the jewes silver—

.   .   .   .

He was an archangel of hevene, on of Godes knights
He was loveliest of sight, after our Lord,
Till he brake buxomness thorow boast of himself
Then fell he with his felawes, and fendes becomen,
Out of heaven into hell hobleden fast
Summe in the eir, summe in the earth and summe in hell
    deepe
But *Lucifer* lowest, ligeth of them all.

Here, however, Lucifer and Satan are not blended, though they are thoroughly in agreement. Satan even flatters Lucifer with the clever way in which—

Nat in forme of a feonde, but in form of an adre

he enticed Eve to eat of the forbidden tree. For it is Lucifer who is wily. Satan is the strong one. He is the spirit who urges war, the barring of the gates, and—a strange light upon Milton, whom we know was well acquainted with the greatest middle English satire —eggs on Astrot to manufacture gunpowder and cannon to *lette* the Lord of light,

Ere we thorow brightness be blent.

But the *dukes* of the *dim-place* must needs give way,
and Piers Plowman also tells us of that rescue of the
Patriarchs from hell which forms a convincing episode
of the fourth canto of the Inferno.

This catholic tradition was overwhelmed by the
new heaven and earth created for English literature
by the pagan dramatists of the Elizabethan renaissance. The Christian Devil and his attendant Vice
found little consideration at the hands of Shakspeare
and his brethren. Marlowe, the self-acknowledged
scoffer, used him, it is true,—but he never troubled to
analyze him, or to embody him in any horrible per-
sonfication. Mephistopheles is the symbolisation of
German scholarly scepticism; and it is not strange that
the whole German literature, born of the Elizabethan
drama, offers no deep analysis of spiritual good and
evil. Even Goethe, original and vast as he undoubtedly is, clung very closely to the mocking Marlowe,
and his intellect is so untouched by the fiery zeal which
burns in the soul of Æschylus, Milton and Dante, that
it is not irksome to him to introduce the Author of all
evil in a jesting colloquy with the Spring of all good.
With the Elizabethan both the Hebrew and the classical myths are obliterated; and though Achilles, Hector
and the Hellenic gods and goddesses gleam through
double translations, their features are blurred, their
characters modernized, and but for their names, so
Englished as to be almost beyond recognition.

Under this mountain, from three convergent sources

flowed the stream by which sat the muse of Milton. The religious continent of the imaginings of the poet of *Paradise Lost* was, however, no longer catholic. It was localized. It was puritan. It was untouched, unsoiled, by the grosser devil which in the mediæval mysteries ran howling about the mouth of hell. With him the Jehovah of the Hebrews became the All-father; the Devil of the mediæval mysteries an evil power of the first magnitude, while the gods and goddesses of Greece and Rome were allowed no higher sphere than that of attendant spirits to the supreme ill. But Milton's Satan is not the Christian Lucifer. Shelley says of him with perfect truth: "This character engenders in the mind a pernicious casuistry which leads us to weigh his faults with his wrongs and excuse the former because the latter exceed all measure." In other words, the sympathy of the reader is with Satan. He is very human, not at all horrific. The sublime pageantry which surrounds him only adds zest to the pity for his magnificent sufferings. How inexpressibly human and touching is the passage,

> To speak
> Thrice he assayed, and thrice, in spite of scorn,
> Tears such as angels weep burst forth.

Compare these tears with those of Lucifer in the last canto of the Inferno—

> With six eyes did he weep and down three chins
> Trickled the tear-drops and the bloody drivel.

Is it possible that these two beings are the same or akin? The answer would seem to be,

> My Master pleased to show me
> The creature who once had the beauteous semblance;

and shortly afterwards

> Were he as fair once as he now is foul
> And lifted up his brow against his Maker.

Here Dante gives us two distinct references to the legend upon which the great spirit of the *Paradise Lost* is built. But the second reference is uttered as an hypothesis—there is almost a doubt of the truth—for though Milton's soul has taken hold of the tradition, has cast out the coarser features and beautified the whole, the fire of his imagination transmuting it; yet Dante's genius working in the same way has produced a heavier metal. The starting place of both poets is the earth. Milton's soul in the *Paradise Lost* rises and finds Satan next to God. Dante's genius goes down into the bowels of the earth and in the uttermost abyss discovers—Dis.

The consideration of a more modern poet may perhaps help us to understand the action of the imaginative fire of a great poet's intellect. It is commonly considered as creative. It is not so. The imagination of the multitude creates. The intellect of the poet transmutes. Such an imagination was Shelley's. His mind was instinct with the legends of the Trojan Epos, his spirit was fed on the heroic and dramatic poetry of Greece and Rome. To his imagination there were no bounds set by the supreme sanction of religion, though he was in another sense supremely religious. Such a soul, if it worked like Milton's, upward, should transmute devils into gods; if its action was like Dante's, downward, it should deify some influence, perhaps some element.

Now in the *Prometheus Unbound,* Shelley borrows the machinery of Æschylus. He transfers the Apollo wholly from the Greek to the English almost without change. His furies, however, are more elemental than those of Æschylus. There is no suggestion of their conversion into Eumenides. Prometheus here is God suffering for man; Jupiter is the essence of Evil,—and behind the whole broods the shade of the Demogorgon —which reminds us very strongly of the Fata of Dante's master, Virgil.

Religion may be called the continent of imaginings. It was religion which bound Milton to the Jehovah of the Hebrews. The religious awe in the soul of Aeschylus led him to make Apollo a mere regulator of the furies, and eventually in the Eumenides, forced him to convert even them into benefactors of the race they had tormented. He, too, undertook the unthankful task which Milton proposed to himself—

> To assert eternal Providence,
> And justify the ways of God to men.

The failure or success of both we discuss later. Shelley proposes to himself no such labour. In his first drama—or goat song, as he calls it, so emulative

of the Hellenic spirit is he—the religious continent of
his imaginings is his worship of the great literature
and genius of the Hellenic peoples. He does not
wander essentially from the example set him by
Æschylus. In the Christian mythology, however, his
spirit has no confining limits. It is, perhaps, unfortunate that when he treats of the Christian Deity and his
antagonist Lucifer, he forsakes the drama for the
Spencerian stanza and canto. But he says enough for
our purpose—

> Two Powers o'er mortal things dominion hold
> Ruling the world with a divided lot,
> Immortal, all-pervading, manifold,
> Twin Genii, equal Gods,—

> O'er the wide wild abyss two meteors shone,
> A blood-red Comet and the Morning Star
> Mingling their beams in combat—as he stood,
> All thoughts within his mind waged mutual war,
> In dreadful sympathy—when to the flood
> That fair Star fell, he turned and shed his brother's
>   blood.
> Thus evil triumphed, and the Spirit of evil,
> One Power of many shapes which none may know,
> One Shape of many names; the Fiend did revel
> In victory, reigning o'er a world of woe,
> For the new race of man went to and fro,
> Famished and homeless, loathed and loathing, wild,
> Hating good—for his immortal foe,
> He changed from starry shape, beauteous and mild,
> To a dire Snake, with man and beast unreconciled.

> And the great Spirit of Good did creep among
> The nations of mankind, and every tongue

Cursed, and blasphemed him as he passed; for none
Knew good from evil, though their names were hung
In mockery o'er the fane where many a groan,
As King, and Lord, and God, the conquering Fiend
did own.

As Shelley has taken this transmuted Lucifer from
Milton's Satan; deified him a little more; as he has
borrowed the gods and furies of the *Prometheus Un-*
bound only slightly changed from the stage of Æschylus, so Æschylus himself has borrowed his gods and
goddesses from the Heaven, Earth and the Shades of
Homer. But though these in the *Iliad* and *Odyssey*
have passed through the transmuting fire of Homer's
imagination, they have not there emerged thoroughly
purified. Not only are they anthropomorphic,—not
more or less than deified men,—but their original, elemental character continually appears. Zeus, the All-
father, is still the sky, Neptune has no being apart
from the ocean; while Hephaestos, as we have seen,
was cast out of heaven by his father, Zeus, and as the
god of fire, has become a good-natured, harmless fellow, the friend of man and the prototype of the
Prometheus.

Not only is this so, but the most solitary and grand-
est figure in the literature of Ancient Greece calls
attention to it, emphasises it, and is so fiercely indig-
nant of it, that we feel this very indignation responsible
for much of the grandeur of his creation. There has
been faction and betrayal among the gods. A new
dynasty has seized on Olympus. Zeus, the All-father,

even he had a father, who is now—where? And a
son shall come to him, as Æschylus knows. And yet
cry the Erinyes, "My ancient honours remain to me—
though possessing a station beneath the earth and
sunless darkness."[1]

Even Mercury, the courier of Jove, is a mere menial,
to Prometheus and Æschylus—the overseer of the
tyrant.

> ἀλλ' εἰσορῶ γὰρ τόνδε τὸν Διὸς τρόχιν,[2]
> τὸν τοῦ τυράννου τοῦ νέου διάκονον·
>
> But yonder I behold the scout of Zeus,
> Of this new potentate the servitor;

And the Erinyes themselves despise him with all the
rancour of aged servants overlorded by a young
parvenu.

> ἐπεὶ καθιππάζει με πρεσβῦτιν νέος·
> Since *young* you ride down me in years.

The creator of all these gods was the brooding imagination of prehistoric man. Such deities were born
of the wind and sea, in the sky and the clouds, in
the storm, and in the memory of inundation and cata-
clysm. Thus, the primitive intellect, with its tendency
to personification, knows one of the impulses as Or-
muzd, the other as Ahriman. The Greek intellect,
thrown upon itself, takes refuge in the conception of
Moira, ruling even the gods, a hybrid of good and its
opposite.

When we say that the Greek intellect personified the

[1] *Eumenides*, 371-374.   [2] *Prometheus*, 962-963.

forces of nature and worshipped personifications as gods, we state absolute truth. But few things are so misleading as absolute truth. The Greek thinker became intelligible to himself and to others only in so far as he availed himself of the prevailing mode of thought. Otherwise, he was unintelligible. Whatever his private opinion may have been on the subject of the myths and the cosmogonies, he found them a convenient basis of thought. Hence we see the physical experience and the intellectual experience of the Greeks accumulating in harmony for centuries, with no peril to the state religion. The multitude could have dwelt in their world and the philosophers could have dwelt in their world forever without the development of conflict, but for one circumstance. That circumstance was the accumulation of spiritual experience. Of spiritual experience, in our sense, the Greeks were, of course, destitute, but that they were vouchsafed a quality of it, we can detect almost as far back as Homer. It culminated in Socrates.

This spiritual experience, such as it was, lagged far behind the physical experience, and farther still behind the intellectual. Æschylus struggled with it, but the Greek mode of thought was inadequate to its expression. He made himself intelligible to his contemporaries, but the audiences for whom Euripides wrote would have found the *Prometheus Vinctus* a riddle. This seems to be the clue to the obscurity of Æschylus. He is conscious of a mighty force at work, destined one day to hurl the gods from their thrones. But he has 'that within which passeth show,' and he cannot render intelligible the message whose purport fills him with gloom. The Greeks gazed in awe, and we may conjecture that they felt uncomfortable. Certainly they took refuge in a more congenial atmosphere. Æschylus became the theologian of antiquity, and Euripides became the successful playwright.

At first, as we have said, these gods were only personified elements; but passed through the minds of the priestly poets, Homer, Hesiod, Æschylus, and among the Latins, Virgil, who appear as the recording memories of past times, they become gods like men, and then men like gods. Meanwhile, the demand from below for the mere elemental gods must be satisfied: the gods of tempestual destruction, the gods of the trouble cf the soul. Of this demand are born Harpies, the Erinyes of Æschylus, the Fates of Virgil, the Furies of Shelley—perhaps even the Hounds of Hell, which in the *Paradise lost* are the incestuous offspring of Sin and Death.

It would be interesting to follow to his elemental origin the Mercury whom we find regulating the Furies in the *Prometheus Unbound* of Shelley. Unfortunately, concerning him there is much mystery. It is certain that he is the Apollo of Æschylus, who is the Phoibos Apollo of Homer. But even the name has given rise to discussion as to its origin. It is interesting, however, to note here that the Puritan, John Bunyan, uses the word in the sense of destroyer. Apollyon is the name of his great adversary.

This should assure us that the dimmed glory of Milton's fallen archangel borrows some of its light from the winged messenger of the older gods, who yet to Æschylus are parvenus. Though he has lost the bond which bound him to the element, it is at least probable that in the prehomeric days he was the personification of the pestilence, the desert, or the storm —a horrible vision startling the minds of men. He is always the Minister of Vengeance. Wolves followed him. He carries in his hand the arrows of destruction; and even in the *Iliad*, Achilles still calls him "the most pernicious of all the gods."

The Erinyes of Æschylus are the ministers of blood vengeance. The black Night is their mother. Their office, given perfect from the gods, is to track forever the steps of the murderer of his fellow, to suck the blood from his limbs, to bear him alive below. In their station beneath the earth in sunless darkness they are called Evils. And what form are they given? Old women? No. Gorgon? No. They are wingless to behold, black and altogether abominable; out of their eyes they distil a horrible rheum. And their dress is not worthy to be worn either at the shrines of the gods or in the dwellings of men.[1] Awful these, indeed, and yet these have an office not easily set aside. These retain their ancient honours, though possessing a station beneath the earth in sunless darkness.

The religious sanction which bounded the imaginations of Æschylus and Milton to endeavor to justify

[1] *Eumenides,* 48-61.

the ways of God to men,—that rule of the Anarch, Custom, through which Shelley breaks with such startling cries,—lays heavier upon Dante than on all. With him, however, there is no attempt at justification. It is sufficient for him that these things are so. He is catholic. The continent of his imaginings has no leak; the walls are thin only where he lightly touches upon the fabled deities and false of his master, Virgil.

Dante is too much of a Latin, too much a Roman, to relegate, as Milton does, the whole family of the pagan gods to the nethermost abyss. The rigid faith in him forces him downward; his leader is the great Roman poet; and if for no other reason than this, he must leave the false Olympians behind him. Yet there is no doubt that because of this lightness of touch he feels the rigour of the religious bond much tighter. The fact that the gods of Virgil are false, makes him so much the more merciless in his dealing with the damned, and adds another circle to the infernal realm.

The last canto of the *Inferno* is a climax to a gradual procession downward. In this descent, however, the genius of Dante has worked on the same principle as we have seen that of Æschylus working, that of Milton, that of Shelley. But the order is reversed. In this poem we find the infernal deities of Greece and Rome—Minos, Plutos, the Furies, the Minotaur and the Harpies—ruling different circles of the shades. When the eighth circle is reached, the mansion in Hell called Malebolge, the list of the infernal deities is exhausted. This place is so awful that in all the poet's wide reading there is no devil damned black enough to rule. Before the ninth circle is passed, however, we meet the giants, Nimrod, Ephialtes and Anteus, titanic men, whose names appear on the dim horizon of history. The transmuting fire of the poet's imagination begins to work. Nimrod was a mighty hunter before the Lord, sprung from the knowledge or creative imagination of the Hebrews. He was responsible and is punished for the tower of Babel, and the division of human speech ere the continents were subdivided.

Ephialtes was the Hellenic child of the earth. These and Briareus stand at the boundary of the eighth circle and the ninth. In Hell they are the landmarks between the speakable and the unspeakable, as in the time they divided the recorded from that which has not been written.

For we are not at the bottom yet. There is yet to be seen

> . . . the abyss which swallows up
> Judas and Lucifer.

In this lowest region of all, whence then can Dante derive his imagery? On what material will the transmuting fire, the demiurgic genius of the poet work? The most fearful descriptions in the *Aeneid* are of Charon:

> Portitor has horrendus aquas et flumina servat
> Terribili squalore Charon; cui plurima mento
> Canities inculta jacet, stant lumina flamma
> Sordidus ex humeris nodo dependet amictus;
>
> *Aeneid VI, 298.*

> A grim ferryman guards [servat] these floods and rivers,
> Charon of frightful slovenliness; on whose chin a load
>   of hair neglected sprouts.
> His eyes flame. His vestment filthy hangs from his
>   shoulders by a knot.

And of

> Cerberus haec ingens, latratu regna trifauci
> Personat adverso recubans immanis in antro.

And of immense

Cerberus [who] with three-throated bark makes this knigdom
to resound—stretched enormously along the cave.

> Cui vates, horrere videns jam colla colubris.

To whom when the priestess saw his neck to bristle with
horrid snakes.

Deeper horrors are not described, and the Latin poet
confesses like the Greek dramatist his inability; and
dedicates in these lines the further work, the further
labour, to one who should come after him, one mightier
than he:

> Non mihi si linguae centum sint oraque centum,
> Ferrea vox, omnes scelerum comprendere formas,
> Omnia poenarum percurrere nomina possim.
> Were there to me a hundred tongues, a hundred mouths,
> A voice of iron, it were not possible to me to comprehend
>   all their crimes, or to enumerate all their punishments.

So he can no longer borrow from his teacher Virgil.
As deep as this the older poet never ventured. This
terrible vision cannot therefore be seen through Virgil.

> He [Virgil] from before me moved and made me stay,
> Saying: Behold Dis and behold the place
> Where thou with fortitude must arm thyself.

We have learned how the wolf-leading, man-destroying personification of the pestilence became in Homer, Phoibos Apollo; how this light-bearing god became the regulator of the ministers of vengeance in the Eumenides; how Milton's Satan borrows some of his light from that same Apollo, and finally, how the demiurgic fire of Shelley's imagination makes of this Satan the benefactor of man and the light of the world. By a similar process working in the inverse order, the genius of Dante has produced the morning-star, Lucifer, the creature who had once the beauteous semblance.

The materials were ready at his hand,—he was born among them; they were of him and he of them. The very name gives us the cue: Dis, that is Dives, riches, Plutus, Orcus! In Romanesque folklore Orcus, is a black, hairy, man-eating monster. In the Old Testament, the Hebrew word *sa-ir,* translated "devils," is literally "hairy-ones." The Etruscan god of Death was a savage old man with wings and a hammer.

And thus Dante describes him in the thirty-fourth canto:

> Underneath each came forth two mighty wings
> Such as befitting were so great a bird;

And later:

> At every mouth he with his teeth was crunching
> A sinner in the manner of a brake;

And later still:

> And when the wings were open wide apart,
> He laid fast hold upon the shaggy sides.

The hugeness and horror are lost in quotation. But what of it? The worst of it is indescribable.

> How frozen I became and powerless, then,
> Ask it not, reader, for I cannot write it,
> Because all language would be insufficient.

The whole canto is of hint; the imagination of the reader is left to do the rest. It is a climax. As Virgil steps aside and says to Dante:

> Ecco Dite!

So Dante moves out of the way and says to the reader:

> Behold the King of Hell!

Pausanius, a Graeco-Roman writer of the second century, with whose *Descriptio Graeciae* Dante was probably well acquainted—in his third book describes at length the gods and sacrifices of the ancient Archæans. In one place they sacrifice in a manner that may not be spoken. In another, he saw the images of gods, which he regarded as the oldest deities of Greece. One was the three-eyed Zeus, and another the three-headed Artemis. And so Dante—

> Oh, what a marvel it appeared to me
> When I beheld three faces on his head!

Let us note here a fact heretofore we believe unnoted —that Dante is fully conscious of the utter degeneracy of the language he uses. He knows, and none better than he, that a people is as its speech is. For this reason he chooses Virgil as his master; Virgil, whose epic epitomises the glory of the country and times of Dante's forefathers. For this reason he has chosen to write in the tongue of his time, conscious that the day of the Latin is passed, and that the new Roman must speak a new Latin. Hence comes the cry with which he enters the city of Dis:

S' io avessi le rime ed aspre e chiocce,
. . . .
Nè da lingua che chiami mamma e babbo.[1]

It is not a child's tongue that can describe the foundation of the universe. It is not a language about to be born from the putrefaction of the imperial tongue of Rome that he would choose were the choice his. Upon what times has he fallen for such a song! One epithet of Greek, one old Roman adjective, would express what his Italian brethren coined a line to carry. In these days the very word *horrendus* has lost its bristling meaning, and even Virgil ascribes it indifferently to Charon and to the serpent-hairy neck of Cerberus.

[1] See *Inf.* c. *32*, ll. 1-9.

PART II

Lucifer in Dante's Inferno

τίς οὖν 'Ανάγκης ἐστὶν οἰακοστρόφος;
Μοῖραι τρόμορφοι μνήμονές τ' 'Ερινύες.
—*Prometheus, 523, 524.*

Who then is helmsman of Necessity?
The triform Fates and the remembering Furies.

IN connection with this horrible vision of Dis it would be interesting to consider the fearful triform god of the Hindoos and other Asiatic peoples. But we have here only time to hint at it. The grovelling imagination of degenerate multitudes has carved the eidolon of Brahma, Vishnu and Siva from the legends and fables of their Buddhist priests. But Buddhism stands in the same relation to the original Brahmanism, as Italian stands to Latin, or Protestantism to Catholicism; and the basis of Brahmanism, its sacred literature, is the Veda. And what of the Veda? It is a collection of hymns older than the oldest Greek, older than Sanscrit; it is the fountainhead of the literature of the Aryan peoples. Here Zeus the All-father, in Latin Jupiter, is Dyans; the all-embracing god of light is Varuna, the Greek ὄσρανός, and related to him Mitra, the bright sun of day. Another name for the same conception is Aditi, the infinite. His opposite is Diti, the bound, of whom there is no conception except the personification of Night—decay, destruction and death; signifying also the place of destruction—Nir-riti, the Abyss and the Mother of Hell.[1]   Was it for these deities that the soul of Æschylus hungered when he pictured the man-loving Titan bound down by the might of the new servants of the gods to the thunder-beaten crags of the Asian desert?   For these and more.   Into the heart of Prometheus there has crept a greater conception— that of Love; not the mere brutality of passion such as the new ruler of the gods had for Io.   Not this, but in strong contrast to this.   Æschylus repudiates the heroism of slaughter and the apotheosis of incestuous amours of gods and men.   For this he suffers, and his cry goes up:

> Oh, divine Æther, and ye swift-winged breezes,
> ye fountains of rivers, and ye uncounted
> laughters of the waves of the deep; Oh, earth,
> thou mother of all, and ye all-beholding circle
> of the sun, I call you to behold me, what I a god
> suffer at the hands of the gods.[2]

For Æschylus is conscious that in his awful mythology there is something lacking.   The rulers of the minds of men are changing.   Better the godlike Æther and the uncounted laughters of the waves of the deep; better to worship, better to call upon the great, glorious Earth, the mother of all, gods and men; better return to the deities of the prehomeric days than take these. And why?   The whole drama of *Prometheus* is the answer to this query.   Love is nobler than bloodshed; the philanthropist is greater than the soldier.

[1] See Max Müller, *Origin of Religion,* 131.
[2] *Prometheus,* 88-93.

Herein is the greatness of Æschylus; he has conceived Love,—love suffering for others; has typified it, expressed it under bodily and visible form. But this greatness is limited; with love there is a coequal, Justice. Æschylus has also conceived justice, but herein he is lacking that he has not expressed it in like figure as he has philanthropy.

In the Eumenides of Æschylus, outward shape, power and being are given only to the spirit of vengeance roused against a matricide. Yet here the difference between the power of Æschylus and that of the earlier mythmakers is plainly shown. This embodiment is primarily of the inner, not of the outer nature, and there is, moreover, a distinct artistic knowledge of and delight in such embodiment. This knowledge and delight is expressed repeatedly. It is put into the mouths of the Erinyes themselves:

> τίς οὖν τάδ' οὐχ ἅζεται
> τε καὶ δέδοικεν βροτῶν,
> ἐμοῦ κλύων θεσμὸν
> τὸν μοιρόκραντον ἐκ θεῶν
> δοθέντα τέλεον;
>
> —*Eumenides, 367.*

Who then of mortals dreads not and fears not these.
Hearing our office confirmed by fate, given perfect
    from the gods.

But the keynote of the *Eumenides* is that to which we have given an outline, and which is expressed in the verse in which Athena refers to the Erinyes:

These possess an office not easily set aside.[1]

[1] *Eumenides,* 455

This office is to satisfy the demand for justice, the human cry for a right recompense for evil. That he failed to express, to symbolise, to personify this, Aeschylus himself confesses in the very drama in which he endeavoured to do so. For though perhaps not in execution, yet in conception, the Eumenides falls far short of the noble Prometheus; even while the latter proves that but for an accident Æschylus would have embodied this very demand. The Eumenides are the ministers of blood-vengeance, as we have seen. In the drama they track a mother-slayer to his doom. We have considered the excellence, the faithfulness, of their embodiment in the Erinyes. But the transformation of these into Eumenides of name and word is in itself a confession of failure. There is an evil beyond these, which Æschylus does not attempt to portray— an evil which demands a more fearful personification than any fury Æschylus could conceive.

> δεινὴ γὰρ ἐν βροτοῖσι κἀν θεοῖς πέλει
> τοῦ προστροπαίου μῆνις, εἰ προδῶ σφ' ἑκών.
> —*Eumenides, 224.*

Dire to men and to gods is the wrath of a suppliant
If willingly I should betray him.

The same note is sounded in the *Prometheus*

> πῶς με κελεύεις κακότητ' ἀσκεῖν;
> μετὰ τοῦδ' ὅτι χρὴ πάσχειν ἐθέλω·
> τοὺς προδότας γὰρ μισεῖν ἔμαθον.
> κοὐκ ἔστι νόσος
> τῆσδ' ἥντιν' ἀπέπτυσα μᾶλλόν.
> —*Prometheus, 1087.*

How urgest thou me to practise baseness?
With him I choose to suffer what is decreed,
For *traitor,* I have learned to despise,
    and there is *no* evil
Which I hold a greater abomination.

So cry the chorus of sea nymphs, daughters of ocean

ποντίων τε κυμάτων
ἀνήριθμον γέλασμα,

—the uncounted laughters of the waves of the deep.
But who shall take this greatest abomination of all
abominations—*treason.* Personify it; give it head,
body, wings and purpose; raise in the human mind such
an unutterable disgust for it as it deserves. Easy is
the descent to Avernus. But who shall go down to the
bottom of the bottomless and discover this? Æschylus dared not attempt so vast a creation. The predecessors of Æschylus had not conceived it.

It has been well said that the legend of Prometheus
lives in the poetry of Æschylus and Shelley, and that
the power of one poet can scarcely be measured but by
the equality of the other. If this be true, it would
seem that we might look for the continuation of the
work of Æschylus in the Prometheus Unbound. But
there we do not find it. Shelley was so overcome with
the consciousness of the power of love, of love divine,
suffering for others that the conception of the justice
of punishment has slipped wholly by him.

Shelley is so charmed by the laughter of ocean that
he forgets the murderous grin of the surf; and that

those also are real who "for the sake of evil were born, who evil darkness inhabit, Tartarus beneath the earth, hated both of men and the Olympian gods." Even in the horrible Cenci, where the motive is similar to that in the Eumenides of his master, there does not appear another aspect of the greatest abomination of all.

The more we consider that face of Shelley which is turned towards Æschylus, the more we are bound to feel that his light is of the moon and not the sun, is borrowed and not refulgent. Shelley's Prometheus is the Prometheus of Æschylus; his Furies are the Eumenides as they appear.

> Abhorred virgins, children of eld, whom none of
> the gods or man or beast at any time embraces.[1]

Into his nymphs he has put new life. They are his own. But for the continuation downward, of which Æschylus himself knew, there is not in Shelley a hint.

As we have said, the genius of the Elizabethan poets and the limitation of their stage monopolised and in one sense dwarfed the literary genius of the English people. The drama of the Renaissance allowed of no attempt at any personification on the lines mapped out by Æschylus. Marlowe might have attempted such an embodiment of all evil. He had the daring. But mocking Marlowe's soul was not bound to any such depth as this; while, perhaps fortunately, the muse of Shakespeare was too human. If it could have been done in England, Milton alone was left to perform it.

[1] *Eumenides,* 68-73.

His experience surely fitted him for the work. He passed through storm scenes, where perfidy and war were as ever mingled. His Puritan training showed him many men whom he must have considered arch traitors to God, their country and humanity. His last days, like Dante's, were of defeat and exile. Vice rose triumphant, mocking at his poverty and blindness. Latin and Greek versification was a recreation to which he turned as a relief from his life-work.

He was familiar with Italian poetry; was familiar equally with the *Divine Comedy* and the symbolism of the earliest English satirist—the only Englishman who in intensity of symbolisation is to be likened to the poet of the nethermost deep. We have already seen the glory only dimmed of Milton's Satan. We have seen him weeping tears such as angels weep; we can see no-where in the *Paradise Lost* the horror of treason portrayed in its deformity. Sin springs from the head of Satan a beautiful being—this is the sin of ambition. Ambition and sin bring forth death, and these a horrible brood of hellhounds.

The conception and the workmanship is mighty; but Milton has no more than transferred the Trojan Epos to grander and more spiritual battlefields. *"Et souvent avec Dieu balance la victoire"* is the measure of Milton's failure. Milton is the Puritan Homer. There is no comparison of him with Æschylus, and in no one sense is he the continuation of Æschylus, any more than the vast pile of a mediæval cathedral is a continuation of the simplicity of an Ionic pillar.

Let us here recapitulate. The crowning poet of Ancient Greece is Æschylus; in this, that he has given life and palpable being to the idea of Love in *Prometheus,* and through the hint and shortcoming of the Eumenides, he left it as a legacy to his successors, to as well typify and adequately portray the horrible vision of inexorable justice claiming and punishing the most abominable of all sin—betrayal. In other words, the spiritual successor of Æschylus must embody in a form living for all time the vision of this sin working its own punishment. All the ancients, summed up in Dante's master, Virgil, left this work untouched; Shelley, repudiating punishment, and overcome by the intensity of his love, did not even know that such a task remained. John Milton knew of the task and emulated it. But the puritan, the pure philosophical desire in him to

Justify the ways of God to men,

led him after a false light. We have seen with what power. Sin and death the offspring of the arch traitor, and the hellhounds, who are their offspring, mutually torment themselves. Satan himself is not smirched; the deceiver of mankind still holds his glory and his star; still weeps

Tears such as angels weep.

Nor will the puritan and philosophic doubt in Milton's soul allow him to bind mere men such as Judas, Cain and Wentworth, in a punishment which cherubim endure. For in Satan, Milton has drawn us a princely sinner, a Lucifer of the intellect with slightly tarnished glory. Instead of loathsomeness, there is that in him which speaks home to the noblest of our attributes and leaves a thrill of sympathy.

> High on a throne of royal state, which far
> Outshone the wealth of Ormus and of Ind,
> Or where the gorgeous East with richest hand
> Show'rs on her kings barbaric pearl and gold,
> Satan exalted sat.

The Satanology of the Rabbis contributed little to conception of The Fallen God. Largely derived, as Doctor Kohut has shown, from Parseeism, it makes no mention of a Kingdom of Satan. In the *Talmud* the power of evil is not contrasted with that of good, nor is Satan represented as the enemy of God. Rabbinism viewed the "great enemy" only as the envious and malicious opponent of man, the spiritual element was eliminated. Instead of a powerful principle of evil we have only a clumsy, often a stupid hater. This holds equally true in regard to the threefold aspect under which Rabbinism presents the devil: as *Satan* or *Sammael;* as the *Yetsen haka* or evil impulse in man personified; and as the *Angel of Death*. In other words, as the Accuser; Tempter and Punisher. But there is nothing here which had not been told and better told by Æschylus.

Dante, and Dante alone, is the true successor of Æschylus; a greater than Æschylus. He alone has in some measure attained to and completed what Æschylus essayed. His conception of Lucifer is the supreme intellectual conception of the Fallen God. Nothing in ancient or modern literature has, or perhaps ever will, equal it. With him Lucifer is as repulsive as Milton's Satan is fascinating. All glory is alien to him; all things of sin are a part of and have their source in him. All the multitudinous aspects of his being are varying reverberations and revelations of a single thing—Evil, pure and infinite. He is All-evil; the author of all the sin mankind endures. Every allusion to the former state of Lucifer, is in the *Inferno,* veiled and oblique; and in the last canto, the unfathonable spiritual loathsomeness is so strongly insisted upon, that it would be physically repulsive, did not Dante, by consummate art transmute the realism with an intensely imaginative symbolism. The one faint gleam of apparent ideality left to Lucifer is his name; but, in fact, even that is only darkness visible, ironic emblem of what once he was—Ecco Dite!

> . . . il punto
> Dell' Universo, in su che Dite siede.

Then, too, with his hugeness of person, which is made a measurable loathsomeness, and with all his acts, whose vileness is infinite, there goes, paradoxically, infinite imbecility. Though his influence beats through hell and into the world, and gives to the realms of sin all their being, his motions have all the futility of perfect machinery with no other function than to express utter lack of function, when there should be supreme

function.   Only in this case of Lucifer, this dead activity in place of glorious activity is not mechanical, but
spiritual.   Such is the death-in-life Lucifer (that is,
Evil), all-fulfilled of self, has brought upon himself.

This conception that, although Lucifer is strangely
living, he is also strangely dead, is strengthened by
Farinata's reply to Dante's question as to the kind of
knowledge the damned possess.

> Noi veggiam, come quei c' ha mala luce,
> Le cose, disse, che ne son lontano:
> Cotanto ancor ne splende il sommo Duce.
> Quando s' appressano, o son, tutto è vano
> Nostro intelletto; e,s'altri nol ci apporta,
>
> Nulla sapem di vostro stato umano.
> Però comprender puoi, che tutta morta
> Fia nostra conoscenza da quel punto,
> Che del futuro fia chiusa la porta.
> —*Inferno, c. 34, 100-108.*

We see, like those who have imperfect sight,
The things, he said, that distant are from us;
So much still shines on us the Sovereign Ruler.
When they draw near, or are, is wholly vain
Our intellect, and if none brings it to us,
Not anything know we of your human state.
Hence thou canst understand, that wholly dead
Will be our knowledge from the moment when
The portal of the future shall be closed.

Even these few faint beams from God's far-off
radiance will at the day of doom be withdrawn.   Then
the living death will forever settle down upon the
dolorous realm.

A consideration of several passages from the last canto of the *Inferno* will serve either as concrete illustrations or as refutations of what has just been written; revealing at the same time the marvellous variety in the severe unity of Dante's conception of Lucifer and Evil.

Dante and Virgil have entered the Judecca, the fourth and last division of the ninth circle, which contains those who were traitors to beneficent lords. Here.

> . . . l' ombre tutte eran coperte,
> E trasparèn come festuca in vetro.
> Altre sono a giacere; altre stanno erte,
> Quella col capo, e quella colle piante;
> Altra, com'arco, il capo a' piedi inverte.
> —*Inferno, c. 34, 11-15.*

> . . . where the shades were wholly covered, and showed through like a straw in glass. Some are lying; some stand erect, this on his head, and that on his soles; another like a bow inverts his face to his feet.

A world of meaning lurks in the opening verse of this canto as spoken by Virgil in the depths of hell.

> Vexilla Regis prodeunt Inferni.
>
> The banners of the King of Hell advance.

These words must, with the reminiscences they arouse, pierce the heart of the three traitors—Judas, Brutus and Cassius. They hint of the far-off pageants of the church militant and triumphant, making by contrast

present horrors more horrible; and their apparent
solemn utterance of praise is, at the closing word, inverted to a grim and almost sacred mockery of evil in
the heart of the empire.

Then follows a passage, full in its music, and suited
in its imagery to the gloomy majesty of Lucifer when
seen from afar.

> Come, quando una grossa nebbia spira,
>   O quando l' emisperio nostro annotta,
>   Par da lungi un mulin che 'l vento gira;
> Veder mi parve un tal dificio allotta.
> —*Inferno, c. 34, 4-7.*

As a mill that the wind turns seems from afar when
a thick fog breathes, or when our hemisphere grows
dark with night, such a structure then it seemed to
me I saw.

This soon changes, with terrible irony, to a revelation
of Lucifer as he really is when seen close.[1]

Thus the banners have become the vast batlike wings
of Lucifer, which in their swift rise and fall seem to
advance, all the more because the poets are rapidly
moving toward them. All the toil of scholars has not
made clear the meaning of the three faces. Says
Longfellow: "The Ottimo and Benvenuto both interpret the three faces as symbolising Ignorance, Hatred
and Impotence. Others interpret them as signifying
the three-quarters of the then known world, Europe,
Asia and Africa." Miss Rosetti says the faces are "a
symbol of Lucifer's dominion over all reprobates from

[1] See verses 28 to 69, Lo imperador to aven veduto.

the three parts of the world, the complexions being respectively of Europe, Asia and Africa." Blanc (quoted by Vernon) "thinks that Dante has certainly intended to present Satan with his three faces as a direct antitype of the Holy Trinity."

May not the last two conjectures both be right? Since Dante, like Shakespeare, is fond of a reduplication of meaning, often even in a single word. To the objection to this view, that these three bestial faces are the direct antitype of God in his three-fold unity, to wit, that it too greatly dignifies Lucifer, it may be replied that Dante may once again be employing his figure in direct irony against sin, and that Lucifer's form may be a grim and tormenting parody of the antitype he desired to be when he resumed to attempt to rival him, who in his infinity and incomprehensibleness can have no antitype. Then even to Lucifer himself, his physical being would be a bitter mockery. At any rate, even though Lucifer is the complete antitype of God, Dante deliberately suppresses all mention of the fact. This in itself may be the finest irony.

Brutus, Cassius, Judas Iscariot! These are the three arch sinners whom Satan's teeth are champing. The first is the betrayer of his king; the second is the betrayer of his friend and king; the third is the betrayer of his friend, his king and his God.

We now come to the difficult passage, describing the real ascent, but apparent descent of the poets as they climb over Lucifer.[1]

[1] See verses 70-93.

"This point is the centre of the universe; when Virgil had turned upon the haunch of Lucifer, the passage had been made from one hemisphere of the earth —the inhabited and known hemisphere—to the other, where no living men dwell, and where the only land is the mountain of Purgatory." [1]

The symbolic meaning of this description is, as it seems; that Dante typifies the human soul, journeying through the snares of evil toward salvation; that is, toward the love of God. Hell is the realm of sin, and Purgatory that of absolving penance, whereto true repentance is the portal. Figuratively, then, the moment Dante turns round upon the exact centre of Lucifer, the focus of evil, the world and the universe, and begins the climb toward Purgatory, toward atonement, a spiritual crisis has been passed. A bewildering change comes upon the physical universe, corresponding to that which comes upon the soul when its new life is begun. By the soul's new vision all things, old and familiar, are made so strangely new, with altered or inverted importance, that at first its perplexity is greater than its enlightenment.

The monotonous beating of Lucifer's wings, the ceaseless champing of his teeth, his impotence to utter a word or to make other than mechanical motions, the desolation of a land of ice and life-congealing winds, the intense darkness of the vast cavern below the earth's surface, in which the solitary voices of Dante and Virgil sound alien, hoarse and hollow,—all these

[1] Norton.

things present a picture more terrible than mere solitude and silence, and a life more dead than death.

Yet so austere and restrained is Dante's imagination, and so intense the underplay and overplay of
spiritual meaning, direct or indirect, that although the
grotesque hideousness of evil is fully revealed, the
revelation is noble; nor do we ever, as sometimes in
reading Shakespeare, feel as though we were too close
to the borders of madness, prompted by visions.

> That lawless and uncertain thought
> Imagine howling.

Now the painful upward journey begins; light from
the better world dawns faintly; and spiritual death and
all that make for death, are left behind in their "deep
backward and abysm."

> Salimmo su, ei primo ed io secondo,
> Tanto ch' io vidi delle cose belle,
> Che porta il ciel, per un pertugio tondo:
> E quindi uscimmo a riveder le stelle.
> —*Inferno, c. 34, end.*

> We mounted up, he first and I second, till through
> a round opening I saw of those beauteous things
> which heaven bears, and thence we came forth to see
> again the stars.

In the life of every man two beings struggle ve-
hemently for mastery—the Flesh and the Spirit. The
function of the Intellect, during the struggle, is
strangely impartial. It accomplishes no more than to
afford man a more or less adequate comprehension of

the internal conflict. Crowning itself *pontifex maximus,* the intellect proclaims its divine right and infallibility as judge in the domains of faith and morals, and from man's intellectual impartiality in the confrontation of good and evil, is born—Lucifer. The Greek intellect was impotent in the presence of evil; whereas the meanest hireling may and does, when he will, overcome Satan. For, like every vital thing, the conception of Lucifer—the fallen god,—source of all evil, himself All-evil, has and is having its organic development. The Greek mind conceived of personifications of guilt, of the stings of guilty conscience; personifications even of Evil itself. But its evil was destitute of spiritual significance. This element of spirituality is the informing principle which imparts to Dante's Lucifer his importance, his significance, his reality.

How far it is possible to go in this development of the conception of the fallen god is indicated by Henry Mills Alden when, in view of the "restoration of all things," he says: "Lucifer is light-bearer, the morning star, and whatever disguises he may take in falling, there can be no new dawn that shall not witness his rising in his original brightness."

AVIGNON

AVIGNON

CHILD of the Midi, son of Provençe, surely thy dwelling place is the Promised Land. How exquisite is this view, the Rhone and its banks below. Here is a boat ferrying itself across, for the solitary occupant is asleep in the stern. The great rudder is turned so as to keep the craft aslant the stream; through its prow passes a wire stretched to either bank, and the river's current striking the boat's side pushes it towards Villeneuve on the opposite bank.

Surely we have been asleep and awakened in the fourteenth century! From that solitary tower watch is keeping upon the troops of warrior popes in their little Avignon kingdom. From that castle and its citadel we shall see issuing gaily caparisoned steeds and floating banners and beautiful ladies. For this is Provençe, and only a dozen miles away at Tarascon, King Réné of Anjou holds sway. Perchance, that patron of minstrelsy, whose lofty old castle is barely discerned in the distant purple haze and shimmering sunlight, will to-day offer prize to him who shall most sweetly sing his mistress' beauty and his heart's passion.

We turn our backs on the Cathedral of *Nôtre Dame des Doms* and its monument to Pope John XII. In other towns are to be found old churches and monuments, but where else the Durance, winding a silver thread, and embroidering so vast expanse of spring-time green? Beyond lie the Alps, mantled in snow, and in the foreground these old towers and their cita-del asleep in purple mist and lap of legends old.

But having come here as a pilgrim of Love, and thinking on Francesco Petrarca and his Laura de Noves, a gentle sadness casts its shadow over the scene's joy. It is only a little way to the Rue Joseph Vernet. In the rear of the garden at the back of the Musée Calvet is the monument erected many years ago by Mr. Charles Kensall to the memory of Petrarch's Laura. Her tomb was formerly in the *Eglise des Cordeliers,* but was destroyed during the Revolution. Though this is Southern France and Northern Italy the home of love, and its people the children of the old Minstrelsingers and Troubadours, and the *langue Provençeal,* the language of love; yet do these very children destroy the tomb of Laura, and neglect the monument erected by a stranger from the cold and sunless north-land. One might think they knew nothing of true love, for on the train when leaving Avignon, I remarked to an Italian, that it was the home of Laura, he replied—"Oh, yes, Laura, the mistress of Petrarch! But he was careless to let her have so many children." I told him that Petrarch was twenty-two years of age, and she but in her nineteenth year, when in 1326, in the Church of the Nunnery of Saint Claire the passionate and poetic young Italian first beheld her beauty; and though he never touched her lips,

probably not even her hands, and though during his
eight years in Avignon he never received the slightest
token of her regard, yet whether there or when writing
these touching sonnets at the Fountain of Vaucluse,
or in his weary years of wandering up and down the
world, always his heart was dedicate to her. The poor
man smiled in pity on my northern credulity, and lift-
ing his hands and shrugging his shoulders, replied,
"A pretty story, but impossible. Petrarch was not a
saint, but a man and an Italian. I tell you she was his
mistress." We forget this unworthy worlding at the
remembrance of poor Laura dying at the age of forty,
tired of bearing children, and of an unhappy marriage,
and glad of the tomb, for it brought rest. And poor
Petrarch, to live on after her for nearly thirty years,
faithful to her memory, and enriching the world by
those touching lines to his heart's idol. That mistress
from whom he had not even known one kiss. Ah me!
not for these poor lovers was it given to mingle their
lives.

> In one attempered stream, or side by side,
> So near that scarce a foot-pace may divide,
> Their separate paths, and this maybe is best;
> Or maybe in each other lost,
> In calm or tempest tost,
> One broad full river, they roll on to the sea.

And yet why poor Petrarch? It was his loving
heart and poetic imagination which created the mistress to whom he sang. Laura was simply a personage, a mortal whom he clothed with all the bright

imagery of his fancy and the tender poetry of his heart. the creature whom he loved was of his own creation, immortal, spiritual, and therefore free from human failings. It was of her he wrote, the Laura of the Kingdom of Love. Had he in fact embraced the Laura of Avignon, the wife of Hughes de Sade, the mother of many children, the household drudge, the Laura of flesh and blood, of failings and failures, perchance vain and without poetry, spirituality or imagination, there would have been a rift within the lute, the music would have turned to discord, and we should have missed those sonnets which touch the heart, and sing themselves within the soul of every true lover.

But there is an Avignon other than the Avignon of Petrarch, though the towers are the same, and the town is the same, and is encircled with the same walls, and the same Rhone flows peacefully at the foot of the *Rocher des Domes.* That lofty, gloomy pile, with huge towers and walls thirteen feet thick and a hundred feet high, is the Papal Palace, erected by Clement V. and his successors. This is the Avignon of the Popes. In that *Tour de Trouillas* Rienzi was imprisoned at the same time that Petrarch was dining an honoured guest in the palace hall. That great square tower rising above all the rest—*Le Glaciere,* was the prison of the Holy Inquisition.

A thousand years have passed since those cruel tortures, and, looking back through the eyes of Alfonse Daudet, we forget the scenes of sadness in the brighter light on these old towers. It is impossible long to have gloomy thoughts and for long to dwell on sad pictures when all the world is bathed in this warm air and golden sunshine, and we know *qui n'a pas vu Avignon du temps des Papes, n'a rien vu.* We enter into its gaiety, its life, its animation. The succession of *fêtes,* the processions from morning till night, the flowers and draperies from windows and balconies on the arrival of the cardinals and the gorgeously attired soldiers of the Pope.

He who has lived in Provençe knows the gaiety, and the chatter, and the gossip, and the roar, and the bells, and the tambourines, and the striking of the clocks, and the shoutings to the mules and to the donkeys. And *"La Mule du Pape":* can we not see the good Boniface? Oh, the tears that fell in Avignon when he died! Behold the blessed father upon his mule, going out to his little vineyard, planted by himself among the myrtles of *Château Neuf.* How piously he passes the hours in little drinks, sip and sip, of the old wine, until the bottles are empty, and the dying of the day reminds him of his return to Avignon. Is it a wonder that after his love for the wine of *Château Neuf* he should love beyond all the world his black mule, sure of foot and of glistening coat, which so safely carried the worthy saint? On the animal's back securely he sits and sleeps the gentle sleep of a good man after his ardent labours of the day with his bottles.

To-day one would not find in Avignon the descendants of the miserable *Tistet Védéné,* for he was kicked into a thousand pieces by the *Coups de sabot* of the much injured beast. But of the mule's relatives there are many, and of equally long memories, in this quaint old town of sunshine and shadow, of joy and sadness, Avignon—court of the popes and home of Laura!

FINIS.